Patterns of Learning

*New Perspectives
on Life-Span Education*

Cyril O. Houle

Patterns of Learning

Jossey-Bass Publishers

San Francisco • Washington • London • 1984

PATTERNS OF LEARNING
New Perspectives on Life-Span Education
by Cyril O. Houle

Copyright © 1984 by: Jossey-Bass Inc., Publishers
433 California Street
San Francisco, California 94104
&
Jossey-Bass Limited
28 Banner Street
London EC1Y 8QE

Library of Congress Cataloging in Publication Data

Houle, Cyril Orvin, 1913–
    Patterns of learning.

    (The Jossey-Bass higher education series)
    Includes bibliographies and index.
    1. Self-culture—Addresses, essays, lectures.
2. Continuing education—Addresses, essays, lectures.
3. Learning and scholarship—Addresses, essays, lectures.
4. Formal discipline—Addresses, essays, lectures.
I. Title. II. Series.
LC32.H68   1984   374   83-49264
ISBN 0-87589-597-2

Passages excerpted from *The Complete Works of Montaigne:
Essays, Travel Journal, Letters,* translated by Donald M.
Frame, with the permission of the publishers, Stanford
University Press. Copyright 1943 by Donald M. Frame,
© 1948, 1957, 1958 by the Board of Trustees of the Leland
Stanford Junior University.

Manufactured in the United States of America

The paper in this book meets the guidelines for
permanence and durability of the Committee on
Production Guidelines for Book Longevity of the
Council on Library Resources.

JACKET DESIGN BY WILLI BAUM

FIRST EDITION

Code 8411

The Jossey-Bass
Higher Education Series

Special Adviser
Adult and Continuing Education
ALAN B. KNOX
University of Wisconsin at Madison

To my fellow students of adult education at
The University of Chicago, 1935–1978

Preface

Prior to the middle of the nineteenth century, learning was accepted without question as a lifelong activity. Even in highly developed societies, only a relatively small number of people secured a basic education, and they did so in an unsystematic fashion that depended largely on individual opportunity and initiative. But it was understood that those who mastered the rudiments of scholarship would, if they wished, use their competence to enhance their further learning, alone or in groups, guiding their own study or accepting tutelage, and using whatever resources were available. The education of the young had primacy because basic skills and knowledge could be most readily inculcated in youth, but it was seldom forgotten that learning in childhood served as the basis for deeper study in adulthood—if one wanted to undertake it and had the means to do so.

This balanced view of learning was distorted by the rise of a cultural democracy centered largely on the provision of primary, secondary, and higher education for all young people. According to legend, an exuberant Ohio backwoodsman told a

European visitor in the 1850s that "we already have a grammar school, next year we'll have an academy, and we're cutting the logs for a college." This egalitarian spirit spurred both by the creation of American institutional forms and by the borrowing and adaptation of foreign theories and systems gave the schools and colleges of the country a central place in educational thought and action that has lasted to the present time.

Though the practices and institutions of adult education were eclipsed, they endured, they grew, and they proliferated. After the end of World War I, their importance began to increase because of a self-identified movement that built its strength in many ways. It was especially aided by meeting the successive challenges created by the Great Depression, World War II, and the strains and opportunities of the post-war world. Ever larger numbers of young people who had achieved a sound basic education and wanted to build on it provided even more impetus for the growth of adult education.

By 1970, educators began seriously to rethink learning as a lifetime activity, rather than as one restricted to childhood. The assumed continuity that had been adequate in by-gone years would not suffice to provide articulation for the intricately complex systems of education that had been developed first to serve children and youth and later to serve adults. Rigidities and discontinuities impeded learning in many ways that will be illustrated in Chapter One. Their nature can be suggested by a simple though widely experienced example. In completely youth-oriented schooling, it is assumed that the students should learn everything that they will need to know throughout their lives. The curriculum is therefore crowded with content, much of which will later prove to be inadequate or incorrect and some of which creates no spark of interest in the learners because it appears irrelevant to the urgent problems they expect to face upon graduation. When opportunities for learning in adulthood were minimal and when knowledge did not increase rapidly, it may have been prudent to try to compress all education into a short span of years near the start of life. Today it is not. People can learn to cope with the new kinds of responsibility that adulthood brings at the time they need that knowledge, thus freeing time in youth for a sounder and broader mastery of fundamentals. Thus any concept of lifelong learning requires reciprocal changes in the present sequence of education.

Since 1970, a substantial and steadily increasing body of literature has appeared exploring the implications of this and other examples of how basic and continuing education need to be integrated. However, as the subtitle of this book, *New Perspectives on Life-Span Education,* suggests, this topic needs to be examined in different ways than have been applied in the past.

To begin with, the literature on life-span education does not differentiate among underlying points of view. For example, some analyses deal with the personality attributes related to the nature and extent of continuing learning in people's lives. Some try to discern the educational implications of the successive stages of human life. Some are concerned with how the institutions that provide education can extend their programs to serve new age cohorts of students. I have tried to distinguish each of the ways of examining and using the broad concept of lifelong education and have constructed a simple taxonomy that I hope will be strengthened and amplified by those who use it.

Second, in analyzing and working with current theories, it has become apparent that most of them are concerned only with how the longitudinal aspect of life influences learning from birth to death. Many such examinations look solely at some single kind of institutional participation or form of inquiry, asking, for example, how age influences attendance at a university or alters the habit of serious reading. But learning has depth and breadth as well as length. At any given time in one's life, a person is likely to be engaged in several different kinds of learning. The pattern these activities make is apparent only when they are seen as interwoven life experiences. Patterns change as life proceeds. This conception of life-span education, called the *sequential patterns of learning* approach, will be presented in this book. Its nature, implicit throughout, is most fully stated in Chapter Ten.

Third, the term *pattern of learning* implies that each individual is simultaneously engaged in several kinds of consciously

educational experience. Each of these is here called a *method*,
or some synonym of that term. Most of them are familiar, including participating in a class, studying with a tutor, attending
a lecture, or reading a sequence of books. An examination of
learning as an inherent part of the fabric of life reveals, however, that while some methods would probably be universally
accepted as educative, they are not frequently considered as
parallels of more familiar forms of learning. Among them are
the self-directed improvement of performance at work, deliber-
atively educative travel, and scholarly companionship. The
analysis of such methods (particularly as components of patterns of learning) therefore becomes a central theme of this
book.

Fourth, the essential methods of education have remained the same throughout history since they are based on
fundamental forms of personal and social experience. The importance of this truth is sometimes forgotten by those who are
bemused by an invention and who highlight its distinctive advantages without paying due attention to its essential similarity
to earlier processes. It seems essential, therefore, to use the
people and practices of earlier times in pursuing the inquiries
that make up the substance of this book. By looking at the
past, we can gain a perspective on the present; this fact is particularly true of adult educators, most of whom have little
sense of their historical antecedents.

Fifth, the nature of life-span learning suggests that, at this
stage of the inquiry, the universal can best be discerned by a
close study of the particular; therefore most of this book is devoted to specific case reports. For example, since a pattern of
learning centers on the experience of a single person, Chapter
Two is focused upon the life of Michel de Montaigne, who revealed with elaborate explicitness how the processes of his education occurred in the structure of his life. Similarly, in Chapter
Six, the nature of a single complex method of learning, educative travel, is studied in terms of one center of culture, Florence.
It is certain that more comprehensive ways will be found of
studying sequential patterns of learning (one such way is mentioned in Chapter Ten), but the basic ideas underlying this ap-

proach require more explicit and detailed analyses now than will be the case later.

Finally, it is possible to make a general inventory of how patterns of learning are related to experience. An overview of this sort is presented in Chapter Nine, using three different approaches, all of them based on the writings of people who lived prior to the nineteenth century. How should education fit into one's life? What are the basic reasons why people, particularly adults, should learn? What are the fundamental methods by which they do so? The answers to these questions provide a culminating synthesis for the more specific inquiries reported in earlier chapters.

It is fair to ask of this book as of any other, For whom is it written? The brief answer is, For anyone interested in education during the whole span of life, but particularly during adulthood. Some people simply want to know more about this topic, but many others are motivated by a desire for action. Some want to plan learning programs for themselves or for other people. Some want to conduct research to find out why and how people learn. And some want to prepare themselves for careers as practitioners or scholars. While *Patterns of Learning* does not chart any specific course for the future, it suggests that education is a far more complex process than it is usually thought to be. I hope this work will provide to observers and to present and future activists incentives for thought and action.

Acknowledgments

The central purposes of this book, as they are defined in Chapter One, began to take shape in my mind in the early 1960s, but it has required until now for them to reach their present form. A number of the chapters were originally prepared as separate essays, although each has since been substantially revised. Chapters One and Ten tie together the specific themes presented in the other chapters and suggest their underlying synthesis. References are given at the end of each chapter.

My gratitude is expressed to the Chicago Literary Club, where Chapters Two, Three, Five, Six, and Seven were first read to the membership and which was kind enough to publish Chapter Three; to Oxford University, where Chapter Eight was first presented; to Syracuse University (and particularly to Chancellor William H. Tolley), where Chapter Four was first read and which later published it as a small separate volume; and to *Perspectives in Biology and Medicine,* which published Chapters Three and Eight. Permission to reprint has been secured where necessary. Seven of the ten chapters are here published for the first time.

A large number of people have read or listened to parts of this book and many have commented on it, sometimes more freely than I liked. But I have profited substantially from their observations and have made many changes in the manuscript as a result. Colleagues, research associates, and librarians have helped greatly in identifying sources and suggesting others. Bruno Bettelheim provided encouragement at a time when it was much needed. Alan B. Knox and Robert Hencey read the first draft of the book and appraised it with their usual acuteness. Other friends and critics have also been generous with their suggestions for change, some of which I have gratefully accepted. Connie Tomak and Leona Gilson supervised the production of the manuscript. The many drafts were typed with infinite care by the Word Processing Center of the W. K. Kellogg Foundation. I thank all of them for their help but insist that all deficiencies in the book are my own.

Battle Creek, Michigan   Cyril O. Houle
January 1984

Contents

The Author

Cyril O. Houle is senior program consultant at the W. K. Kellogg
Foundation and professor emeritus of education at the University of Chicago. He was awarded both the bachelor's and master's degrees at the University of Florida in 1934 and the Ph.D.
degree at the University of Chicago in 1940, all three in the
field of education.

Houle served in various teaching and administrative positions at the University of Chicago from 1939 to 1978; his major
academic interest was adult and continuing education. He was
also a visiting faculty member at the University of California at
Berkeley, the University of Washington, the University of Wisconsin at Milwaukee, Leeds University, and Oxford University.
In various capacities, Houle has studied adult education in
thirty-five foreign countries and has served as a member of national and international commissions and as consultant to governmental and private organizations in the United States and
abroad. He is a member of the National Academy of Education
and has been awarded honorary doctorates by Rutgers Univer-

sity, Florida State University, Syracuse University, New York University, De Paul University, and Roosevelt University.

He is the author of numerous books and other publications, including *The Effective Board* (1960), *The Inquiring Mind* (1961), *The Design of Education* (1972), *The External Degree* (1973), and *Continuing Learning in the Professions* (1980), winner of the Imogene Okes Award presented by the Adult Education Association. Houle now lives and works in both Battle Creek and Chicago.

Patterns of Learning

New Perspectives

on Life-Span Education

1

Variety, Not Uniformity

I

Describing English life in the last half of the eighteenth century, G. M. Trevelyan observed that "in spite of the decadence of the only two Universities that then existed in England, in spite of the decay of the endowed schools specially charged with secondary education, the intellectual life of the country was never more brilliant, and the proportion of men of genius per head of population in the irregularly educated England of George III was immensely greater than in our own day. It would seem that the very highest products of the human mind are the outcome of chance and freedom and variety rather than of uniform organization" (1942, p. 367). If Trevelyan had wanted another example to illustrate his thesis, he need only have looked across the Atlantic, where, in the same period, an extraordinary galaxy of leaders was creating a new nation. Eighty-nine men signed the Declaration of Independence, the Constitution, or both; of that number, only thirty-six had been graduated from the primitive colonial colleges. The rest of them, Lawrence Cremin has noted, "represented every conceivable combination of parental, church, apprenticeship, school, tutorial, and self-education, including some who had studied abroad" (1970, p. 550).

Chance and freedom and variety do not provide learning but only the opportunity and stimulus for it, a fact that Trevelyan implied and Cremin demonstrated. The flow of experience unorganized by forethought makes a continuing profound impact upon every individual, bringing knowledge and understand-

1

ing, reinforcing habits and attitudes, and altering personality in ways that may be immediately felt or that may not become apparent until later. In addition, activities purposefully undertaken for profit or enjoyment, because of a sense of duty, or arising from any other motive may also have unforeseen educative consequences. But while learning is often a result of conditioning or a by-product of actions pursued for other purposes, substantial accomplishments are usually achieved as a result of sustained and earnest effort.

Exceptions to this rule, such as Joan of Arc's mastery of military strategy and Wolfgang Amadeus Mozart's grasp of musical theory, come readily to mind as does the apparently inborn talent of an idiot savant. But an examination of the careers of those who accomplish greatness, those who strive for it, and those who seek merely to fulfill their personal potential shows that they have used ordered and systematic processes of preparing themselves for their accomplishments. Every such individual finds ways of learning that are congenial to his or her temperament and circumstances of life and uses them to master content, acquire skills, or increase sensitiveness.

Little comparative or analytical study has been made of these personal patterns of learning or of the methods that compose them. Biographies and autobiographies include some mention of how the person described used education to become what he or she wanted to be, and some psychological case studies do the same thing. A group of scholars, most notably Allen Tough (1971), has focused on self-generated episodes of study and speculated about why and how they occur. But the basic methods of learning, most of which have been used through the centuries of recorded thought, have had surprisingly little analysis, either generally or in their intricately varied applications.

II

The first purpose of this book therefore is to explore several of the ways by which learning processes are provided and used, both separately or in a simultaneous or sequential fashion, in order to achieve personal and social ends. The intent here is not to be either comprehensive or precisely analytical but to evoke by the use of illustration a sense of the nature and diversity of educational methods. The book presents accounts of some of the ways in which learning has been central to the lives of people during the long history of culture. The effort throughout is to describe the general by examining a few particulars in the hope that details will reveal what the smoothing hand of generalization often obscures.

In Chapter Two, the focus is upon Michel de Montaigne, the sixteenth-century Frenchman who, in a life filled with the performance of civic duties and the demands of estate management, found ways to enlarge his horizon by scholarly companionship, reading, travel, and involvement in affairs of state. His essays (a literary form that he created) and his journals show how systematically he studied and how that study enriched the literature he produced.

Chapter Three is devoted to the ways by which a great poet, despite almost unimaginable adversity, used tutorial guidance, self-directed disciplined study, and the companionship of gifted associates as the methods by which he brought his genius to fruition.

Chapter Four considers still another author, Henry David Thoreau, a nineteenth-century handy man and pencil maker in a small New England town, who was fortunate enough to have as good a formal education as his country could then offer but who scorned it in favor of other means of learning: the direct observation of nature and of the people of his village, close self-examination, and small-group discussion. The unorthodox consequences of these methods of sharpening his talents have been profoundly felt throughout the world.

In the foregoing examples, the emphasis has been upon the individual learner, but some methods of education are inherently collective. Of them all, the oldest and most widely used is spoken discourse. To catch the essence of this method, attention should be centered upon the deliverer of the message, not upon its often myriad recipients. Chapter Five is therefore focused upon Billy Graham and especially on how he achieves the effects that have made him the most widely heard orator in history.

Another method of both individual and collective learning is travel. Here the focus may appropriately be geographical. Chapter Six deals with Florence, a center of culture to which people (including Montaigne) have gone for centuries in order to learn from its astoundingly deep and varied resources. What kinds of people go there and what can they hope to learn? The answers to these questions turn out to be remarkably complex.

In the past two hundred years, methods of learning such as those already mentioned have come to be considered largely in terms of their relationship, if any, to systems of instruction, particularly schools, colleges, and universities. Chapter Seven sketches how this formal system grew up in the nineteenth century, using as a point of reference the career of Edward Everett. As it happens, he was one of the greatest political orators of the century and might have been the subject of the chapter on spoken discourse rather than Graham if enough were known about how Everett achieved his command of vast audiences. But the central purpose of his career was to establish systems of high-quality education for people of all ages, and this is the endeavor described here.

In a more specialized way, William Osler, a Canadian physician, sought, in the United States and England as well as in his own country, to establish the importance of both didactic and practical education for doctors throughout their lives. Chapter Eight describes how he carried out this task, both by reforming medical schools and by establishing such basic systems of continuing education as journals, study clubs, local associations with libraries, and, most important, instruction in hospitals and other places where sick people are cared for. His work has proved to be profoundly influential for other professions as well as for his own.

These studies of individual people and places would be incomplete without a broader and more schematic examination of the patterns of learning recommended and used throughout the history of Western civilization. People have considered education to be part of an entire design of life, they have thought deeply about its values, and they have proposed or used its basic methods. Chapter Nine summarizes many of these concepts and processes.

Chapter Ten suggests some of the implications of these case studies for those who plan and administer educational activities, for those who do research in the field, and for the people who are interested in or profit from the work of such practitioners and scholars.

III

The second purpose of the book is to suggest that modern educators of adults might, by pondering illustrations of their long and rich tradition, be able to escape from some of the limitations imposed by dominant prevailing practices. Everett, Osler, and their colleagues turned out to be more successful in founding institutions for young people than in establishing patterns of learning for the later years of life. In egalitarian societies, the desire to achieve cultural democracy gave rise to enormous and continuing expenditures of time and money that made universal schooling central to the educational thought of people everywhere. The schoolroom and the laboratory became the major places of instruction with the result that the teaching of classes grew to be the chief (and, many people assume, the only) way of learning. The overformalization of education was an unintended consequence of the earnest desire of worthy people to serve all of the educational needs of youth and achieve many other social purposes as well.

The institutions that are now parts of these systems were originally intended for separate and distinct purposes. The university was for advanced research scholars and professionals, the college for future leaders of society, the secondary school for young people who wanted to enter a university or college, the elementary school for the culminating education of the common people, and the kindergarten and nursery school for the acculturation of small children. But as these institutions grew, two major developments helped give them an ever greater dominance over other structures and processes of learning.

First, each kind of institution expanded in scope and function to become much more comprehensive than before. For example, the university vastly enlarged its goals and services so that it almost seemed to wish to be omnicompetent, becoming a multiversity or a communiversity. Its originally narrow off-shoot, the junior college, flowered in the mid-twentieth century into the fascinatingly broad community college. This develop-ment is only the most recent example of a long-standing move-ment of outreach whose most prominent previous American form was the land-grant college. Similar expansion occurred at other levels; the elementary school has added several kinds of social reform to its original purpose of teaching basic language and arithmetic skills, and the secondary school now has many curricula, not just one.

Second, institutions that were originally distinct in scope and purpose have been rationalized into a sequence that, in its fullest expression, leads an individual onward from entry into a nursery school to the achievement of the doctorate. Thus a monolithic system has been created, one which, despite all its diversity, is capable of being understood by everyone, even those who do not share deeply in its benefits. The creation and support of this majestic enterprise have given it a central place in all educational thought. Individuals have continued to find other ways, often self-directed and self-monitored, to change themselves to achieve the goals they desire, but these countless private ventures seldom challenge the orthodoxy of the system. Even where public libraries, museums, apprentice-ship plans, youth groups, and other institutions flourish, all of them with strong educative purposes, formal schooling remains the dominant pattern of learning.

The system was given an added unity because, no matter how diverse its purposes became, it relied from beginning to end on the mode of instruction. It is true that a long line of influ-ential philosophers, most recently John Dewey, has stressed the value of learning as an interactive process of inquiry by teacher and students; but while such thought has deeply influ-enced the practice of some educators, schooling has remained essentially a master-pupil system, exemplified in different ways in various types of institutions but retaining a structural frame-work by which well-established content, skills, and appreciation are conveyed by instructors (variously identified and defined) who know what is to be learned to students who do not. The classroom or its equivalent is the dominant learning site of the nursery school, the university, and all the formal institutions between them in a laddered system of education.

Because this schooling was provided primarily for people from the ages of two to twenty-five, education came to be thought of as a youth-related or even a youth-bound activity. The belief (accepted throughout all earlier history) that learning should extend during the whole span of life was gradually forgotten by most people so that when theories and practices of adult education were formulated in the first quarter of the twentieth century, they were hailed in many countries as innovations, not as rediscoveries. In the ensuing years, great strides have been taken to increase the opportunities for learning available to men and women. As yet, however, adult education has not freed itself from the dominance of the formal school system and of the use of the mode of instruction as virtually the only way by which education can occur.

A few examples will suggest the nature of this inhibition. It is widely believed, for instance, that the practicing members of professions should keep abreast of new theories and practices, but such continuing education and the credentials for which it provides a basis usually require some form of organized instruction and are not necessarily linked in any close way to improvement in performance. In fact, all those who seek degrees or other credentials are usually expected to acquire their knowledge in formally organized, sequentially ordered classes; new systems and patterns of acquiring certificated knowledge have as yet made relatively slow headway. In addition, the so-called educational programs of associations, libraries, museums, labor unions, hospitals, religious institutions, industrial and commercial organizations, the armed services, and other institutions are often adapted from the methods used in formal instruction and have an air of didacticism about them. Finally, learners who do not achieve their goals by formal study often either feel belligerent and profess contempt for academic study or feel inadequate and apologize because their knowledge or ability was not achieved in what is accepted by society as the only correct system of education.

One way to escape from the conceptual prison of the

classroom and the school is to examine the relative values of
alternative ways of learning. The essence of a basic method can
readily be identified, although every time it is employed it is
adapted to the customs of its age and the specific circumstances
of its use. Listening to spoken discourse, for instance, has occurred throughout the history of culture whenever and wherever
someone has delivered a systematic address to another person
or to a group of people. It also takes place when the voice and
image of a person are recorded and transmitted by microphone,
camera, satellite, cable, television set, videotape, and all the
complex mechanisms that link them so that the message can
later be heard and watched at the convenience of a learner who
is perhaps half a world away. Other methods have other varied
forms. Socrates used a visual aid in the *Meno* when he drew
with a stick on the sand; medieval and Renaissance muralists,
tapestry designers, and creators of stained glass windows often
wanted their pictures and designs to convey messages; and modern inventors have devised intricate pictorial ways to stimulate
the acquisition of knowledge. Yet in both examples—spoken
discourse and the use of a visual aid—the essence of the method
remains the same despite the uniqueness of each usage.

IV

The third purpose of this book, transcending the first
two, is to suggest that, in the light of the illustrations presented,
life-span learning should be considered in a broader framework
than has yet been the case. The idea that education should occur at all ages of life from birth to senility or death is not new
and has often been taken for granted, as Plato did in planning
the careers of the philosopher-kings. But as adult education began about 1920 to spread as a world-wide movement, it gradually created or enlarged its institutions and activities until they
became a powerful cluster of forces that needed to be recon-
ciled, both theoretically and practically, with the education of
children.

Many ways of approaching this topic have been suggested.
A first answer, arising in central Europe, was that a science of

andragogy (the study of the teaching of adults) should be created that would be parallel to pedagogy (the study of the teaching of children), the two being thought to be essentially different because of the biological and social differences between adulthood and childhood. Often the theories were proposed as being antithetical to one another; whatever was effective for adults was bad for children and vice versa. In the 1960s and 1970s, however, different theories arose that stressed the fact that education is continuous throughout the life span, though constantly evolving in purpose and procedure. Several different variations on this theme were proposed, each of them with a distinctive designation, by the European members of international organizations. The United Nations Educational, Scientific, and Cultural Organization preferred the term *lifelong learning,* the Organisation of Economic and Cultural Development preferred *recurrent education,* and the Council of Europe preferred *permanent education,* a term that loses a great deal in its translation from the original French expression *l'education permanente.* The subtle differences among the theories that underlie these terms have not yet been adequately analyzed, but the general idea that they all express has been well accepted and is now most commonly called *lifelong education.* Even the proponents of the science of andragogy find little or no discomfort in accepting the overarching theme, noting that they are concentrating on the study of but one part of the life span and are no longer focusing on contrasts with pedagogy.

The broad sweep of the central idea of lifelong education captured the imagination of many people, particularly because of the eloquence with which it was expressed in such works as *Learning to Be* (Faure and others, 1972). Educators began to identify existing programs of education that exemplified the idea and to devise new ways of putting it into effect. The following models suggest some of the varied ways by which this synthesizing approach has been used:

The public library has long been successful in moving individuals through the levels of reading material in the children's room, then on to the young adult collection, and subsequently to the general collection. The visible presence of people of all ages using the same institution reinforces the continuity of both purpose and method.

Each of the armed services has planned career sequences for its officer corps in which people alternate formal training with field duty throughout their entire period of service, the degree of success in each episode of education or action determining both the nature and the quality of the next assignment. Meanwhile, during field duty, many opportunities are provided for supplementary study, so that the officer at every career level regards himself or herself as being engaged in both sequential and simultaneous patterns of learning.

The community-school movement has sought to tie the school curriculum closely to community problems, the purpose being not only to solve these problems but also to relate young students to older people, thus fostering continuity of contact.

Community education has opened up the public school system so that its resources are available at all hours of the day with programming designed to meet the learning needs of all age groups.

The land-grant universities have developed the Cooperative Extension Service, in which the learning of people is aided from the time they join 4-H clubs as children until the ends of their lives. Although this system formerly dealt only with rural families, particularly those on farms, it has broadened its scope of services in recent years.

The junior college, which began as an institution offering the first two years of postsecondary academic and occupational training, expanded in the 1960s and 1970s into the community college, which, in its fullest expression, offers education for everyone from adolescent years onward and has, in fact, assiduously sought out new audiences to serve.

Some teachers and schools have tried in many ways, under the generic term of *the open classroom,* to include a variety of experiences for young people, thus accepting the idea of a diversified pattern of educational methods and laying a foundation for subsequent breadth of view toward learning.

Some authors have suggested that all schools should be eliminated so that everyone can learn "naturally" by independent study, interactions with other people, and through the use of voluntary learning centers, tutorial arrangements, and other methods of inquiry—all of which would start early in life and flow uninterruptedly to its end. This idea of "deschooling" has proved to be too radical for society to adopt except in a few hotly contested circumstances, but its followers have created some exciting new systems of voluntary adult learning.

A great deal of thought is now being given in various professions to shifting the ages at which content should be presented to learners. Do people preparing to be engineers require training in administration, or should it be taught to them later on when they know they need it? At every stage of the education of physicians—premedical programs, undergraduate medicine, graduate medicine, preparation for specialty certification, and continuing education—challenges are being made to both the content of the curriculum and its sequencing in the career pattern.

However significant these and other models have undoubtedly been, they are specialized as to institution, function, or stage of life and do not deal with an ultimate conception of life-span learning that is based on the full array of learning activities of the individual throughout a lifetime. A sixteen-year-old girl may spend 1,250 hours a year in school but still have about 4,500 waking hours to do other things, some of which may be purposefully educative. By choice, she may join clubs, learn to play a musical instrument, gain skill in several sports, and persuade her friends to teach her things they know. Meanwhile habit establishes other unconsciously systematic ways of acquiring knowledge and insight, increasing skill, or deepening sensitivity; she watches television, listens to the stereo or radio, and reads books, magazines, and newspapers in a more selective fashion than she may realize. Similarly, a forty-year-old professional man learns from the self-analysis of his work, from the comments of peers and supervisors, from conferences and short courses, from the improvement of his recreational skills, from systematic travel, and (like the sixteen-year-old) from his individualistic use of the mass media.

The personal pattern of learning shifts with age and circumstance. Both the sixteen-year-old girl and the forty-year-old man have had earlier learning patterns and will have later ones. But precisely how age and circumstance exert their influence is not known. Individuals may appear to be wholly idiosyncratic in their succession of patterns, but it is likely that deeper study would show that commonalities can be found. A great deal of analysis has been made of specific stages in the life span, with close and detailed attention being given to infancy and childhood and less to later life. Such stages are thought to be significant for determining the purposes and selecting the content of education but may be equally influential for choosing methods of learning.

Since relatively little investigation has been made of many of the basic methods of learning, it is not known to what extent they may be age-related. Reading would appear to be equally useful from about the age of five onward, although it may increase in relative emphasis during the latter part of adulthood. Travel may be different. As Chapter Six reports, powerful voices have declared that it may be educative in childhood and again in mature adulthood but that it should not be undertaken in later adolescence or young adulthood, which are precisely the times when it is presently most encouraged.

In seeking to fulfill its three purposes, this book is intended to stimulate not prescribe. Its readers should draw their own conclusions, either from the total presentation or from specific incidents. "History," said Osler, "is simply the biography of the mind of man; and interest in history and its value to us is directly proportionate to the completeness of the study of the individuals through whom this mind has been manifested" (1909, p. 211). The inquiries reported in this book were carried out in the spirit of this comment. In order to be evocative, many facts are included that do not, initially at least, appear to bear directly on the processes of learning. Bare-bones case studies have no power of allusion; they cannot indicate how intimately the pattern of learning adopted by a person or a group arises out of a totality of personal actions and interactions. For example, the heredity and idiosyncrasies of Montaigne influenced deeply the way he applied his mind to his own improvement, and the richness of Florence as a place to learn cannot be indicated without supplying a wealth of information about its past and present. In discussing these chapters with readers and audiences, I have found that details that some people regard as extraneous often bring forth a powerful response in other people, helping them to comprehend either the nature or the result of a pattern of learning as it occurs within the total framework of a life.

Chapter Ten does suggest some of the implications that a complex view of educational method may have for the future development of life-span learning, particularly that portion of it that occurs in the adult years. But the pathways into the future summarized in that chapter reflect the tentative ideas of only one person. It is my hope that the lines of inquiry and action initiated by this book will be developed and expanded in ways that lie beyond my present comprehension.

References

Cremin, L. A. *American Education: The Colonial Experience, 1607–1783*. New York: Harper & Row, 1970.

Faure, E., and others. *Learning to Be: The World of Education Today and Tomorrow*. Paris: United Nations Educational, Scientific, and Cultural Organization, 1972.

Osler, W. *An Alabama Student and Other Biographical Essays*. New York: Oxford University Press, 1909.

Tough, A. *The Adult's Learning Projects*. Toronto: Ontario Institute for Studies in Education, 1971.

Trevelyan, G. M. *English Social History*. London: Longmans, Green, 1942.

2

Michel de Montaigne

Profiting from

Scholarly Companionship, Reading,

Travel, and Affairs of State

I

Supreme accomplishment in art, as in science, almost always results from sustained, sequential, and often collective effort. Innovators attract followers, early ventures lead finally to masterpieces, and members of schools of thought evolve principles collectively. Seldom does a new art form—full, complete, and enduring—arise from the work of a single person and establish itself so permanently that while later followers may use the same pattern, they never equal the power of the original. In literature, I know of only two examples: Homer in the creation of the epic poem and Michel de Montaigne in the establishment of the essay. We cannot be absolutely sure about Homer, for he may have had precursors now lost in antiquity, and, despite much research on the subject, it is still not certain that one person wrote the entire body of work now credited to him. But Montaigne was a man of modern times; more is known about

14

him than about most long-established literary figures. He knew he was creating a new kind of work of art, and it is possible to trace the powerful influence he continues to exert.

His distinctive device is the relatively short, discursive paper, intended to whet interest and provoke thought. To such a work he gave the whimsical name by which it has been known ever since, the *essai*—that is to say, the attempt, the trial, the exploration. It is intended to be tentative, interesting, stimulating, personal, but never definitive or complete. And yet, his apparently modest and fragile effort turned out to have a surprising strength and has lasted through the centuries. Even today, four hundred years and thousands of authors later, Montaigne's use of the art form he invented has never been paralleled in scope or quality. Let us then look closely at the short, thick-set, dark, bald figure of Montaigne, whom Virginia Woolf called the "subtle, half smiling, half melancholy man, with the heavy-lidded eyes and the dreamy, quizzical expression" (1925, p. 91). In a tower on a hill in Gascony, he spent much of his life, surrounded by his thousand books, sometimes leaning back in his chair to read, his feet as high as his seat or higher, sometimes jumping up to pace about or to dip into books but coming back to write a passage that people still ponder.

His works achieved fame almost at once in both France and England. The *Encyclopaedia Britannica* refers to the essay as "a peculiarly English thing" and as "one of the glories of English literature" but admits that it was not native but naturalized. The first French edition of Montaigne appeared in 1580; in 1597, Francis Bacon's first ten essays were issued. In 1603, John Florio's English translation of Montaigne appeared and, for a long while, almost every year found some new author presenting his own work in essay form. Shakespeare was indebted to the observations and anecdotes he found in Montaigne; both his and Ben Jonson's copies survive. And in every era since, Montaigne has had his followers and admirers. In the nineteenth century, Charles Sainte-Beuve called him "the wisest Frenchman who ever lived" (1863, p. 177), and, in the twentieth, T. S. Eliot said he was the most essential author in the modern history of French thought (1936, p. 156).

His ideas came from many sources. His extraordinary father and the early regime he set for his son laid the groundwork for sustained inquiry in which Montaigne examined every aspect of his own life and his association with others. Two very different traditions of European history (the established landowner and the exiled Sephardic Jew) met in and were assimilated in him. As feudal lord, as local and national politician, as a traveler driven by the quest for health, and as intimate companion of one of the leading intellectuals of his time, he had varied and rich experiences. He is chiefly remembered, however, as a serious reader, partly because that is how he sometimes wanted history to view him. In the entire pattern of lifelong education that refined the man and his essays, reading is a central thread.

II

Boiling up within Montaigne were countless ideas, each of which he felt the urge to record. "Let me begin with whatever subject I please, for all subjects are linked with one another" (III:5, p. 668).* But what links them? Jottings alone are not enough; they must have some form or some unity of thought. He found his central theme, or pretended to have done so, in an incident he witnessed: "One day at Bar-le-Duc I saw King Francis II presented, in remembrance of René, king of Sicily, with a portrait that this king had made of himself. Why is it not permissible in the same way for each man to portray himself with the pen, as he portrayed himself with a pencil?" (II:17, p. 496). In his preface, he says, "I want to be seen here in my simple, natural, ordinary fashion, without straining or artifice; for it is myself that I portray" (p. 2). Such a desire does not fit into any form of discourse that imposes a predetermined structure of presentation upon thoughts that rise up afresh in the mind. Their expression requires directness of speech. Ralph Waldo

*Quotations from Montaigne are here cited by volume and chapter, a practice traditionally followed in both the French and translated editions. In addition, page references are here given to the English translation by Frame, which is listed in the References for this chapter.

Emerson would observe three centuries later, "Cut these words, and they would bleed; they are vascular and alive" (1883, p. 161). It also requires a constant shift of position and of ideas, for people do not think logically but by a stream of associations and also they change as they grow older. Moreover, if Montaigne were to describe his own personality, it would require vividness, irony, paradox, and the constant use of imagery. "We are all patchwork," he said, "and there is as much difference between us and ourselves as between us and others" (II:1, p. 244).

As could be expected, even his basic point of view shifted. In his later days, Montaigne came to realize that, in describing himself, he was to some extent describing humankind. His final book is based on the proposition that "each man bears the entire form of man's estate" (III:2, p. 611). For example, he was a licentious man and professed not to be able to remember when he lost his virginity. He dwells frequently and vividly on the delights of Venus, recounting, for example, the story "of a woman who had passed through the hands of some soldiers: 'God be praised,' she said, 'that at least once in my life I have had my fill without sin!' " (II:3, p. 257). Emerson fretted about Montaigne's directness of speech and excused it on the ground that in the sixteenth century only men read books, ignoring the fact that all of the dedications of the essays were to women and some of the language is directly addressed to them. Library copies of Montaigne sometimes open almost automatically to the most explicit essay on sex, which is rather improbably called "On Some Verses of Virgil." Montaigne knew he was licentious; he later came to believe that all people are or would like to be equally so. He wrote: "I know well that very few people will frown at the license of my writings who do not have more to frown at in the license of their thoughts" (III:5, pp. 641-642). If posterity disagreed with him, he noted at another place, "I shall have a neat revenge; for they will never be able to be so indifferent to me as I shall then be to them" (quoted in Lowenthal, 1935, p. 11).

As insights grew with age and experience, he moved into the world of universals, not particulars, while still insisting that he had not moved at all. T. S. Eliot observed, "What makes

Montaigne a very great figure is that he succeeded, God knows how . . . in giving expression to the scepticism of *every* human being" (1936, p. 158). Eliot thought that the author himself "very likely did not know that he had done it—it is not the sort of thing that men *can* observe about themselves, for it is essentially bigger than the individual's consciousness" (p. 158). But one may wonder. This seemingly simple man who dwells often on his laziness, his short attention span, his hungers, his rural habits, his bowel movements, and other similar matters can suddenly flash forth with a noble sentiment or a penetrating insight. Should we accept Montaigne at face value as a pedestrian self-teacher accidentally scaling the heights of grandeur? Or did he know precisely what he was doing in building a majestic edifice of thought with a scope and sweep paralleled in French literature only by Honoré de Balzac and Marcel Proust? The debate has gone on for four centuries. It will not be concluded here.

The epithet most often applied to Montaigne is *skeptic*; Emerson treats him as the prototype of this point of view. The skeptic is the natural enemy of the true believer of a doctrine. During Montaigne's life and for some time after it, his ideas seemed safe from attack, but as they reached a wider circle of readers, they provoked opposition. In those days, the most likely arena of conflict was religion. Montaigne was a professing Roman Catholic all his days, but his essays left room for the suspicion that his observance of practice was not necessarily supported by belief. Certain ambiguous comments, indeed certain lengthy passages, gave rise to doubts, and the subtle minds of the learned doctors of the Church detected conscious or unconscious heresies. Blaise Pascal, for one, believed that Montaigne's ideas must be destroyed, and he set out to do so, a hard task, for, as Eliot justly observed, "you could as well dissipate a fog by flinging hand-grenades into it. For Montaigne is a fog, a gas, a fluid, insidious element. He does not reason, he insinuates, charms, and influences; or if he reasons, you must be prepared for his having some other design upon you than to convince you by his argument" (1936, p. 156).

Silence can be imposed, however, without analysis or refutation. In 1676, eighty-four years after Montaigne's death, his work was placed on the Church's Prohibitory Index. Centuries later this fact gave rise to an ironic event. A cherished niece of his, Jeanne, had been in danger of following her mother into Calvinism. Montaigne intervened, had her removed from her mother, and saw to it that she was brought up as a Catholic. She performed many miraculous works and was canonized in 1949. On that occasion, Pius XII expressed the hope that some day the work of the new saint's uncle might be removed from the Index. After all, the Pope said, "it is thanks to him that the little girl became a Catholic" (Frame, 1965, p. 32).

III

The paternal family of this complex man has been traced back as far as the tenth century; as part of the rising middle class of Bordeaux, it had grown increasingly prosperous. Michel's great-grandfather amassed a sufficient fortune to buy the castle of Montaigne and thereby, as a landowner, rose somewhat above the bourgeois class. For four later generations, the family name of Eyquem was retained; Michel was the first to drop it and to emerge with the full grandeur of nobility. The family was Gascon, and the people of that region have long been famous for the extravagance of their pretensions; the word *gasconade* was coined to describe their manner of speech. D'Artagnan of *The Three Musketeers* was a Gascon, and Bergerac, whence came the famous Cyrano, is only five leagues from the chateau of Montaigne.

But Michel was not true to type. His father, "the best father there ever was" (II:12, p. 320), was far more flamboyant than he. The son said of his father that he was "very well suited to the service of the ladies, both by nature and by art" and described him as "a small man, full of vigor, and straight and well-proportioned in stature. An attractive face, inclining to brown. Adroit and distinguished in all gentlemanly exercises. I have even seen some canes filled with lead, with which they say he exercised his arms to prepare for throwing the bar or the stone, or for fencing, and some shoes with leaded soles to train him to be lighter in running and jumping. . . . I have seen him, past sixty, put our agility to shame: leap into the saddle in his furred gown, do a turn over the table on his thumb, hardly ever go up to his room without taking three or four steps at a time" (III:2, pp. 247–248).

This remarkable man married remarkably. His wife was descended from Sephardic Jews who had been expelled from Spain, had prospered, had been converted to Catholicism, and had gallicized their name from Lopez to Louppes. Of her, as of his own wife, Montaigne says almost nothing (a remarkable silence for one so quick to describe himself and others), but surely, either genetically or culturally, he was profoundly influenced by being part Gascon, part Jew.

Michel's father had unusual theories about childrearing. In the child's infancy, he was sent to live with rough peasants so that he would absorb a feeling for the common people. Later, to alleviate the rudeness of awakening each morning, he was roused by the sound of a musical instrument. When it came time for him to learn to speak, his tutor was fluent in Latin, and the boy was allowed to hear and speak only that language until he was six. His parents, his other relatives, the servants, and the peasants with whom he came in contact all had to learn at least a rudimentary Latin, and he later observed, with amusement, that the Gascon dialect spoken around his home long remained contaminated by the ancient language.

When Michel began more serious studies, his father put him under the care of tutors chosen chiefly for their good natures and easy-going dispositions. "The first taste I had for books," said Michel later, "came to me from my pleasure in the fables of the *Metamorphoses* of Ovid. For at about seven or eight years of age I would steal away from any other pleasure to read them, inasmuch as this language was my mother tongue, and it was the easiest book I knew and the best suited by its content to my tender age" (I:26, p. 130). As a consequence, he read none of the children's books of his time. More important, he began, even so young, to escape the confinement of his own century and to accept as contemporaries men who had lived fifteen hundred years before. "At that point," he said, "I happened by remarkable good fortune to come in contact with a

tutor who was an understanding man, who knew enough to con-
nive cleverly at this frivolity of mine and others like it. For by
this means I went right through Virgil's *Aeneid,* and then Ter-
ence, and then Plautus, and some Italian comedies, always lured
on by the pleasantness of the subject. If he had been foolish
enough to break this habit, I think I should have got nothing
out of school but a hatred of books, as do nearly all our noblemen. He went about it cleverly. Pretending to see nothing, he
whetted my appetite, letting me gorge myself with these books
only in secret, and gently keeping me at my work on the regular studies" (I:26, p. 130). Later Montaigne encountered enough
pedants to make him scorn theories about education that are
based, as so many are, chiefly on ideas about what not to do.

His choice of a career, taking for granted the fact that, as
Lord of Montaigne, he must be an overseer of property, was
limited to arms, the Church, or the law. His father judged that
the third of these best fitted the young man's temperament.
Somewhere, perhaps at Toulouse, he studied jurisprudence, and
sometime in his early youth he started visiting Paris, which became his most deeply beloved city. For thirteen years, beginning at the age of 24, he was a councilor in the Parlement of
Bordeaux and began to achieve that access to the seats of power
that was to be an increasingly important part of his future life.
He was later to serve as mayor of Bordeaux, as his father had
before him, and was accorded the rare honor of a second term.
But essentially he worked behind the scenes as confidant, emissary, advocate, and negotiator. He knew and was trusted by
Catherine de Medici and her three kingly sons, by Mary Queen
of Scots when she was queen of France, by Pope Gregory XIII,
and by Henry IV. Most of Montaigne's life was taken up either
with official duties or with political intrigues, and the notion
that he was a recluse reader, absent from the world of affairs,
was never true, however much this image persists.

As the names just mentioned suggest, Montaigne lived in
a bloody time. Constant battles between Catholics and Protes-
tants split families, laid waste the countryside, encouraged as-
sassinations, and reached a peak in the Massacre of St. Bartholo-
mew's Day. The bubonic plague was recurrent, as were other

pestilences. Montaigne's was an agitated, stormy, and anarchic period, with no sure refuge and no certain way to tell a friend from an enemy. He said, "I have gone to bed a thousand times in my own home, imagining that someone would betray me and slaughter me that very night" (III:9, p. 741). One of the most ghastly attributes of the times was the hardening of antagonism into callousness, then cruelty, then sadism. The greatest favor of life, Montaigne said, was to permit an enemy to "die suddenly and insensibly" (II:27, p. 524).

An extraordinary mildness or nobility of manner seemed to protect Montaigne himself. He left his house open and unguarded. He likened himself to Lycurgus, the Spartan, "who was the general depository and guardian of his fellow citizens' purses" (III:9, p. 738). "Amid so many fortified houses, I alone of my rank in France, as far as I know, have entrusted purely to heaven the protection of mine" (II:15, p. 468). "Any defense bears the aspect of war" (II:15, p. 467). Twice Montaigne was the victim of plots designed to kill him and capture his treasures. Those who seized him (and once his entire household) could have done anything they wished. Yet in both cases, his demeanor was such that at the last moment, just before a sword thrust ended everything, they suddenly withdrew, scrupulously giving back to him not only his life but all his possessions (III:12, pp. 812-814). He has no explanation of this behavior other than his innocence of manner. Search as we may, we have no alternative suggestion.

His last years were gravely afflicted, however, not from without but from within. Michel's father had developed kidney stones, after which he dragged out an agonizing existence until his death seven years later. Montaigne developed a horror of this malady, one of the most feared of all the torments in antiquity and in his own time. Michel was sure that although he was twenty-eight years old when his father had his first attack, the ailment was inherited, and, in a passage remarkably prescient of modern genetics, he asks, "Where was the propensity to this infirmity hatching all this time? And when [at my birth, my father] was so far from the ailment, how did this slight bit of his substance, with which he made me, bear so great an impression of it for its share? And moreover, how did it remain so concealed that I began to feel it forty-five years later?" (II:37, p. 579).

From this affliction came much pain but also a deeper sense of himself: If I can bear this torment, I can bear anything. Others might not have the same iron control as he, but on the whole he thought most people did. From the very fierceness of the desire for life springs the indomitable quality of humankind. Early editions of his essays lack this spirit; later ones are filled with it. They are filled, too, with the insights his travels brought him, and that travel was intended chiefly to find the spa whose waters would give him most relief. The travel journal kept for his own remembrance and not intended for publication is filled with keen observations of people and places and also with clinical details of his ailments that have fascinated modern medical historians and led them to give him excellent advice centuries too late.

Montaigne might have paid no attention to this advice if he had heard it, for he had also inherited from his paternal ancestors an antipathy to physicians. The essay called "Of the Resemblance of Children to Fathers" (II:37) is an excellent piece of good-natured but telling invective on the subject. An abundance of anecdotes is used. A Greek, for example, "was asked what had made him live healthy so long. 'Ignorance of medicine,' he replied" (p. 582). An unskilled wrestler became a doctor. " 'Take heart,' Diogenes said to him, 'you are right; now you will bring down those who brought you down before' " (p. 582).

As he developed his position as a stoic, Montaigne came finally to the belief that pain and death had to be accepted and endured as impassively as possible. "If you don't know how to die," he remarked, "don't worry; Nature will tell you what to do on the spot, fully and adequately. She will do this job perfectly for you; don't bother your head about it" (III:12, p. 804). Death of old age, he thought, was a rare and wonderful triumph; yet, at the end he came near to achieving it. He faded away at his castle, finally being carried off by an attack of quinsy at the age of fifty-nine, his family at his side, with a final mass having been sung for him.

IV

Why has this complex, wandering, influential, busy, and ailing man come down to us as a bookish hermit in a tower? The answer seems to be that the results of that part of his existence were so powerful that they have erased the memory of the other things he did. He feared that such would be the case and said from time to time how little and how sporadically he read and how often and eagerly he left his tower. But on this—as on other matters—he contradicted himself, a fact made fully evident by the essays themselves.

His mature study began when he was thirty-eight years old. The groundwork was prepared earlier during his four-year friendship with Etienne de la Boétie, the closest relationship of his life other than that with his father. La Boétie was slightly older than he, married, a scholar, and author of a treatise attacking tyranny. The friendship of the two young men was instantaneous and complete, one which, Montaigne says, "together we fostered, as long as God willed, so entire and so perfect that certainly you will hardly read of the like, and among men of today you see no trace of it in practice" (I:28, p. 136). On what was this friendship based? Montaigne examined the obvious possibilities, including homosexuality, and rejected them all. In the first edition of the essays, he concludes this inquiry by saying, "If you press me to tell why I loved him, I feel that this cannot be expressed"; but, in his old age, he added "except by answering: Because it was he, because it was I" (I:28, p. 139).

La Boétie's death, caused by an infection, was described in minute detail by Montaigne in a letter to his father and was the great trauma of his life, one from which he never wholly recovered. The event threw him immediately into two years spent in those practices that are supposed to bring forgetfulness, particularly to young men. Then, following his father's advice, he entered into an arranged marriage. Three years after that, his father died and Michel became Lord of Montaigne. Giving up his position in the Bordeaux parlement he returned home, taking with him the library of La Boétie, who had bequeathed it to him, as Michel said, "with such loving recommendation, with death in his throat" (I:28, p. 136). There, in the famous tower, in a study next to the library, he caused the following inscription in Latin to be placed on the wall: "In the year of Christ 1571, at the age of thirty-eight, on the last day of February, anniversary of his birth, Michel de Montaigne, long weary of the servitude of the court and of public employments, while still entire, retired to the bosom of the [Muses], where in calm and freedom from all cares he will spend what little remains of his life now more than half run out. If the fates permit, he will complete this abode, this sweet ancestral retreat; and he has consecrated it to his freedom, tranquility, and leisure" (Frame, 1965, p. 115).

Fortunately this devout wish was not to be carried out. Though dutiful, he was not house-proud enough to "complete this abode," particularly since the improvements the old castle needed might make it desirable enough to invite pillage and invasion. And, lethargic though he pretended to be, he could not spend all his time in reading. In that direction, he told himself irritably, lay idleness or pedantry. Unless, he said, you keep minds "busy with some definite subject that will bridle and control them, they throw themselves in disorder hither and yon in the vague field of imagination" (I:8, p. 21). To rid himself of wildness, ineptitude, and strangeness, he concluded that he must "put them in writing, hoping in time to make my mind ashamed of itself" (I:8, p. 21).

What was he to write? Formal and didactic treatises, long or short, would limit his freedom of thought. He had no intimates to whom he might send letters. He did not wish to subject himself to the discipline of poetry. Moreover, he wanted, as he said, to "consider the various tastes of a whole public" (I:40, p. 186). And so, choosing some topic that occurred to him—in meditation, in discourse, in a dream, or in action—he set down his ideas, weaving in with them quotations from the authors he had been avidly reading since he was seven, and sometimes pacing his rooms or riding his horse until he could get a thought clear and stated with crispness and wit. These were not rounded and finished works. "My language is in every way," he confessed, "too compact, disorderly, abrupt, individual" (I:40, p. 186).

In the centuries of world-wide scholarship based on Montaigne's work, many overall plans, themes, and progressions of viewpoint have been proposed for the essays, but the author himself denied that he had any conscious structural design. Sometimes he explored a new topic, sometimes an old one, "I take the first subject that chance offers. They are all equally good to me. And I never plan to develop them completely. For I do not see the whole of anything; nor do those who promise to show it to us . . . I give it a stab . . . as deep as I know how. And most often I like to take it from some unaccustomed point of view" (I:50, p. 219). That beginning might be a witticism. He starts his essay "Of Three Good Women" with the observation that "they don't come by the dozen, as everyone knows" (II: 35, p. 563). He opens his essay "Of the Disadvantage of Greatness" with "Since we cannot attain it, let us take our revenge by speaking ill of it" (III:7, p. 699). The essay "Of Names" starts disarmingly with the observation that "I am here going to whip up a hodgepodge of various items" (I:46, p. 201). And often he uses an anecdote, as when in "Of the Vanity of Words" he gives the response of a Greek when asked whether he or Pericles was the better wrestler. " 'That' he said 'would be hard to establish; for when I have thrown him in wrestling, he persuades those who saw it happen that he did not fall, and he wins the prize" (I:51, p. 221).

Despite Montaigne's intentions recorded on his wall, most of his active career as political leader, negotiator, and traveler lay before him. But he kept at his study and writing for twenty-one years until his death in 1592. His first two books of essays were published in 1580, but even as he worked on the third, he kept adding to the earlier versions, and these changes were incorporated into subsequent editions. When in 1588 all three books were published, the first two were far more substantial than they had earlier been, and the third book had both a largeness of conception and a depth of penetration that the earlier ones lacked. But Montaigne was far from finished, for, from 1588 until very near his death, he kept adding to his own copy of his work, sometimes only a word or two, sometimes an apt quotation he had just discovered, sometimes a whole passage.

He seldom deleted anything, and often the new passages were digressions, unwieldy distensions, or contradictions. Thus one of his earliest essays is entitled "That to Philosophize Is to Learn to Die" (I:20), but later he wrote that "it is philosophy that teaches us to live" (I:26, p. 120). Diversity of viewpoint can be tolerated in an essay, and the reader of Montaigne must expect to find it, for this final personal copy has become the definitive source of later editions.

Modern collections of the essays distinguish in some fashion the material published before 1588, the material added in that year, and the material written by Montaigne on the margins of his own copy or on slips of paper. His writing grew more subtle and requires the reader to pay closer attention than is necessary for the earlier works. It is worthwhile to read at least one of the substantial essays three times, concentrating on each version separately. In later versions, tightness of structure is diminished and so is clarity of perspective, but the gain lies in the qualities that made Montaigne great: profundity of insight, brilliance of expression, vividness of imagery and anecdote, and sharpness of wit. He constantly grew as a result of both his experience and his reading; his education was essentially an adult one. In the ten years beginning with his thirty-eighth birthday, he learned to be great; in the next eleven years he learned to be immortal.

V

Both experience and literature were woven into his works, but since we can share only the books, let us concentrate upon his use of them. What books meant to Montaigne is hard to determine, for he has, in accommodating fashion, provided a text for every position possible, and scholars have made elaborate textual exegeses, traced attributions to sources, and made estimates about how much of the author's work was original and how much was derived from other sources. Ultimately this research suggests three governing propositions. Montaigne's thought was deeply rooted in literature, particularly classical literature. He used it for adornment, for evidence, and for author-

ity. His greatness arises because he brought to that literature his
experiences, his thoughts, and his literary skill.

As already noted, Montaigne had been a reader from an
early age and was fortunate to have the resources to range widely. Books were precious objects in those early days of printing,
and anyone who took them seriously usually became thoroughly immersed in them. His friendship with La Boétie was based
on their common love of literature. "I do not travel without
books," he said, "either in peace or in war. . . . I cannot tell you
what ease and repose I find when I reflect that they are at my
side to give me pleasure at my own time, and when I recognize
how much assistance they bring to my life" (III:3, p. 628). He
was familiar with the nuances of language, having translated
(before he began to write his own works) the thousand pages of
Raymond Sebond's *Theologia Naturalis* for his father, a man he
thought to have "very clear judgment for one who was aided
only by experience and nature" and not by reading (I:35, p.
165).

Almost every page of Montaigne's essays sparkles with
quotations. As time went on and revision followed revision, new
jewels were constantly added. One might use against him his
anecdote about Diogenes, who, when asked what sort of wine
he liked best, answered "other people's" (III:9, p. 726). Sometimes other people's comments are from new books; more often
they are from old ones, for, as their user observed, "books that I
revisit always smile at me with a fresh newness" (I:9, p. 23).
"In my youth," he also said, "I studied for ostentation; later, a
little to gain wisdom; now, for recreation; never for gain" (III:3,
p. 629). A reader might well conclude that all these thousands
of quotations, inserted with steadily increasing skill in the body
of his own work, were actually employed for all four ends.
Montaigne, at that moment, would not agree. Yet, at another he
would begin an essay on Seneca and Plutarch by saying that his
own work had been "built up purely from their spoils" (II:32,
p. 545).

One essay that seems remarkably free of quotation is his
description of cannibals, one of whom had recently been
brought to France and subjected to the author's close scrutiny.

Here, scholars have said, is the pure Montaigne, building his conclusions from his own experience. Not so, says the modern
scholar Bernard Weinberg. Going back into the literature available to Montaigne, Weinberg discovered the work of an author
who had lived in Brazil, from whose writings two other authors,
also once resident there, had borrowed heavily for their own
books. Montaigne, in turn, had used all three. Hardly a passage
of his essay is not close in content or language to one of these
sources, and yet his emphasis and balance are consistently different from theirs. As Weinberg says, "He cares less than they
about cannibalism, gore, items of idle curiosity; he cares more
about morals, virtue, and a way of life that might illustrate the
philosophical points that he was making" (1968, p. 278). But
that he used the books, though without citing them, there can
be no doubt. Weinberg concludes, "Whether he went back to
his books by rereading and consulting, or whether he made
reference only through the memory as stimulated by . . . conversations, I cannot be sure. But I think that both probably
took place" (p. 279). What Montaigne brought to his reading
made his essay immortal; his three sources are known only to
specialists.

     A novice might believe that Montaigne, one of the best-
known readers of all time, had a consistent theory about the
value of reading. On other subjects—such as the evils of medicine—he certainly did. But on books and their study and enjoyment he presents many contradictory views. In one of my
readings of his essays, I copied more than a hundred aphoristic
statements that deal generally with books and reading (ignoring observations on particular authors or on such literary areas
as history or poetry). These statements ranged on the spectrum
of enthusiasm from "the study of books is a languishing and
feeble activity" (III:8, p. 704) to books are "the best provision I have found for this human journey" (III:3, p. 628).

     Despite the range of these points of view, those who
have studied Montaigne most deeply in all his varied patterns of
belief have usually believed that books were central to his
thought. Bayle St. John, an Englishman writing in 1858, observed simply, "Montaigne, then, was essentially a reader" (p.

60). And R. A. Sayce, an American writing in 1972, agrees that "if his own mind and the world refracted through it are Montaigne's subjects, the instruments he uses to measure and grasp them are primarily books" (p. 25).

The ultimate truth seems to be that, for Montaigne, reading always was an activity as natural and necessary as eating. Some books were better than others, some suited his tastes while others did not, and variety was best of all. When one had not been able to read for a time, books were seized on ravenously; when one was satiated, one turned away from them to another resource or experience. But life could not be sustained without them; the mind could not grow in their absence.

VI

In this respect, as in so many others, "each man bears the entire form of man's estate" and the ways most serious learners acquire knowledge may be essentially habitual and blend together in ways unforeseen by them. When, at the age of thirty-eight, Montaigne designed his own further education, he chose reading as his paramount method, but perhaps that choice had already been ordained by the fact that it was an integral part of his life as indeed were the other ways—travel, discourse, politics, and estate management—by which his knowledge was increased. Perhaps it was only in retrospect that he saw that all of them were important. His motto was "What do I know?" and he chose as the epigraph for the culminating edition of his work "He acquires strength as he goes." He must have understood that personal power develops through knowledge gained from the steady and judicious use of experience, including reading. He also knew that, in writing of himself, he was describing fundamental aspects of the human condition.

References

Eliot, T. S. *Essays Ancient and Modern*. New York: Harcourt Brace Jovanovich, 1936.

Emerson, R. W. *Representative Men*. Boston: Houghton Mifflin, 1883.

Frame, D. M. *Montaigne, A Biography*. New York: Harcourt Brace Jovanovich, 1965.

Lowenthal, M. (Ed.). *The Autobiography of Michel de Montaigne*. Boston: Houghton Mifflin, 1935.

Montaigne, M. de. *Complete Works*. (D. M. Frame, Trans.) Stanford, Calif.: Stanford University Press, 1967.

St. John, B. *Montaigne, the Essayist*. London: Chapman and Hall, 1858.

Sainte-Beuve, C. A. *Nouveaux Lundis*. Vol. II. 1863.

Sayce, R. A. *The Essays of Montaigne: A Critical Exploration*. Chicago: Northwestern University Press, 1972.

Weinberg, B. "Montaigne's Readings for *Des Cannibals*." In G. B. Daniel (Ed.), *Renaissance and Other Studies in Honor of William Leon Wiley*. Chapel Hill: University of North Carolina Press, 1968.

Woolf, V. *The Common Reader*. New York: Harcourt Brace Jovanovich, 1925.

3

"He"

Using Tutors, Colleagues, and Self-Disciplined Practice

I

The theme of this chapter, as of the previous one, is the nurturing of genius. Some of those who possess it, like Mozart or Shakespeare, seem to flourish without forethought or care, but most of the gifted must cultivate their powers, although they may suggest—and even believe—that the natural force that created their brilliance also disciplined it. A few of those who go far beyond normal accomplishment not only use a carefully mastered craftsmanship but are eager to write about what they have learned. Among the greatest of them was a man who chose a narrow framework for the expression of his art, but, by ardent labor, so expanded its scope that his thought influences the lives of all of us—literary artists, scholars, or common folk.*

This chapter was previously published as Club Paper 78, Chicago Literary Club, 1970, and later appeared in *Perspectives in Biology and Medicine*, 1971, *15* (1), 94–109. Used with permission.

*This chapter was written as a paper to be read at the annual ladies' night celebration of the Chicago Literary Club and the title was picked with that fact in mind. A pleasant tradition of the Club leads many authors

He was, it has been said, "easy to hate, but still easier to quote" (Birrell, 1888, p. 55). He was equally easy to love, and it is well to begin this account with the story of one who did so.

II

When Edith Sitwell was eleven years old, she was required to memorize *Casabianca,* the poem that begins: "The boy stood on the burning deck / Whence all but him had fled." The Victorian era has been noted for the violence of the revolutions mounted against it, but perhaps not even the emotion that motivated Karl Marx or Sigmund Freud was stronger than the choked fury of little Edith when compelled to master this piece of verse. Her revolt took an interesting form: She fell deeply in love with the next poet whose work she read (Sitwell, 1965, pp. 38-39). He seemed to her to be incomparably graceful, blending profundity of feeling with mastery of content and sureness of touch. For him, she developed a lifelong crush excessive even in a schoolgirl but odd indeed when expressed by the awesome Dame Edith, whose intimidating force in English letters led her to call herself "an electric eel in a pond of catfish" (Brophy, 1968, p. 10).

By the age of forty-three, although the flame of her adoration had still not dwindled to a steady glow, she was able to set down a biography of the man she worshipped. The frontispiece is an engraving of a slender and willowy but mature Edith, gazing deeply into the eyes of a bust of her hero and wreathing him with a garland of laurel. The object of her adulation was, she concedes, a "little, deformed creature," a "crippled hunchback" who was "liable to bursts of fury," who was "tortuous in his dealings" and "capable of suppressing or altering passages in his letters which might not exhibit him in the

---

to select obscure or ambiguous titles whose meaning is revealed somewhere within the paper itself. In the present case, this tradition is carried to its ultimate conclusion. The readers of subsequent drafts of the paper were as intrigued by its unconventionality as were the earlier auditors; therefore this chapter retains the original form. Anybody who does not want to play the game has only to look at the last two words of the chapter.

light in which he wished to appear," who was "uncandid," and who lived "in an atmosphere of spells, enchantments, and fairy tales," many of them created by himself. And yet, she adds, he was a "creature of genius," "the purest of our artists," "beyond all praise," "perhaps the most flawless artist our race has produced," and with "the most subtle and sensitive feeling for beauty of form" of any English writer. She speaks glowingly of "the greatness, the fire, the supreme music" of his poems. All this is said before she has reached the twentieth page of her long book—and her ardor does not diminish as she proceeds (Sitwell, 1930).

Many other literary artists have had as pronounced a view of her hero as did Dame Edith, although some have stressed the positive and some the negative side of his work and character. Even in the nineteenth century, when his reputation fell so low that Matthew Arnold and others denied that he was a poet at all (Strachey, 1925, p. 11), he had his defenders. Charles Lamb said he could read him "over and over for ever" (Tillotson, 1959, p. 29). William Thackeray called him "the greatest literary *artist* that England has seen" ([1853], 1911, p. 141). G. K. Chesterton believed that "in all the forms of art which peculiarly belong to civilisation, he was supreme" (1903, p. 47). Countless other authors and critics have found new depths in the work of the master, flying to his defense, celebrating his virtues, regarding him with astonishment, and, in generation after generation, starting up again the drum beats of praise.

In recent years, as literary criticism has become a major industry, the mills of the academic gods have ground his work exceedingly fine. The earnest reader is now provided abundantly with treatments of and special approaches to his life, his character, his poetic technique, his documentary sources, and his literary debts and associations. Every year from thirty to fifty studies are centered on him and his work. His narrow shoulders have lifted many a scholar to the doctorate or even to academic tenure.

It cannot be said that large numbers of readers are intimately familiar with his poems. But his words and thoughts pervade our culture, so that, in addition to the high road traveled by one genius recognizing another and the low road of the researcher delving into roots and sources, the byway of chance leads less specialized men and women to him. Again and again some occurrence calls up a line or pair of lines that states a point of view so perfectly that no other words can say it so well. He aimed at precisely that effect. See how much better he put the thought than I have just done: "True Wit is Nature to advantage dressed, / What oft was thought, but ne'er so well expressed."*

He can thrust himself into our consciousness anywhere. We wander across an ancient Greek plain, straggling along behind the guide. He seats us on the rocks, points to a disagreeable-looking seeping-up of moisture, says that it is the Pierian Spring, and starts off on one of his rigid recitations. But our minds wander. The Pierian Spring. Where have we heard of it? Surely not in this Homeric context of sea-blue sky or rust-brown boulders. A sentence shapes itself: "Drink fully or avoid the Pierian Spring." Not right. Not right at all! Then suddenly it comes, perfect and full blown: "A little learning is a dang'rous thing; / Drink deep, or taste not the Pierian spring."

Again, years after an elective course in Shakespeare, we remember and quote with approval reinforced by age the rhymed couplet with which Polonius ends his speech to Laertes: "Be not the first by whom the new are tried, / Nor yet the last to lay the old aside." We are told that we have misidentified the quotation. We scoff, we back our memory with money, and we lose the money, for it was not Polonius who said it nor Shakespeare who wrote it.

Again and again the examples come:

> For Forms of Government let fools contest;
> Whate'er is best administered is best.

> To err is human, to forgive, divine.

> Men must be taught as if you taught them not,
> And things unknown proposed as things forgot.

---

*All sources of poetry are listed by first line in the References at the end of this chapter.

Hope springs eternal in the human breast.

Nature, and Nature's laws, lay hid in night,
God said, *Let Newton be!* And all was light.

For Fools rush in where Angels fear to tread.

Lo, the poor Indian! whose untutored mind
Sees God in clouds, or hears him in the wind.

Know then thyself, presume not God to scan;
The proper study of Mankind is Man.

Then, for more than a few readers, his shadowy figure moves from the rear of the stage to full center. Take my case: I was idling along the shelves of a bookstore after lunch one rainy day, avoiding an overhasty return to work. A book with a bright yellow cover caught my eye. I reached over to pick it up, a passer-by jostled my elbow, the book dropped to the floor into a puddle of water left there by a dripping umbrella, and, at the same moment, the clerk caught my eye and, with a frown, moved severely toward me. An astonishing combination of events: the color, the movement, the passer-by, the puddle, the stern glance, the sinking realization that I would have to buy the book. It must all have been chance—or so my literal mind insists. But back at my desk, as I looked idly at my new purchase, a hunchbacked figure rose from its pages, flicked the tails of his greatcoat, fixed me with his viperous glare, and, in his melodious voice, began to put his marvelously compressed bits of wisdom into the larger contexts in which they first appeared.

It is the brilliant writing itself that most fascinates the reader, whether it is viewed as a series of perfectly framed one- or two-line statements or as a group of epic essays and narratives. But two other elements add to its author's compelling power. His character was so arresting that it colored everything he thought and said and all that has since been thought or said about him. And his was a talent so laboriously perfected that he stands forever as the model of the self-taught genius. Not for him the instant careless perfection, the unblotted line. He got the effect of spontaneity, but he worked hard to do so.

Perhaps it is this last attribute that has so powerfully attracted later authors, particularly poets, who, like the members of any other profession, are deeply interested in shoptalk. How can words and pauses, vowels and consonants and punctuation marks, lines, meters, and rhythms, allusions and references all be brought together into the harmonious whole that expresses an idea and a mood with the greatest possible feeling of freshness and originality? Perhaps nobody has ever achieved this universal aspiration more perfectly than Dame Edith's darling.

III

He was born in 1688, the only child of his parents' union, and he lived for fifty-six years. All his life was spent in England, most of it in London or in the countryside not far away. He had only a sketchy schooling, but his self-taught learning was prodigious. He never married, but he had a multitude of friends and acquaintances—and of enemies. He was a Roman Catholic at a time when the members of that faith were subjected to unceasing restraints and persecutions. Yet the chief obstacle that both nature and society required him to surmount was the grotesqueness of his body, a fact that nobody who knew him could forget and that we must constantly remember.

His father had a curved spine and his mother had racking headaches; he inherited both, the doctors of the time said learnedly. When he was three, he was knocked down, trampled, and gored by a cow. Beginning at the age of twelve, he had a progressive degeneration of the spine. At his full growth, he was only four feet, six inches high. His contemporaries said that he had a "little, tender, and crazy carcase" (Sitwell, 1930, p. 43), that he was a "young, short, squab gentleman," and that he was "protuberant behind and before" (Johnson, [1781], 1936, p. 307). Samuel Johnson reported that "when he rose, he was invested in bodice[s] made of stiff canvas, being scarce able to hold himself erect till they were laced, and he then put on a

flannel waistcoat. One side was contracted. His legs were so
slender, that he enlarged their bulk with three pair of stockings,
which were drawn on and off by the maid, for he was not able
to dress or undress himself, and neither went to bed nor rose
without help. His weakness made it very difficult for him to be
clean" ([1781], 1936, p. 308).

His head was noble but ravaged with suffering. Sir Joshua
Reynolds reported that "he had a large and very fine eye, and
a long handsome nose; his mouth had those peculiar marks
which always are found in the mouths of crooked persons; and
the muscles which run across the cheek were so strongly marked
as to appear like small cords" (Prior, 1860, p. 429). Louis
François Roubiliac, who sculptured a bust of him, noted that
"his countenance was that of a person who had been much afflicted with headache" and went on to say that even if he, Roubiliac, had not been told of this suffering, he would have detected it by "the contracted appearance of the skin between the
eyebrows" (Prior, 1860, p. 429).

The poet was tiny, he was misshapen, he was in constant
pain, he was a member of a persecuted religious group—and he
was far from being purified into saintliness by his suffering. Dr.
Johnson's analysis of the darker side of his character occupies
ten close-packed pages, and even those who loved him most
could not close their eyes to his faults. He was vain, demand-
ing, self-indulgent, constantly engaged in intrigues, capriciously
resentful, miserly, snobbish, deceitful, and discontented. He had
no firm conception of the truth as far as the facts of his own life
were concerned and was ready to conceal, to embellish, or to lie
to aid his reputation. He spent much of his genius in savage and
vindictive warfare, sometimes attacking men so inconsequential
that they are now remembered only because of his hatred. His
great passages of invective are the purest distillations of literary
vitriol imaginable. One celebrated quotation will illustrate the
point:

>   Yet let me flap this bug with gilded wings,
>   This painted child of dirt, that stinks and stings;
>   Whose buzz the witty and the fair annoys,

> Yet wit ne'er tastes, and beauty ne'er enjoys: . . .
> Eternal smiles his emptiness betray,
> As shallow streams run dimpling all the way.
> Whether in florid impotence he speaks,
> And, as the prompter breathes, the puppet squeaks;
> Or at the ear of *Eve,* familiar Toad,
> Half froth, half venom, spits himself abroad,
> In puns, or politics, or tales, or lies,
> Or spite, or smut, or rhymes, or blasphemies.

Without resorting to example, let it also be said that the poet was sometimes obsessed with the orifices of the body and their discharges, with venereal diseases and disorders, and with the more extreme effects of nausea. He called himself a spider, and he could be a poisonous one.

But although no valid balance sheet of his or any other person's character can be drawn, it must be said that few people of his time had a larger or more diverse circle of friends and acquaintances than did he. Some were attracted by his great fame, but many were drawn by his kindness, his luminous discourse, or his considerateness. He was a faithful friend, he disciplined himself far more than he did other people, and he could be very kind to those in trouble or in need.

He was also a man of hard, shrewd business sense. He had to be, for his father left him little or nothing, his religion (which his name called constantly to mind) barred all customary roads of advancement or compensation in government or the established church, and his misshapen body was too weak to allow any imaginable work other than that which he actually undertook. He was the first man of letters to earn his livelihood —indeed, to make a small fortune—solely from the royalties that came from the sale of his works. Earlier authors had inherited or married money, had lived on the favor of rich patrons, had had governmental or religious sinecures, or had starved. He was fortunate enough to appear just at the time when publishers had built up enough wealth to permit them to undertake substantial ventures and to pay their authors appropriately. He took full advantage of his situation. The publishers helped him become

famous by the age of twenty-five; then he used his fame to drive
shrewd bargains with them. His modest wealth permitted him
to be fiercely independent. He rejected the patronage offered
him by noblemen and politicians, even when they promised to
keep their benefactions secret. He refused large bribes from
those who wanted to buy immortality by being mentioned in
his work. He did not want to have it influenced or even thought
to be influenced by any person or party, for, as Dr. Johnson so
justly asked, "of what could he be proud but of his poetry?"
([1781], 1936, p. 314).

IV

The most extraordinary fact about his literary artistry
was the narrowness of its framework. He could have used any of
the vast array of poetic forms created in the classical tradition,
in which he was firmly rooted, or by the English and continen-
tal authors whose work he knew so well. But not for him the
variety offered by Homer, Horace, Dante, Spenser, Shakespeare,
or Milton. All his notable work was cast in the simple framework of the rhyming couplet, each line made up of five iambic
feet. He had only two lines of ten syllables each to work with,
and the final syllables of each pair of lines had to have the same
sound. Occasionally, to show his virtuosity or to make a point,
he would add an extra syllable or cut one out; or he would shift
the meter or use an extra foot; or he would resort to assonance
rather than rhyme. But mostly he limited himself to uniform
twenty-syllable sets. A single poem might have hundreds or even
thousands of couplets, every one of them separately fashioned
and then linked with all the others in a smooth flow of meaning. He once spoke with amusement of a "fellow that spent his
life in cutting the twelve apostles in one cherry-stone" (Quennell, 1968, p. 186), but his own form of expression sometimes
seems almost as limiting as that of the sculptor. His accomplishment lay in the infinite variety he achieved, as he made the
poetic couplet truly heroic.

The constant use of this one form, even in his masterful
hands, can lead to monotony. The tripping rhymes and rhythms

and the cadence that seldom breaks its step and is used to deal with both the loftiest and the meanest thoughts cause many readers finally to flee, pursued by the incessant tinkling of the beat. In a moment of despair he may even have had the same feeling. "I should be sorry and ashamed," he wrote, "to go on jingling to the last step, like a waggoner's horse in the same road, to leave my bells to the next silly animal that will be proud of them" (Quennell, 1968, p. 96).

But to the sensitive ears of his poetic followers, he seemed to enlarge the unvarying structure until it comprehended the universe, producing an endless array of nuances of rhythm, speed, and depth, and catching every mood of people and nature, from the glistening insubstantiality of a cobweb to the thunder of doom. He could write:

> The sprightly Sylvia trips along the green,
> She runs, but hopes she does not run unseen.

But he could also write:

> She comes! she comes! the sable Throne behold
> Of Night primeval and of Chaos old!

V

Having chosen this form, he devoted his life to its perfection, beginning early in his childhood. His was an isolated home near Windsor Forest, and his parents were simple folk. His father gloried in his ability to grow artichokes, and his mother's portrait reminded Dame Edith "of all kind, homely things—of cold sheets and of home-made bread and butter, and sweet dews on a field of cowslips, and moonlight that is smooth and cold as amber" (Sitwell, 1930, p. 33). (I do not know who painted this remarkable portrait.) But the parents of the solitary boy had standards. His father was not often pleased by his early poems. "These are not good rhymes," he would observe and require the boy to do them over (Quennell, 1968, p. 1). Later that son would write, "My Father taught me from a lad, / The better art to know the good from bad."

By his own testimony, not always reliable, there was never a time when he did not plan to be a poet.

> Why did I write? What sin to me unknown
> Dipped me in ink, my parents', or my own?
> As yet a child, nor yet a fool to fame,
> I lisped in numbers, for the numbers came.

By the age of twelve, he had already achieved his ambition to see the great John Dryden. Not too many years later, he was himself famous. But the intervening years, like those that followed, were filled with the incessant labor required to perfect his powers. With only indifferent instruction, he had mastered the rudiments of a classical education. His Catholicism barred him from good schools or from study at a university. The cultivation of his genius lay almost entirely in his own hands and at his own initiative. How did he do it?

VI

One way was to seek out men and women who had had broad worldly experience and to probe deeply into their minds and memories. His extraordinary talent for reaching the hearts of those who could help him was first demonstrated when Sir William Trumbull, a sixty-year-old ex-ambassador and minister of state, settled down near Windsor, admired the artichokes, and was at once seized upon by the teenage poet so powerfully that the learning, wit, and worldliness of the older man were drawn into the mind of the younger. Another close associate was William Walsh, a member of Parliament but also a poet, who not only taught his young friend about the world but also constantly urged him to revise and correct his work—and was as a consequence later apostrophized:

> Such late was Walsh—the Muse's judge and friend,
> Who justly knew to blame or to commend; . . .
> This praise at least a grateful Muse may give:
> The Muse, whose early voice you taught to sing,
> Prescribed her heights, and pruned her tender wing.

Trumbull and Walsh were but the first of the lifelong line of intimates who knew the world and could interpret it. Beyond them lay the great country houses of England and the literary lights of London.

In one area of his new life the budding poet needed particular instruction. He moved into a free-and-easy, outspoken society whose interest could not long be held by dainty pastorals and hymns to rural nymphs. And so he sought out the company of rakes and ladies of the town, perhaps to gain an understanding of the lustier human passions, perhaps to feel the vicarious thrill that may have been the only kind his grotesqueness allowed. After a disastrous experience or two in company with young sports, he tended to choose as his companions the older gallants. They could accept the poet, smile at his sniggering pretensions to share their amorous adventures, and kindly protect him—as younger men had not—from being put to the test of performance.

He had a wide acquaintance among gentlewomen, and with a few the relationship became both close and long. Its exact nature in each case has never been accurately defined. Though he constantly suggested that his liaisons were of the closest physical sort, the ardor of his letters tended to increase with his distance from his feminine correspondent. The society of his own age gossiped about him—could he or couldn't he?—and modern Freudians have learnedly dissected the complexity of his emotional attachments with a vivid explicitness perhaps better known to them than to him. When one remembers his physical presence, it is possible to believe that, no matter how strong his passions, nothing very intimate ever transpired. He was, perhaps, a safe man in whom a woman could confide, for, in the ordinary way, he could neither offer a hope nor pose a threat. Meanwhile he could probe deep into her emotions and viewpoints, building insights and perceptions to be revealed in his poetry.

He also had close and continuing associations with his fellow professionals. With such men as William Wycherley, William Congreve, Joseph Addison, Sir Richard Steele, Jonathan Swift, John Gay, and Voltaire he discussed the nuances of poetry and gained the advantages of comparison, criticism, col-

laboration, and occasional competition. His contact with these
men was sometimes casual, as when they met one another at
dinners or in the coffeehouse intellectual society of the time. It
could also be close, as when he spent weeks on end with Walsh
studying ancient and modern poetry. That was an era, too,
when literary men were much given to forming clubs to discuss
and criticize one another's work. The young man from Windsor
soon joined in and through his whole life remained a member of
one or another study circle. Even when a group of poets met to
lampoon hilariously the failings of their lesser contemporaries,
each taught the others what not to do.

VII

However much the poet's erudition might be enlarged or
his skill refined by association with other people, study and
writing are solitary pursuits and their hardest lessons must be
self-taught. The boy was bookish and the man remained so, por-
ing over ancient and contemporary volumes, acquiring the knowledge of both classical and modern sources that would be reflected in his poems. His "appetite for knowledge" was "too
eager to be nice," according to Dr. Johnson ([1781], 1936, p.
239), and in borrowing ideas from Lord Bolingbroke or editing
Shakespeare, the poet showed his lack of scholarship. But he
read avidly, and the results of that reading were all too clear in
his early work. Like many another budding author, he began
by imitation and by experimenting with technique. Between the
ages of twelve and fifteen, he was hard at work on an epic
poem, of which he later said, "There was Milton's style in one
part and Cowley's in another, here the style of Spenser imitated and there of Statius, here Homer and Virgil, and there
Ovid and Claudian" (Spence, 1966, p. 18). This work he later
destroyed, probably prudently, as he came to realize that the
task of the poet is to be original.

Most writers who reach this conclusion turn away from
their models and seek inspiration wholly in themselves. But
there is a diametrically opposed way of working that requires
the discovery of fundamental principles of an art and their

study and conscious use. Such was the aim of the young genius. The public, he well knew, expected poetry to rise solely through inspiration and liked to think that "fluent Shakespeare scarce effaced a line." But as far as he could read the ancient masters of literature, "they constantly applied themselves not only to that art, but to that single branch of an art, to which their talent was most powerfully bent" (1769, p. xi). As for himself, he freely confessed his need to take pains: "I have served myself all I could by reading;... I made use of the judgment of authors dead and living;... I omitted no means in my power to be informed of my errors, both by my friends and enemies" (1769, p. xi).

His major learning period began at the age of twenty and was a truly adult education. William Warburton, who knew him well, describes it in this way: "He went over all the parts of his education a-new, from the very beginning, and in a regular, and more artful manner. He penetrated into the general grounds and reasons of speech; he learnt to distinguish the several species of style; he studied the peculiar genius and character of each language; he reduced his natural talent for poetry to a science, and mastered those parts of philosophy that would most contribute to enrich his vein. And all this, with such continued attention, labour, and severity, that he used to say, he had been seven years (that is, from twenty to twenty-seven) in unlearning all he had been acquiring for twice seven" (Spence, 1966, p. 22).

The work that made the young poet famous was a report on his continuing researches into the essence of a poetic style, and he returned to this topic again and again, giving its rules, showing their application, and ridiculing the bores and dunces who did not follow them. His age self-consciously patterned itself on the life, literature, and art of the Roman era of Augustus, believing that the lessons of the ancients had been forgotten and that no new canons had arisen to take their place. The announced purpose of the young poet was to give form and style to poetry, to study the unchangeable laws of language that provide opportunity, challenge, and discipline to those who follow them. Lord Bolingbroke, the great Tory leader, reinforced the poet's aim, assuring him that Homer had laid the groundwork for Greek, Virgil had established Latin, and that, while English was still in flux, the young man from Windsor would "contribute to fix it" and so "deserve to be translated three thousand years hence into languages perhaps as yet unformed" (Quennell, 1968, p. 200).

The recipient of this praise thought he could perceive the true source of poetic art. It was nature. Modern scholars have counted the number of times he used the word and have elaborated the variations of its meaning as derived from its context. We cannot here follow all these twists and turns. In general, he held that all life has an inherent harmony that people must seek to understand.

> Unerring Nature, still divinely bright,
> One clear, unchanged, and universal light,
> Life, force, and beauty, must to all impart,
> At once the source, and end, and test of Art.

Some of nature's universal truths have been revealed, he claimed, particularly to poets:

> Those Rules of old discovered, not devised,
> Are Nature still, but Nature methodized;
> Nature, like Liberty, is but restrained
> By the same Laws which first herself ordained.

He believed that one must therefore learn those rules by study, by application, and by constant experimentation.

But he, who had been told to fix the language, sought to interpret nature by discovering the rules that govern poetic statement when nature speaks English. This he did in abundance and detail. Thus, he said, "*Monosyllable-Lines,* unless very artfully managed, are stiff, or languishing: but may be beautiful to express Melancholy, Slowness, or Labor." He objected to "the *Repetition* of the same rhimes within four or six lines of each other, as tiresome to the Ear thro their Montony." He noted that in a ten-syllable line there is usually a pause after the fourth, fifth, or sixth syllable and said that "to preserve an

exact Harmony and Variety, the Pause of the 4th or 6th shou'd
not be continu'd above three lines together, without the Inter-
position of another; else it will be apt to weary the Ear with one
continu'd Tone, at least it does mine" (Sherburn, 1956, p.
23). For each kind of poetry he sought to write, he was careful to establish the particular principles; thus he prefaced his
early pastorals with a discourse on the rules that he had followed in writing them. Again and again he stressed his belief
that a poet can learn only by studying the greatest masters:

Be Homer's Works your Study and Delight,
Read them by Day and meditate by Night,
Thence form your Judgment, thence your Maxims bring,
And trace the Muses upward to their Spring.

Later generations have tried to trace his own genius upward to its spring. Scholars have worked over almost every line,
drawing diagrams, making comparisons, and deriving principles
that are sometimes too rarefied to be easily understood. A particularly fruitful field for study has been the comparison of various drafts of some passages. He left behind his work sheets and
many versions of his poems; the task of comparing them has
never ceased to fascinate his successors. Thus, a rough draft of
one important couplet reads: "The stern Pelides' rage, O goddess, sing / Of all the woes of Greece the fatal spring." The finished version reads: "The wrath of Peleus' son, the direful
spring / Of all the Grecian woes, O goddess sing!" To Dame
Edith, "the reason for most of these alterations is obvious. The
'i' sound in Pelides, quickly followed by the 'a' in rage, un-
hinge the line by giving too violent a lifting movement to the
middle of the line. The word 'direful' with its huge fiery smoky
sound, is obviously better, in its place in the line, than the
smaller and rather tinny sound of 'fatal,' which is not heavy
enough" (Sitwell, 1930, pp. 115-116).
　　His profoundest rule of composition was one to which he
referred in many places and that he applied with unparalleled
mastery throughout the whole body of his work. Its most celebrated statement was "The sound must seem an Echo to the

sense." The use of this principle within the limitations of the simple rhyming couplet gave him full opportunity to display his virtuosity. Thus, in three successive couplets, he conveys tranquility, storm, and toil:

> Soft is the strain when Zephyr gently blows,
> And the smooth stream in smoother number flows;
> But when loud surges lash the sounding shore,
> The hoarse, rough verse should like the torrent roar;
> When Ajax strives some rock's vast weight to throw,
> The line too labours, and the words move slow.

He seemed capable of catching the sound of almost any mood or phenomenon:

> The spider's touch, how exquisitely fine!
> Feels at each thread, and lives along the line.

> Shut, shut the door, good John! Fatigued, I said,
> Tie up the knocker, say I'm sick, I'm dead.

> A needless Alexandrine ends the song
> That, like a wounded snake, drags its slow length along.

> Now lap-dogs give themselves the rousing shake,
> And sleepless lovers, just at twelve, awake.

> The Muse but served to ease some friend, not Wife,
> To help me through this long disease, my Life.

The poet must keep all such rules as these, grand or small, vigilantly in mind to retain his or her powers, for the very action of time will otherwise erode them:

> Years following years, steal something every day,
> At last they steal us from ourselves away;
> In one our Frolics, one Amusements end,
> In one a Mistress drops, in one a Friend:

> This subtle Thief of life, this paltry Time,
> What will it leave me, if it snatch my rhyme?
> If every wheel of that unwearied Mill
> That turned ten thousand verses, now stands still?

Thus it was that the researches of the poet and his effort to illu-
minate principle lasted all his life as he set ever more lofty goals
for himself:

> Late as it is, I put myself to school,
> And feel some comfort, not to be a fool . . . .
> Not to go back, is somewhat to advance,
> And men must walk at least before they dance.

VIII

But although he could teach anybody how to walk, neither he nor anyone else could teach the untalented how to
dance. He knew this truth from his own experience, for he long
studied the art of painting from his friend Charles Jervas. Now
Jervas had no shadow of a doubt concerning his own brilliance.
To amuse himself he once copied a painting of Titian; when he
saw how much the imitation excelled the original, he remarked,
"Poor little Tit, how he would stare!" (Sitwell, 1930, p. 81).
Yet not even Jervas could help the poet learn how to paint. "I
comfort myself," the poet wrote his friend Gay, "that I have
not broken the commandments, for my pictures are not the
likeness of anything in heaven above, or in the earth below, or
in the waters under the earth" (Sitwell, 1930, pp. 100-101).
However important his processes of self-education, the essence of his success cannot be found within them. His work
stood firmly on the high plateau of poetic rules and principles
to which he had so laboriously climbed, but his own achievement was a peak that towered above it. If there are rules that
governed his ultimate art, neither he nor any of the multitudes
of his admirers has known how to express them. He met the last
highest test that he himself set:

Let me for once presume t' instruct the times,
To know the Poet from the Man of rhymes:
'Tis he, who gives my breast a thousand pains,
Can make me feel each Passion that he feigns;
Enrage, compose, with more than magic Art,
With Pity, and with Terror, tear my heart;
And snatch me, o'er the earth, or through the air,
To Thebes, to Athens, when he will, and where.

Lord Byron, also crippled but different in every other way from the little genius, once called him "the most *faultless* of Poets, and almost of men," and later said, "I have always regarded him as the greatest name in our poetry" (1901, pp. 109, 274). His appeal, in his own time, as now, is so broad that it can be felt by both the sophisticated and the simple.

About 1740, the young Joshua Reynolds went one day to a crowded auction to attend a sale of pictures. Standing near the front, he presently noticed a bustle at the rear and heard the name of the poet whispered throughout the room. The company drew back in awe and made a passage for the little man who labored his slow way forward, bowing to right and to left. Reynolds saw him plain and clear, touched him, and never forgot the magnificence of the moment (Prior, 1860, pp. 428-429).

One summer, perhaps in that same year, a villager and his son were walking on a path near Twickenham when they passed a tiny hunchback in drab and ancient clothes limping to some unknown destination. "Poor man!" said the boy, filled with pity. "Poor man!" his father exclaimed; "that is no poor man. It is the great Mr. Alexander Pope" (Sitwell, 1930, p. 192).

References

Birrell, A. *Obiter Dicta*. (2nd series.) New York: Scribner's, 1888.

Brophy, J. D. *Edith Sitwell: The Symbolist Order*. Carbondale and Edwardsville: Southern Illinois University Press, 1968.

Byron, G. G. *Letters and Journals*. Vol. 5. London: John Murray, 1901.

Chesterton, G. K. *Varied Types*. New York: Dodd, Mead, 1903.

Johnson, S. "Pope." In *Lives of the English Poets*. Vol. 2. World Classics Edition. Oxford: Oxford University Press, 1936. (Originally published 1781.)

Pope, A. *Works*. Vol. 1. London: Bathurst, 1769.

Prior, J. *Life of Edward Malone*. London: Smith, Elder, 1860.

Quennell, P. *Alexander Pope*. New York: Stein and Day, 1968.

Sherburn, G. (Ed.). *The Correspondence of Alexander Pope*. Vol. 1. Oxford: Clarendon Press, 1956.

Sitwell, E. *Alexander Pope*. London: Faber and Faber, 1930.

Sitwell, E. *Taken Care Of*. New York: Atheneum, 1965.

Spence, J. *Observations, Anecdotes, and Characters of Books and Men*. Oxford: Clarendon Press, 1966.

Strachey, L. *Pope*. Cambridge, England: Cambridge University Press, 1925.

Thackeray, W. M. *The English Humorists of the 18th Century*. Boston: Ginn, 1911. (Originally published 1853.)

Tillotson, G. *On the Poetry of Pope*. Oxford: Clarendon Press, 1959.

Poetry Cited

References to Pope's poetry have been standardized in the various editions of his works. If a work is divided into parts, the roman numeral indicates the part in which the quotation is to be found and the arabic numeral or numerals indicates the line or lines within that part.

"True Wit . . ."—*Essay on Criticism*, II, 297-298.

"A little learning . . ."—*Essay on Criticism*, II, 215-216.

"Be not the first . . ."—*Essay on Criticism*, II, 335-336.

"For Forms of Government . . ."—*Essay on Man*, III, 303-304.

"To err is human . . ."—*Essay on Criticism*, II, 525.

"Men must be taught . . ."—*Essay on Criticism*, III, 574-575.

"Hope springs eternal . . ."—*Essay on Man*, I, 95.

"Nature, and Nature's laws . . ."—Newton's epitaph in Westminster Abbey.

"For Fools rush in . . ."—*Essay on Criticism*, III, 625.

"Lo, the poor Indian . . ."—*Essay on Man*, I, 99-100.

"Know then thyself . . ."—*Essay on Man*, II, 1-2.

"Yet let me flap . . ."—*Epistle to Dr. Arbuthnot*, 309-312, 315-322.

"The sprightly Sylvia . . ."—*Pastorals, Spring*, 57-58.

"She comes! . . ."—*Dunciad*, IV, 629-630.

"My Father taught me . . ."—*The Second Epistle of the Second Book of Horace*, 54-55.

"Why did I write? . . ."—*Epistle to Dr. Arbuthnot*, 125-129.

"Such late was Walsh . . ."—*Essay on Criticism*, III, 729-730, 734-736.

"Fluent Shakespeare . . ."—*The First Epistle of the Second Book of Horace*, 279.

"Unerring Nature . . ."—*Essay on Criticism*, I, 70-73.

"Those Rules of old . . ."—*Essay on Criticism*, I, 88-91.

"Be Homer's Works . . ."—*Essay on Criticism*, I, 124-127.

"The wrath of Peleus' son . . ."—*Iliad*, I, 1-2.

"The sound must seem . . ."—*Essay on Criticism*, II, 365.

"Soft is the strain . . ."—*Essay on Criticism*, II, 366-371.

"The spider's touch . . ."—*Essay on Man*, I, 217-218.

"Shut, shut the door . . ."—*Epistle to Dr. Arbuthnot*, 1-2.

"A needless Alexandrine . . ."—*Essay on Criticism*, II, 356-357.

"Now lap-dogs give themselves . . ."—*Rape of the Lock*, I, 15-16.

"The Muse but served . . ."—*Epistle to Dr. Arbuthnot*, 131-132.

"Years following years . . ."—*The Second Epistle of the Second Book of Horace*, 72-79.

"Late as it is . . ."—*The First Epistle of the First Book of Horace*, 47-48, 53-54.

"Let me for once presume . . ."—*The First Epistle of the Second Book of Horace*, 340-347.

4

Henry David Thoreau

Engaging in Small-Group Discussion, Self-Examination, and Observation

I

Our theme now turns away from the learning patterns of an individual and focuses instead upon the educative interaction of a man and an institution. A good point at which to begin is an early autumn morning in 1852 when a New Englander sat down at his desk in the bare room at the top of his mother's boarding-house. Whatever else he may have been, he was deeply sensitive to nature. He began the entry in his journal that morning by noting: "A warm rain-storm in the night, with wind, and to-day it continues. The first leaves begin to fall; a few yellow ones lie in the road this morning, loosened by the rain and blown off by the wind. The ground in orchards is covered with windfalls; imperfect fruits now fall" (X:323).* But another kind of imper-

---

*All references to Thoreau's writings are taken from the collected edition published in 1906; the roman numeral designates the volume and the arabic numeral the page.

fect fruit concerned Henry David Thoreau that morning. Plung-
ing forward with the eloquence of deep feeling, he wrote: "We
boast that we belong to the Nineteenth Century, and are making the most rapid strides of any nation. But consider how little
this village does for its own culture. We have a comparatively
decent system of common schools, schools for infants only, as
it were, but, excepting the half-starved Lyceum in the winter,
no school for ourselves" (X:323).

We shall eventually consider the rest of what he wrote
that morning, but a possibly unfamiliar word in the last sentence catches our attention. To Thoreau, as to most educated
people in the gloriously advanced nineteenth century, the
lyceum was too familiar to need explanation. Even today, most
literate people can fetch up out of their memories some kind of
association with the term, but unless they are students of cultural history their perceptions are likely to be half-formed, speculative, narrow, or wrong. For Thoreau, the lyceum was a central element of life, contributing to his ideas about human
association—ideas that are now helping to transform the world.

II

The lyceum was given its nineteenth-century meaning by
a Connecticut entrepreneur, Josiah Holbrook. He was graduated
from Yale in 1810 into a nation already strongly aware of itself
and beginning to feel the need for cultural as well as political
freedom. Ralph Waldo Emerson was later to declare the independence of American thought in his Phi Beta Kappa address at
Harvard in 1837; but, twenty years earlier, Holbrook felt the
stirrings and restlessness of cultivated people, often isolated by
the wilderness, who looked with distaste at their primitive life
almost devoid of intellectual companionship. By 1815, he was
traveling about New England giving lectures, usually on geology,
to groups of people wherever he could find them. He earned his
living by selling scientific equipment. If his intellectual endeavors stimulated the demand for his wares, his audiences
probably approved; he was acting in the best tradition of the
shrewd Yankee trader.

In 1826, he reinforced that tradition by moving into
what, even today, seems like a large-scale enterprise. His travels

had convinced him that all over the Eastern seaboard men and women hungered for learning. In the towns and villages that at best were seaports and could usually be reached only by long journeys on muddy or dusty rut roads, there were squires and parsons and schoolmasters and lawyers and doctors and town clerks and women with inquiring minds who had had some exposure to culture and whose intellectual life was not yet dead. Because these people were not clustered geographically, Holbrook proposed the creation of a network of groups, each to be locally organized but all to come together in state and national federations. These groups would read and discuss, they would hear local or imported lecturers, and they would elaborate such crucial issues as the proper development of the common schools.

What should such groups be called? Why not start with what, to classically educated people, would seem the grand example? Aristotle used for his classroom the shaded walks of a field called the Lyceum because it was near a temple of Apollo Lykeios. Perhaps the idea that every American hamlet should become a new Athens might not have been suggested by a more self-conscious or less patriotic man or one whose defensiveness had not been aroused by European sneers at American lack of culture, but Holbrook was not deterred by any such thoughts. Confidently he announced his plan to create an American lyceum, nationwide in scope, linking together all thoughtful and cultivated people in the continuing pursuit of knowledge. If there were those who smiled at his pretentiousness, they did not do so long. He had correctly assessed the temper of the times, and his energy and organizing ability proved equal to the task he set for himself. In less than ten years, 3,500 local lyceums had been established in sixteen state associations, with annual national meetings. In 1840, this superstructure collapsed, and the lyceums became wholly local, but their number may have continued to grow. Their continuing influence depended on the strength of their local leadership. Aristotles are in short supply, even in Massachusetts, one of whose citizens later observed that there were not ten men in Boston equal to Shakespeare.

Whatever may have happened in individual lyceums, their national influence was great. A nation with 3,500 or more local groups devoted to culture and made up essentially of the leaders of the community is different from a nation that does not have such a resource, not merely in the intellectual life afforded to individuals but also in the opportunity provided to hear about and to discuss social issues. The significance of the lyceums in building the American system of free public education has been carefully documented, and their value in other areas of social life may have been almost as important.

The lyceums were a great success as instruments of mass culture, but they also aided the creation of high culture. In each generation, perhaps, there can be only a few richly talented men and women, but their number is almost certainly augmented by the existence of a sensitive and appreciative audience. The lyceums gave this kind of a hearing (and also a livelihood) to such literary and intellectual leaders of the first half of the nineteenth century as Daniel Webster, Henry Ward Beecher, Horace Greeley, Louis Agassiz, Oliver Wendell Holmes, James Russell Lowell, Nathaniel Hawthorne, and Wendell Phillips. The most famous was Emerson. Late in life, his attitude grew equivocal. In his journal in 1865, he noted: " 'Twas tedious, the squalor and obstructions of travel; the advantage of their offers at Chicago made it necessary to go; in short, this dragging of a decorous old gentleman out of home and out of position to this juvenile career was tantamount to this,—'I'll bet you fifty dollars a day that you will not leave your library, and wade and ride and run and suffer all manner of indignities and stand up for an hour each night reading in a hall;' and I answered, 'I'll bet I will.' I do it and win the $900" (Perry, 1926, p. 310). But he knew that the months he spent each year lecturing to lyceums brought him more than money. He had the opportunity to clarify his ideas before thoughtful audiences and to shape and reshape the expression of his thoughts before they took final form in his great essays.

III

The lyceum at Concord, Massachusetts, came into being early in 1829. At Thanksgiving services in 1828, the Reverend Doctor Ezra Ripley gave notice of a meeting "to take into con-

sideration the expediency of forming a Lyceum in Concord"
and, on December 3, "a large and respectable meeting of citizens of Concord was convened." There was unanimous agree-
ment that a lyceum would be desirable, a committee of distinguished citizens was formed, and a constitution was presented
and discussed at three subsequent sessions and ratified on January 7. The rapidity of movement and the number of meetings
during the Christmas season suggest that the people of Concord
had either great enthusiasm or a lack of other things to do. Perhaps the lack created the enthusiasm.

In the Concord Free Public Library, the constitution and
minutes of the Concord lyceum still exist, the first document
set forth in the fine, clear handwriting (but with the uncertain
punctuation) of Lemuel Shattuck, recording secretary. It starts
out with a flourish: "We the subscribers, desirous of our own
improvement in Knowledge, the advancement of Popular Education, and the diffusion of useful information throughout the
community generally; and believing that these objects can be
more certainly, easily, and fully accomplished by united, than
by individual exertions; agree to associate under the name of
the *Concord Lyceum.*" Thus begins the record of an institution
that, despite occasional interludes and stormy episodes, sur-
vived for more than ninety years.

From the beginning, the Concord lyceum's greatest asset
was the fact that in and around the town and in nearby Boston
lived many of the literary, political, religious, and humanitarian
leaders of the time. A richness of talent was ready at hand that
perhaps no other lyceum in a town of comparable size could
command, then or now. To the lectures by such luminaries were
added debates between them, often on the same evenings, dealing with such issues as whether it is ever proper to offer forcible
resistance to oppression by the government. On this topic, Thoreau and his brother John took the affirmative and Amos Bron-
son Alcott the negative, but, although the subject was carried
over to the second week, the question was never put to the vote,
perhaps because the feelings of the audience were too intense.

The lyceum did not live always on a high intellectual
plane. Occasionally music—a concert by the town band—was in-

troduced into its program. On the evening of November 18, 1842, there was a discussion as to whether the meetings should be given a more social character. On this point the minutes read: "Drs. Alcott and Jarvis advocated the plan and thought such a change would the better promote the object of the Lyceum—but Dr. Tewksbury thought it was detracting somewhat from the dignity of the association to 'introduce soft talk and courting times' . . . into our meetings. The question was finally referred to the directors." The minutes of subsequent meetings suggest that those worthies listened to Dr. Tewksbury, not to his opponents.

As in every enduring human organization (and particularly so in one based solely on local initiative), the lyceum had its moments both of tedium and of excitement. Some evenings it could find no lecturers, or scheduled speakers failed to appear. There were perennial problems in getting members to serve as officers and curators and secretaries. Gaps in the minutes suggest either delinquent secretaries or a moribund lyceum. But there were also occasions of high drama. Here, for example, is the spare and rigidly decorous account of the meeting of March 5, 1845:

> After the lecture, Mr Saml. Barrett moved that the curators be requested to invite Mr Wendell Phillips to deliver a lecture on Slavery before the Lyceum on Wednesday of the ensueing week. Which motion after discussion was adopted by a vote of 21 to 15 as declared by the President.
>
> After the declaration of the vote two of the Curators Messrs Frost and Keyes resigned their office of curators.
>
> It was then moved to adjourn sine die, which motion was submitted to the Lyceum by the President & declared to be a vote. Which vote was immediately doubted, but without calling for the contrary minded or in any way settling the vote, the President left the chair.
>
> After calling for the Vice Presidents, Col

Wm. Whiting took the chair. On motion, Col Whiting was chosen President pro tem. The Lyceum then proceeded to fill the vacancies made by the resignation of Messrs Frost & Keyes. Thereupon Messrs Ralph W. Emerson, Saml. Barrett & David H. Thoreau were chosen curators by ballot.

On the following Wednesday evening, the lyceum listened to a lecture by Phillips on slavery.

Thoreau called the Concord lyceum "half-starved" and so it seems to have been. Its original constitution called for annual dues of two dollars for those living in "the centre school district in Concord" and one dollar for those living outside the district. A later hand has crossed out these figures and written in "one dollar" and "50 cts." Committees were occasionally appointed to collect funds for the further support of the lyceum. In 1839, the program included seven successive lectures by Emerson, at the last of which, Thoreau records in the minutes, "Mr. Frost made some remarks on the favor conferred on us by gratuitous lecturers." But, as Van Wyck Brooks has pointed out, "on evenings when the moon shone, the thrifty Concord folk turned out the streetlamps" (1937, p. 259), and such folk could buy a great deal for little cash. As Thoreau (admittedly a close man with a dollar) put it: "How much might be done for Concord with $100! I myself have once provided a select course of twenty-five lectures for a winter, together with rent, fuel, and lights, with that sum; which was no inconsiderable benefit to every inhabitant" (Sanborn, 1917, p. 316).

As the years went by, the depth of local involvement in the lyceum's program gradually diminished, and it turned into a scheduled series of hired lecturers and entertainment. As it did so, it found money to support its activities, presumably from gifts and bequests. In the curator's report for 1878-1879, it was noted that "not only is the Lyceum enjoying financial prosperity, and, therefore, the ability to procure the best talent in the lecture field, but, from an intellectual point of view, it is believed that the people of our town have gained new vigor of thought with the increased vitality of this institution, and will insist upon keeping this platform fearlessly free and independent of every narrowing influence. In this way only can the Lyceum continue to influence the community for good as it has already done for fifty years" (Low, 1959, p. 41). Thoreau, with his usual perversity, might not have been happy to see such prosperity, for, by its fiftieth year, the lyceum, though rich, had lost its chief resource: the continuing interaction of a group of men and women who were deeply concerned with their own education and felt a personal responsibility for it. What had formerly been provided freely must now be paid for.

IV

In his youth, Thoreau did not seem a likely prospect as a lyceum member or indeed as one much given to human companionship of any sort. As a student at the Concord Academy, he participated for about two years in an academic debating society along with eighteen other boys, aged eleven to thirteen. This dedicated group had a constitution and bylaws, and its successive secretaries left a record that is careful though misspelled. In it, Thoreau is mentioned only three times, always with disfavor. On November 5, 1829, for example, an item in the minutes suggests a good deal not only about Thoreau but also about the lofty moral attitude of the youthful secretary: "The discussion of the question selected for debate next followed, 'Is a good memory preferable to a good understanding in order to be a distinguished scholar at school?' E. Wright Aff. H. Thoreau Neg. The affirmative disputant, through negligence, had prepared nothing for debate, and the negative, not much more. Accordingly, no other member speaking, the President decided in the Neg. His decision was confirmed by a majority of four. Such a debate, if it may be called so, as we have had this evening, I hope never again will be witnessed in this house, or recorded in this book. It is not only a waste of time, but of paper to record such proceedings of wood and oil" (Nyren, 1964, pp. 94–95).

Nor was Thoreau much more responsive to society in his college days. One of his classmates at Harvard recalled him as he had been there: "He was cold and unimpressible. The touch of his hand was moist and indifferent, as if he had taken up something when he saw your hand coming, and caught your grasp upon it. How the prominent gray-blue eyes seemed to rove down the path, just in advance of his feet, as his grave Indian stride carried him down to University Hall! He did not care for people; his classmates seemed very remote. . . . We remember him as looking very much like some Egyptian sculptures of faces, large-featured, but brooding, immobile, fixed in a mystic egoism. Yet his eyes were sometimes searching as if he had dropped, or expected to find, something. In fact his eyes seldom left the ground, even in his most earnest conversations with you" (Atkinson, 1927, pp. 15-16). Those who knew him then could not have been greatly surprised at his later career, with its strong tone of negativeness and isolation, his refusal to pay his taxes, his night in jail, and his sojourn at Walden Pond. But that consistent picture is marred, superficially at least, by his devotion to the Concord lyceum.

He was a loyal and devoted mainstay of the organization throughout his mature life. If, when he returned from Harvard, his first act was to sign off from the church, his second was to join the lyceum. Soon he was elected secretary and curator and at first wrote out full minutes in an elegant shaded script signed, with a flourish, "Henry D. Thoreau, Secretary." Within a year, his minutes for a meeting were reduced to five or six words and signed "H.D.T. Secy." Off and on for the next ten years he served as an officer of the Concord lyceum, and, in the course of his career, he spoke before it twenty times. He attended whenever he was in Concord, even when living at Walden, and when he was away he pined for its meetings.

It introduced him to the only intellectual career open to him. He earned his living first by reducing his wants and then by supplying them through his work as handy man, pencil maker, and land surveyor. He could not seem to make his ideas provide him with a livelihood. New England, he said, "would rather have his surveys than his thought" (Canby, 1958, p. 306). A formal academic career was repugnant to him; when Emerson said that they taught most branches of learning at Harvard, Thoreau said, "Yes, indeed, all the branches and none of the roots" (Albee, 1901, p. 22). Nor could he get money from his writing. "Only *The Ladies' Companion* pays," he wrote, "but I could not write anything companionable" (VI:107-108). But lecturing did offer an avenue for his thoughts and at least a modest payment—the latter not from the Concord lyceum but from its sister organizations in other communities. So throughout his career he announced himself as a lecturer and only rarely declined an opportunity to speak.

In his journal, he recorded his thoughts and ideas and observations, his conversations with townspeople and with hunters and trappers, the anecdotes they told him, and, most of all, the constantly changing face of nature. He also read incessantly in the eight languages with which he had some acquaintance (Wagenknecht, 1981, pp. 38-39). Sometimes he professed to find his speaking engagements an interruption to his processes of self-education. "For some years past," he wrote in 1857, "I have partially offered myself as a lecturer; have been advertised as such several years. Yet I have had but two or three invitations to lecture in a year, and some years none at all. I congratulate myself on having been permitted to stay at home thus, I am so much richer for it. I do not see what I should have got of much value, but money, by going about, but I do see what I should have lost. It seems to me that I have a longer and more liberal lease of life thus" (V:214). "The lecturer gets fifty dollars a night; but what becomes of his winter?" (VI:303). Such observations as these are common in his writing, but his lack of invitations suggests that his comments bear the pungent taste of sour grapes.

The truth seems to have been that he was highly variable as a lecturer. In the right mood, particularly when he spoke on nature and when he allowed free play to his aphoristic wit, he delighted his audiences. When he breathed fire against slavery and in defense of John Brown, he stirred his hearers to action, for or against him. But most of the time he was too transcendental. Unconventional or obscure though his ideas might be, his aim was only to express them, and if he had a hundred different ideas to record in a paper, he set them down one after the other with either sketchy connections between them or none at all. One sees an audience sitting before him, observing his peculiar personality, looking at the top of his head as he bent it forward over his manuscript, hearing his dry voice, with no effort at rhetoric, read a series of unrelated observations most of which were so odd and unfamiliar that they could not be comprehended and some of which were so sarcastic and irritating that they could only be resented. He recorded his own attitude in his journal: "Preaching? Lecturing? Who are ye that ask for these things? What do ye want to hear, ye puling infants? A trumpet-sound that would train you up to mankind, or a nurse's lullaby?" (XVII:324). This viewpoint must almost certainly have been transmitted to his audiences. There can be little wonder that so few of them wanted to hear him.

To those who did, later generations have had cause to be grateful. The raw experience that Thoreau recorded in his journal might never have taken any shape at all if he had not had an audience ready at hand at the Concord lyceum and in other similar groups who were willing to hear him. Thoreau was explicit on this point: "From all points of the compass, from the earth beneath and the heavens above, have come these inspirations and been entered duly in the order of their arrival in the journal. Thereafter, when the time arrived, they were winnowed into lectures, and again, in due time, from lectures into essays" (VII:413). Lectures and audiences might be irritants, but some irritants produce pearls.

The lyceums were not merely means of employment or stimuli to writing. When he left the church, his written declaration said, "Know all men by these presents that I Henry Thoreau do not wish to be regarded as a member of any incorporated society which I have not joined" (Bazalgette, 1924, p. 70). But unsociable though he might seem, one of his central preoccupations throughout his life was the proper relationship of people to one another. His first lecture at the Concord lyceum was not on solitude. It was on society. One cluster of his ideas about society has exploded in the twentieth century like a time bomb. On this point, hear three witnesses.

Mohandus Gandhi: "I read *Walden* first in Johannesburg in South Africa in 1906 and his ideas influenced me greatly. I adopted some of them and recommended the study of Thoreau to all my friends who were helping me in the cause of Indian independence. Why, I actually took the name of my movement from Thoreau's essay, 'On the duty of Civil Disobedience,' written about eighty years ago" (Hendrick, 1956, p. 464).

Martin Buber: "It is now nearly sixty years since I first got to know Thoreau's essay 'Civil Disobedience.' I read it with the strong feeling that here was something that concerned me directly. . . . He addressed his reader within the very sphere of this situation common to both of them in such a way that the reader not only discovered why Thoreau acted as he did at that time but also that the reader—assuming him of course to be honest and dispassionate—would have to act in just such a way whenever the proper occasion arose, provided he was seriously engaged in fulfilling his existence as a human person" (Buber, 1962, p. 55).

Martin Luther King, Jr.: "During my early college days I read Thoreau's essay on civil disobedience for the first time. Fascinated by the idea of refusing to cooperate with an evil system, I was so deeply moved that I re-read the work several times. I became convinced then that non-cooperation with evil is as much a moral obligation as is cooperation with good. No other person has been more eloquent and passionate in getting this idea across than Henry David Thoreau. As a result of his writings and personal witness we are the heirs of a legacy of creative protest" (King, 1962, p. 43).

But one who takes solitude and civil disobedience to be Thoreau's only approach to life drastically oversimplifies. He spent but two of his forty-five years at Walden; even there, as his friend Prudence Ward said, "He has many visitors, whom he receives with pleasure & does his best to entertain. We talk of passing the day with him soon" (Canby, 1958, p. 216). His celebrated stay in jail lasted only one night; he had a roommate there, and if we may believe Thoreau's account, they spent virtually all of that night in conversation. We must see beyond the foreshortenings of history to discover the breadth of his thought on the role of people in society. When we do we shall find that both the source and the expression of that thought may be found in the Concord lyceum.

V

Thoreau is an almost ideal central figure for a literary cult. He was so many different people simultaneously that some aspect of his thought or personality can appeal to everyone. In fact, the conventional way of writing about him is to begin by saying that there are three Thoreaus or five Thoreaus (choose your number as you will) and then to expound on each of them. Every analyst is safe, for there are as many Thoreaus as you want to count, and somewhere you can find a quotation from him that will confirm whatever you believe him to have been.

Today the various and contradictory aspects of his thought have a special appeal to a surprising range of people. He is quoted constantly not merely in literary quarterlies and avant-garde journals but also in popular periodicals, in the daily press, and, although the mind reels at the prospect, in fashionable and sophisticated magazines. He could not write anything companionable, but his writings have found many companions. In his funeral oration for Thoreau, Emerson said, "No college ever offered him a diploma or a professor's chair; no academy made him its corresponding secretary, its discoverer, or even its member. Perhaps these learned bodies feared the satire of his presence" (Emerson, 1892, p. 440). But now in academic and literary circles we discover a minor Thoreau industry. A modern scholar has called him "austere, vituperative, provincial, misanthropic, shrewd, caustic, didactic, suspicious, ill-balanced, idealistic, expectant, eager, full of compassion, tender, patient, serene, and reverent" (Atkinson, 1927, p. 31). How can anyone fail, with such a man, to find distinctive affinity?

Those who make special studies of Thoreau, however, are finding it increasingly hard to locate a fresh approach. "Scholars," he noted, "are wont to sell their birthright for a mess of learning" (I:98). Modern scholars have turned the pages of his writings over and over to find the ultimate key to unlock

Thoreau; as a result the answers grow increasingly abstruse. Visions denied to many are granted to a few. One modern authority, for example, has concluded that "Thoreau's hatred for the state was an extension of his Oedipal hatred for his father and of his occasional dislike (the other side of the coin of love) of his dominating mother." The same author argues that "at the unconscious level Thoreau ended his life of his own accord. He was convinced that he had to die chiefly because John Brown and his father had died. He had to expiate his intolerably increasing load of guilt. Christian contrition was not for him but leaving life represented ample expiation." This authority does, however, note, "I agree with the past biographers that on the conscious level [Thoreau] died of tuberculosis" (Bode, 1962, p. 78).

For the present, the conscious level must suffice. Any attempt completely to explain Thoreau is certain to diminish both him and the explainer. Thoreau left us his ideas, not his personal problems. Gandhi, Buber, and King were deeply influenced by what he said about the way to attack an unjust state, not by why he said it. It will be useful to follow their example as we turn away from his antagonistic and rebellious views to inquire into his more positive conception of the values of society as he gained them from his continuing contemplation of himself, of nature, and of the people who surrounded him.

The key idea is voluntary assent. ("I Henry Thoreau do not wish to be regarded as a member of any incorporated society which I have not joined.") The first requisite for the individual, therefore, is to know oneself, to be aware of one's own potential, to be all of a piece whatever that piece might be. One did not need to be intellectual to win his admiration. He wrote often of Therien, the wood chopper. Of one Minott he said that he "is, perhaps, the most poetical farmer—who most realizes to me the poetry of the farmer's life—that I know. He does nothing with haste and drudgery, but as if he loved it. He makes the most of his labor, and takes infinite satisfaction in every part of it" (IX:41).

But of most people he was less tolerant. "He described some of his Concord neighbors as 'newly shingled and clapboarded,' but if you knock no one is at home" (Canby, 1958, p. 96). When people said that John Brown had thrown his life away, Thoreau asked which way they had thrown theirs (Brooks, 1937, p. 432). And he asked of every lecturer a "simple and sincere account of his own life, . . . some such account as he would send to his kindred from a distant land,—and if he has lived sincerely, it must have been in a distant land to me" (VII:484).

The search to find oneself must be an active one. "How vain it is," he said, "to sit down to write when you have not stood up to live" (VIII:404). For him, at least, solitude and contemplation were one way to stand up. But, he went on, "there may be a lyceum in the evening, and there is a book-shop and library in the village, and five times a day I can be whirled to Boston within an hour" (Paul, 1958, p. 306). In addition, he believed that to find oneself, one must put oneself in the proper frame of mind in order not to miss what one would otherwise discover. "We find only the world we look for" (XV:466). "From the brook in which one lover of nature has never during all his lifetime detected anything larger than a minnow, another extracts a trout that weighs three pounds. . . . Though you roam the woods all your days, you never will see by chance what he sees who goes on purpose to see it" (XIV:192). One begins to understand although not quite to believe Clifton Fadiman's remark that Thoreau could "get more out of ten minutes with a chickadee than most men could get out of a night with Cleopatra" (Krutch, 1948, p. 34).

Another way for one to find oneself is to let one's mind interact with that of another. Thoreau's journals and letters are filled with disquisitions on friendship, with reverberations of the rise and fall of his own friendships, and with accounts of particular meetings. Perhaps the most poignant passage is in a manuscript in the Huntington Library: "I had a friend, I wrote a book, I asked my friend's criticism, I never got but praise for what was good in it. My friend became estranged from me and then I got blame for all that was bad. So I got at last the criticism which I wanted. While my friend was my friend he flattered me, but I never heard the truth from him but when he became my enemy he shot it to me on a poisoned arrow" (HM 13182). Some people, he thought, have nothing to say to us, or at least it seems so at the beginning. "We occasionally meet an individual of a character and disposition so entirely the reverse of our own that we wonder if he can indeed be another man like ourselves. . . . Such was the old English gentleman whom I met with today. . . . Though I peered in at his eyes I could not discern myself reflected therein. The chief wonder was how we could ever arrive at so fair-seeming an intercourse upon so small a ground of sympathy" (VII:48).

It is the depth of communication that matters, not its range. With some people, not many, one can go very deep indeed, and Thoreau's writings have numerous accounts of his conversations. Here is one: "Just spent a couple of hours . . . with Miss Mary Emerson. . . . The wittiest and most vivacious woman that I know, certainly that woman among my acquaintance whom it is most profitable to meet, the least frivolous, who will most surely provoke to good conversation and the expression of what is in you. She is singular, among women at least, in being really and perseveringly interested to know what thinkers think. She relates herself surely to the intellectual where she goes. It is perhaps her greatest praise and peculiarity that she . . . gives her companion occasion to utter his best thought. In spite of her own biases, she can entertain a large thought with hospitality and is not prevented by any intellectuality in it. . . . I never talked with any other woman who I thought accompanied me so far in describing a poetic experience" (IX:113–114).

And so it begins to be clear why, as Thoreau thought beyond personal growth and friendship to social institutions, the lyceum appeared to be the fairest form of all. It was a place where thoughtful men and women could meet together to educate each other and where variety of thought would itself be an inspiration. As Thoreau said: "It is not in vain that the mind turns aside this way or that: follow its leading, apply it whither it inclines to go. Probe the universe in a myriad points. Be avaricious of these impulses. Nature makes a thousand acorns to get one oak. He is a wise man and experienced who has taken many views, to whom stones and plants and animals, and a myriad objects have each suggested something, contributed something" (Channing, [1873], 1902, p. 86).

The depth of Thoreau's appreciation of the lyceum is best highlighted by his contempt for other human associations. The icy disdain for government that he expressed in "On Civil Disobedience" was carried over to other forms of companionship or organization. Here are some of his observations: "Blessed are the young for they do not read the President's Message" (VI:379). "Once at a tea-table, forgetting where I was, I whistled—whereupon the company would not be convinced that it was not meant for a hint that their conversation was frivolous. I thought that their suspicion was the best proof that it was so" (Miller, 1958, p. 118). "I hate museums, there is nothing so weighs upon the spirits. They are catacombs of nature. They are preserved death" (HM 13182, Huntington Library). "Lectured in [the] basement . . . of the . . . church, and I trust helped to undermine it" (XV:188). "What are time and space to Christianity, eighteen hundred years, and a new world?—that the humble life of a Jewish peasant should have force to make a New York bishop so bigoted" (I:67).

His deepest scorn was reserved for those people who set themselves up to improve their fellows. "God does not sympathize with the popular movements," he said (VII:315). Ten years later, in his mother's boardinghouse, he had this encounter: "Here have been three ultra-reformers, lecturers on Slavery, Temperance, the Church, etc. . . . They addressed each other constantly by their Christian names, and rubbed you continually with the greasy cheeks of their kindness. They would not keep their distance, but cuddle up and lie spoon-fashion with you. . . . [One] addressed me as 'Henry' within one minute from the time I first laid eyes on him, and when I spoke, he said with drawling, sultry sympathy, 'Henry, I know all you would say; I understand you perfectly; you need not explain anything to me;' and to another, 'I am going to dive into Henry's inmost depths.' I said, 'I trust you will not strike your head against the bottom' " (XI:263-265).

How different from these associations was the lyceum

and how gratefully he received it. From it, he thought, "a new era will be dated to New England, as from . . . Greece" (I:102). For him, it represented the one form of group association that was tolerable. All of the others, he said, were mere "idling down on the plane at the base of the mountain instead of climbing steadily to its top. Of course you will be glad of all the society you can get to go up with. . . . It is not that we love to be alone, but that we love to soar, and when we do soar, the company grows thinner and thinner till there is none at all. . . . We are not the less to aim at the summits, though the multitude does not ascend them. Use all the society that will abet you" (VI:281). For Thoreau, that society was the lyceum, the direct face-to-face human group where each person brought his or her thoughts, perfected as well as possible, and presented them for the scrutiny of the townspeople, so that they might go up the mountain together, as high as any of them could reach.

One need not agree with Thoreau's strictures against other forms of human association to join in his admiration for this one. As the name of the lyceum itself suggests, the idea that educated and independent people might independently seek to develop their culture is an old belief, and a reading of history shows that it is a pervasive one. Every civilized age has its societies, circles, clubs, and academies, its colloquia, atheneums, and lyceums, its fraternities, associations, and assemblies, and its unions, leagues, and federations. The origins of these groups are diverse; usually at the beginning there is a strong leader or a party of congenial spirits or both. The groups usually succeed, but only for a limited time. After a few years, the members exhaust each other's ingenuity or patience. But a few groups do manage to find within themselves the resources to permit them to continue indefinitely, generation after generation, thereby being supported not merely by learning and companionship but also by tradition.

The values of these continuing associations are many. The individual member acquires a wide relationship with both people and ideas. The angular edges of thought are smoothed by their clash against contradictory ideas. The mind is kept active and alive by being forced to submit its deliberations to the scrutiny of a kindly but critical company. New frontiers of knowledge are explored, and the long reflections of a lifetime are distilled for the benefit of those who can profit from them. People of ability or genius are challenged to perfect their talents and find in the group the raw material of new ideas to refine and develop in solitude. Society as a whole is also the gainer, for such groups preserve and nourish among the leaders of the community those broad and humane values that are the finest fruits of civilization.

Is this all there should be? Friends, a cluster of colleagues to stimulate thought, and other groups one may voluntarily join? For Thoreau, yes, this is all there should be. A spouse, children, the acceptance without choice of church, neighborhood, community, nation, the world? For Thoreau, no—not, at least, as part of a system of thought. Can one build a total conception of society out of his few essential ingredients? Perhaps, but not many people have tried to do so.

But humans do not live by system alone. They turn in need to the idea that will help them and to the writer who most clearly and brilliantly expresses that idea. In Africa, in Asia, in the United States, the thought of Thoreau on civil disobedience today gives strength, resoluteness, and coherence to those who feel themselves oppressed by unjust states. Such people would have rebelled anyway, for such is their nature, but perhaps in a less reasoned, more violent way if they had not been guided by the words of that strange man of Concord who, Emerson said, was "a person not accounted for by anything in his antecedents, his birth, his education, or his way of life" (Sanborn, 1917, p. 1).

VI

It would be as impossible to build a complete social system out of lyceums as it would be to construct a political life based only on civil disobedience. Taken strictly as an idea, though, and not as the focus of a social system, Thoreau's positive conception might prove to be as fertile as his negative one has been. In the modern adult educational movement, the casual, spontaneous, and often transitory circles that have always existed are being amplified and extended to serve all people and to strengthen all society. Let us hear the man of Concord out then as, on that autumn morning in 1852, he wrote the words that, polished and revised in his lectures, finally emerged in his masterpiece, *Walden*:

> We have a comparatively decent system of common schools, schools for infants only; but excepting the half-starved Lyceum in the winter, . . . no school for ourselves. . . . It is time that we had uncommon schools, that we did not leave off our education when we begin to be men and women. It is time that villages were universities, and their elder inhabitants the fellows of universities, with leisure—if they are, indeed, so well off—to pursue liberal studies the rest of their lives. Shall the world be confined to one Paris or one Oxford forever? Cannot students be boarded here and get a liberal education under the skies of Concord? . . . This town has spent seventeen thousand dollars on a Town-House, thank fortune or politics, but probably it will not spend so much on living wit, the true meat to put into that shell, in a hundred years. The one hundred and twenty-five dollars annually subscribed for a Lyceum in the winter is better spent than any other equal sum raised in the town. . . . Let the village . . . not stop short at a pedagogue, a parson, a sexton, a parish library, and three selectmen because our Pilgrim forefathers got through a cold winter once on a bleak rock with these. To act collectively is according to the spirit of our institutions; . . . New England can hire all the wise men in the world to come and teach her, and board them round the while, and not be provincial at all. That is the *uncommon* school we want. Instead of noblemen, let us have noble villages of men. If it is necessary, omit one bridge

over the river, go round a little there, and throw one arch at least over the darker gulf of ignorance which surrounds us [II:120-122].

References

Albee, J. *Remembrances of Emerson.* New York: Robert G. Cooke, 1901.

Atkinson, J. B. *Henry Thoreau, the Cosmic Yankee.* New York: Knopf, 1927.

Bazalgette, L. *Henry Thoreau.* New York: Harcourt Brace Jovanovich, 1924.

Bode, C. "The Half-Hidden Thoreau." *Massachusetts Review,* 1962, *4,* 68-80.

Brooks, V. W. *The Flowering of New England, 1815-1865.* New York: Dutton, 1937.

Buber, M. "Man's Duty as Man." *Massachusetts Review,* 1962, *4,* 55.

Canby, H. S. *Thoreau.* Boston: Beacon Press, 1958.

Channing, W. E. *Thoreau the Poet-Naturalist.* Boston: Charles E. Goodspeed, 1902. (Originally published 1873.)

Emerson, R. W. *Lectures and Biographical Sketches.* Boston: Houghton Mifflin, 1892.

Hendrick, G. "Influence of Thoreau's 'Civil Disobedience' on Gandhi's *Satyagraha.*" *New England Quarterly,* 1956, 460-470.

King, M. L., Jr. "A Legacy of Creative Protest." *Massachusetts Review,* 1962, *4,* 43.

Krutch, J. W. *Henry David Thoreau.* New York: William Sloane Associates, 1948.

Low, A. H. "The Concord Lyceum." *Old-Time New England,* 1959, *50* (2), 29-41.

Miller, P. *Consciousness in Concord.* Boston: Houghton Mifflin, 1958.

Nyren, D. "The Concord Academic Debating Society." In J. H. Hicks (Ed.), *Thoreau in Our Season.* Amherst: University of Massachusetts Press, 1964.

Paul, S. *The Shores of America*. Urbana: University of Illinois Press, 1958.

Perry, B. *The Heart of Emerson's Journals*. Boston: Houghton Mifflin, 1926.

Sanborn, F. B. *The Life of Henry David Thoreau*. Boston: Houghton Mifflin, 1917.

Thoreau, H. D. *Works*. 20 vols. Boston: Houghton Mifflin, 1906.

Wagenknecht, E. *Henry David Thoreau: What Manner of Man*. Amherst: University of Massachusetts Press, 1981.

5

Billy Graham

Developing Oratory as an Art Form

I

Billy Graham's basic method of teaching is perhaps as old as the controlled use of fire or the systematic cultivation of the land. It is world-wide in its application and used by millions of people every day. The presentation of a serious oral discourse to a cluster of listeners began in the darkness of prehistory and is now universal, being found not only in classrooms and auditoriums but in other meeting places throughout society, ranging from small committee rooms to vast arenas. Even discussion groups such as the lyceum may incorporate formal addresses into their meetings and sometimes evolve into organized lecture series with no longer any semblance of interactive responsibility for learning. Modern technology—particularly radio, television, and recording instruments—has adapted this ancient process of instruction but has not changed its innate character.

In the sheer number of people cumulatively reached by Graham's immediate presence, he almost certainly exceeds any other orator in earlier or modern times. The measurement of mass audiences is a notoriously inexact art, and therefore nobody could accurately estimate how many people he has addressed directly. Congregations of thirty to fifty thousand persons are common for him, and he sometimes attracts audiences of more than one hundred thousand hearers. At least one gathering was reliably believed to include more than a million people. In 1966, it was said that he had already preached in person to about fifty million listeners; at that time he was still building his career, and the truly massive throngs had not yet become commonplace. Although in recent years he has become more of a senior statesman than a firebrand, he tirelessly continues to instruct people and seeks to move them to action. Nobody else has such a record, not even those with a purpose different from his, such as entertainment, political persuasion, or the performance of ritual. How has he brought about such a massive achievement?

II

If Graham's method and purpose are to be understood, they need to be seen, first of all, in historical context. For thousands of years (until printing was invented), oratory was the chief means of communicating ideas to the masses, and, until recently, the study of oratory was an important part of a liberal education, for adults as well as young people. Serious advanced analysis of the topic has now almost disappeared except that which guides courses in homiletics in divinity schools. Excerpts from Demosthenes, Cicero, or Daniel Webster may be found in anthologies, but publishers no longer issue those multivolumed compendia of great speeches that were common fifty years ago. Aristotle's *Rhetoric* is still read by students of the classics but by virtually nobody else. The very names of scholarly inquiry into the topic—such as *oratory* itself or *rhetoric, elocution,* or *forensics*—have an antique air. A once-clear discipline has been turned into the murky grayness of "speech" or "communication."

To look back beyond the present age, however, is to recognize that a major force in shaping minds and morals has always been the orator, transmitting a message by the living word, often trying to move hearers to action, but, in the process, at least shaping their beliefs and adding to their knowledge. As Cardinal John Henry Newman said more than a century ago, when men and women "aim at something precise, something refined, something really luminous, something really large, something choice, . . . they avail themselves, in some shape or other, of . . . the ancient method, of oral instruction, of present communication between man and man, of teachers instead of teaching, of the personal influence of a master, and the humble initiation of a discipline. . . . If we wish to become exact and fully furnished in any subject of teaching which is diversified and complicated, we must consult the living man and listen to his living voice" ([1856], no date, pp. 7-8). The orator reaching great throngs is not a classroom teacher or master as such a figure is usually thought of but, in a very old and deep sense, is one of the profound exemplars of the age-old practice of adult education.

Orators are remembered for many reasons. Some, such as Cicero, have left a body of work behind them, and these literary remains serve as their monuments. Some, such as John Wesley, have been the founders of institutions. Some, such as Girolamo Savonarola, have precipitated violent social episodes, while others, such as Adolf Hitler, have changed the course of history. Some, such as Daniel Webster, have grown to be folk figures, remembered as brooding and powerful presences. One sober observer said of Webster that "he was like the mount that might not be touched and that burned with fire" (Lodge, 1883, p. 118); and another man commented of Webster's appearance in the Senate that "he stood there like some time-darkened minster-tower. He was an institution" (Conway, 1904, p. 81).

Although oratory may be studied as literature, as history, or as art, it is always firmly fixed in time and place. The orator speaks not to posterity but to a present audience. Patrick Henry, for example, is remembered for several deathless phrases, but they are embedded in addresses whose allusions can be understood only by people well schooled in American colonial history. More to the point in assessing him as an orator was his effect on his hearers. Of the speech that ended with the words "Give me liberty or give me death," one hearer wrote: "The tendons of [Henry's] neck stood out white and rigid like whipcords. His voice rose louder and louder, until the walls of the building and all within them seemed to shake and rock in its tremendous vibrations. Finally his pale face and glaring eyes became terrible to look upon. Men leaned forward in their seats with their heads strained forward, their faces pale and their eyes glaring like the speaker's. . . . When he sat down, I felt sick with excitement. Every eye yet gazed entranced on Henry. It seemed as if a word from him would have led to any wild explosion of violence. Men looked beside themselves" (Morgan, 1907, p. 193).

Even with so timeless a subject as religion, the relationship of humankind to God, the orator's message reflects the time and the place of its delivery. Let us restrict our examples to the relatively narrow scope of Protestantism in the United States. In the grim theocratic life of colonial New England, in what *Time* has called "the most famous sermon ever preached in America" (Dec. 31, 1979, p. 64), Jonathan Edwards struck a deep, responsive chord when he thundered: "The God that holds you over the pit of hell, much as one holds a spider or some loathsome insect over the fire, abhors you and is dreadfully provoked: His wrath towards you burns like fire; He looks upon you as worthy of nothing else but to be cast into the fire; He is of purer eyes than to bear to have you in His sight; you are ten thousand times more abominable in His eyes than the most hateful venomous serpent is in ours" (Faust and Johnson, 1935, p. 164).

Soon after the start of the nineteenth century, the dominant theme changed to a less accusatory but equally fervent call to salvation, one which was ultimately to be perfected by such thunderers as Dwight Moody and Billy Sunday. At its best, this preaching was intense and exalted; at its worst, it was excited, even orgiastic. Abraham Lincoln suggested that at many revivals and camp meetings "more souls were made than saved" (Oliver, 1965, p. 361). Later on, with the growth of the Victorian ethic, the message was centered on the preservation of solid middle-class values. Henry Ward Beecher, Phillips Brooks, Russell Condon, and many another preacher showed his audiences the way to moral rectitude, to a world whose good things would be shared by everyone, or to the realization that each of us stands amid acres of diamonds and should learn how to mine them.

The camp meeting gave rise to the traveling chautauqua, which rolled through the American hinterland, bringing culture, learning, and the promise of material blessings and salvation to everyone.

Despite the rich traditions of oratory and the biographies of its eminent practitioners, few descriptions can be found of how individual speakers, even the most famous, achieved their effects. How did they inform and move their audiences? Content and social context certainly were important, but neither literary analysts nor observers of contemporary scenes have looked with a candid gaze at precisely how the great orators instructed their listeners or persuaded them to action. Graham is a modern heir of this great and complex tradition and, at least in numbers of people reached, is its greatest figure. How has he reshaped the tradition to fit his own purposes and to respond to those of his times?

III

If you entered the great hall of McCormick Place in Chicago on a June evening in 1971, you were immediately confronted by a long row of tables at which books and phonograph records were for sale, with, for example, a $4.95 authorized biography of Graham going at the special rate of $2.50. Beyond those tables were 38,000 seats, but your choice among them was limited. Some were held for those with "blue and white tickets," whatever that might mean. Some were set aside for groups. Some were reserved for counselors, ushers, and the press. Most of the seats near the door were kept for latecomers. Men with bull-horns were needed to direct the general flow of traffic, but for the most part in-comers were gently urged in one direction by ushers and prevented from going in other directions by barriers. Eventually you came to the place where you could exercise a choice but it was not a wide one. Every seat must be taken, and people were held shoulder to shoulder by linked chairs. When one section was full, another was opened. There must be close, direct, human contact of a physical sort.

The scene and the actions that were about to unfold had

already been replicated many times before and would be many times again. Ten years later in the Memorial Stadium in Baltimore the same basic ingredients would be present and the key personnel would still be the same. Unlike McCormick Place, the double-tiered stadium was open to the soft June air, and countless adjustments were required to accommodate that fact. But anyone present at both Crusades and at others before, between, or after them would have been more struck by the similarities than by the differences in what occurred.

The ushers are indispensable to the entire process. They range from perhaps twenty-five to seventy-five years of age; they are neatly dressed with carefully folded handkerchiefs in their breast pockets; they have fresh haircuts; and they have been either born to their calling or conditioned by years of service on Sunday mornings. Each has four to six rows of seats under his care and sees himself as the kindly shepherd of the people sitting in them. Authority rises above these first-line men in an orderly hierarchy; there are aisle captains and section captains and presumably a floor captain. These men are constantly busy; once the need to seat their flock has been met, they confer with one another endlessly, answer questions from the audience, volunteer information about the evening's program, and, if need be, care for distress or disturbance.

The setting itself is in no sense dramatic, only big. No bold design catches the eye, no banners wave, no striking symbols are to be seen. Later on, there will be no sudden darkenings of the room or the stadium, no beams of light picking out an isolated figure in the darkness, no use of projected images, no hidden electric fans causing banners to wave. No orchestra will play; the only music will be provided by piano or organ. None of the devices of modern industrial design or of the packaging of performance are visible.

The evocation is of something far different and far more familiar. The meeting place feels comfortable to its audiences because it has been made to look as much as possible like customary places of lower- and middle-class pomp and ceremony: the Protestant church, the high school auditorium, or the converted gymnasium or movie theater that is being used for graduation exercises. The people present know where they are because they have been there so often. Only the scale has changed. In Chicago, a banner stretching across the background of the rostrum said: "Jesus said, 'I am the way, the truth, and the life.' John 14:6"; it was fifty feet long. The chorus was made up not of twenty or a hundred voices but of two thousand. The platform was very large. The piano and organ were electrically amplified, so that 38,000 people could hear every note. The runway that projected foward from the platform was edged with the familiar shapes of ferns and ornamental trees. At the base of the lectern was an arrangement of flowers like those at christenings, weddings, and funerals—but incomparably larger. The hall itself was brilliantly lighted throughout, but, in addition, three massed rows of spotlights focused on the platform.

If you had been at the 1971 meeting, you would have noted how the great windows around the upper edge of the hall bring the city into the auditorium: the towers of the Loop to the north and the high-rise apartment buildings to the west and south, the airplanes landing and taking off from Meigs Field, the sky stretching over the lake, and the factories of the Lakeside Press near at hand. God and people thus provide great but familiar visual aids to instruction: the sunset, the moon, the vastness of the sky, the enterprise needed to build the city or, conversely, the dreadfulness of urban blight, the impersonality of a life lived in layered homes, and the wickedness of publishers who offer pornography to the millions. In the sermons to come, these resources will be fully used.

Who is the audience? As with any assemblage of about 35,000 people, almost anybody can be there, but in general it is made up of the white Protestant core of the lower middle class: the people one sees on city beaches, in discount houses and chain stores, or in highway rest stops. They are overwhelmingly white. The spokespeople for the 1971 Crusade estimated that about 4,000 members of an audience of 30,000 were black, but experienced newspaper reporters were skeptical of that figure. The congregations are not made up only of the middle-aged and elderly, as many people seem to think. A large number of young people are present and many repeatedly give the Jesus signal: the right arm raised, the index finger pointing upward.

The programs are recorded for delayed television broadcasting in abbreviated form, and that fact is brought home vividly to the audience in the great hall, making its members feel important and putting them on their best behavior. Heavy television cameras roam the aisles, each with two men to handle its trailing cable, so that the future presence of a vast unseen audience is always evident. There are 35,000 of us, but we are a happy few compared to the millions who will have to look from afar at everything that we can see clearly and at firsthand.

A strong sense of community pervades the hall. It is felt most deeply by the members of a local church congregation who know one another, come from the same community, have planned and undertaken the trip, sit together, and will go home in the same bus. As the service proceeds, the feeling of togetherness spreads to the entire assemblage. We have so much in common. We heard the choir rehearsing before the service. We focused our cameras on the young man who stood silently at the lectern for a half hour before the service; when Billy comes out we are sure to get good photographs. Isn't it wonderful how many people are pouring in? We applaud during the program whenever the success of the Crusade is mentioned. We sing familiar songs. We rise and sit down as directed. We look up passages in the Bibles we have brought. We laugh comfortably at the witticisms. We catch our breaths with astonishment when a celebrity is introduced. We make our financial contributions willingly, eager to help the great Crusade go on. We speak to one another approvingly of the number of young people present this evening. When a speaker makes a telling point, we say "amen." We talk about past Crusades and hope for future ones. We exchange gossip about Billy and the members of his team. We nudge our children and remind them that this is a night they will remember all their lives. We make plans to see all future telecasts, especially the one of tonight's program. We say over and over again how nice it is that Billy has had a chance to come back to Chicago-land, which means so much to him; other people may claim him but he is really one of ours, having gone to one of our colleges and having had his first pastorate here.

When the service begins, its order of events is rigidly fixed. It is conducted by Cliff Barrows, who serves as master of ceremonies, song leader, and offerer of prayers. He has the friendliest, most lilting voice imaginable. In the first fifteen minutes, there is a welcome, a silent meditation while the choir sings, group singing, a prayer by a visiting pastor, and a solo, perhaps by Beverly Shea (a Graham associate), perhaps by a wholesome television performer. A few celebrities are introduced: a preacher, the manager of McCormick Place, and some of the members of the Cubs baseball team. A leader of the Crusade says that money is desperately needed. To nobody's surprise, there is then an offertory prayer, and while organ and piano play "Jesu, Joy of Man's Desiring," the ushers pass the collection buckets back and forth across the aisles. They are, in literal fact, buckets, made of white plastic and having their counterparts in motel ice containers all over the United States. Into them, you can put cash, or if you prefer, you can fill out a blank check or a credit card form that has thoughtfully been included in the printed program.

The pace quickens. With no introduction, Graham bounds to the lectern at the front end of the long runway. He welcomes the group, gives thanks to various people, tells the audience how close Chicago "and the tri-state area" are to his own heart, makes a little witticism, and describes in detail what will be happening each subsequent evening during the Crusade. He is succeeded by several events: Barrows recommending a magazine, a hymn by the choir, another solo by another artist, Barrows recommending a book, a hymn by the choir and audience, and then an introduction of the second most important event of the evening. It is a talk by someone who has found God, often by listening to Graham. The speaker may be a big league baseball player, a handicapped person in a wheelchair, a former member of a youth gang or of the White House staff, or a leader of the advertising profession. This speech is brief, well-rehearsed, and movingly spoken. Then another song by soloist and choir. Then comes the main event of the evening.

As he strides forward, Graham is different in manner from the folksy communicator of his first appearance. He may even wear a different jacket of a darker hue. He begins with a prayer, admonishes the audience: "While you are listening to me, let no one move, no one speak. While I am speaking, God will be speaking." He harks back to the testimony of conversion that has just been presented and leads from it into the passage of the Bible that he has selected as text. The members of the audience who have come with their own Bibles turn to the verses he has chosen.

Almost nobody notices that something significant has just occurred. All previous speakers have been held immobilized at the lectern by the bank of microphones into which they must speak or sing if they are to be heard. Graham in his turn remains fixed while he delivers the prayer. Then slowly, ever so slowly, he draws back. He has escaped from the fixed position that everyone else has had to endure. He is alive, free, dynamic, able to move about and to confront every member of his audience without any change in the power of his voice. It seems almost miraculous until one notices the glint of a neck microphone against his shirt. He has not needed to stand at the lectern at all except to dramatize his escape from it.

He preaches for about twenty-five minutes and then gently he modulates into his appeal for people to come forward "to bear witness for Christ." One knows almost at once what he is doing, and yet he delays and delays and delays. He talks about the importance of a profession of faith; he describes in detail what will happen to those who "come forward"; he assures people the buses will wait for them; he tells how he, too, came forward at an evangelical meeting; he asks the whole audience to remain in a prayerful silence. At some time during this message, a signal is given and the organist begins playing softly; at another signal, the choir starts quietly to sing. Dominating the music, his voice continues its appeal. Then at last, at last, he gives the word ("come now"), and the members of the audience who have been straining toward this moment are finally released and pour forth in a throng. Many of them carry Bibles. The ushers gently detain some of those who press forward; thus the flow is steady. Only one or two are sobbing or otherwise give evidence of an experience of exaltation; most are quiet and withdrawn; and some go forward conversing with one another, even laughing. All this while, Graham stands in prayerful silence.

As the flood of people begins to ebb, he gently urges others who are struggling with their consciences to open their hearts to Christ. He asks the choir to sing again and tells the audience that the night he came forward the choir sang two whole songs and he didn't respond until the final verse of the second song. This appeal brings new recruits. He may make a third or a fourth appeal. He then talks gently to the group that has assembled before him, asks them to pray with him, and tells the whole audience to be faithful in its attendance at the following meetings of the Crusade. Then suddenly, he disappears, presumably down some hidden staircase. Someone gives the benediction and the audience files out, while the counselors take the names and addresses of those who have come forward, thereby establishing contact between them and the Graham organization, as well as providing a basis for a follow-up by a local church.

IV

The man who is the focal point of this elaborate setting and process is taller than his co-workers, erect, and with a springing step. His face is exactly like the one shown in his newspaper photographs except, of course, that it is not black and white but ruddy. His hair sweeps back to a moderate length, its smooth perfection sometimes set off by a little duck tail. His face is lean and his build athletic.

His countenance is mobile, although he never smiles. He uses his hands with extraordinary effectiveness and swiftness and has a large repertoire of gestures, each distinct but flowing into one another with smooth perfection. The right-hand index finger is pointed toward the audience or toward heaven. He clenches one or both fists, or his hands rapidly revolve around one another. A characteristic gesture is made with either hand. It is a swift vertical movement, followed by a swift horizontal one. "He sent his son" (vertical movement) "to die for you" (horizontal movement). The symbolism of the cross must be evident to many and subliminal to others. A frequent mannerism is to thrust his head forward from his body with the chin stretched out as far as possible and the lips tightly pressed. It is a defiant look that says, "I have said something you must hear; if you don't, it is at your cost." His most celebrated posture comes at the end, while he is waiting for people to come forward. Then he stands erect except for a bowed head, his eyes closed, his upper lip resting on his clasped hands.

His voice is vibrant and alive. He knows, as does any orator, that it lies at the heart of his success. While sitting on the platform, he sprays his throat surreptitiously with a hand atomizer, and he takes a sudden last sip of water before he goes forward to preach. His voice has been thoroughly trained, and he uses it to the full limit of its not extraordinary range. His accent is American of the middle-South variety, particularly noticeable in his final "r's" and "o's"; he says "fathuh" and "heah" and "tomorruh." He thunders and he speaks softly and sometimes does one immediately following the other. He can be the great spellbinder, his blue eyes flashing fire. He can speak confidentially. He can be mildly humorous, although only rarely. And yet, although anybody who has ever taken a course in public speaking would realize that Graham is using his voice with great art, he never seems conscious of doing so. The days of the acquisition of mastery are far behind him.

The coming of television has made a substantial difference in Graham's methods of delivery. In earlier years, he used to roam back and forth along the runway, crouching and springing, fronting, in turn, every part of his audience, and often beating his doubled-up Bible against the palm of his other hand. To be seen clearly by thousands of people, he needed to move about dramatically. Now his audience may be many million, but most of those viewers, the ones watching television, will see him in close-up. Although he is still mobile, it is within a much smaller compass, a movement essentially of the shoulders and the head and the backward and forward progression of his body. While he is on, the television audience most often sees his face full front. When he uses the Bible, it is usually held open reverently in his hand or lies on the lectern. When he directly addresses the unseen millions, he gazes full face into a distant camera and speaks conversationally.

But most of the time, he speaks simultaneously to his two audiences, each aware of the other and yet each one feeling that it is primary to him. How he achieves this duality of focus is not easy to determine, but it is presumably the result of many modulations of practice consciously worked into his words and actions until they became second nature.

Throughout the whole address, Graham's discourse is pitched at the lower middle class in both level and content. Cities are not named alone; it is Chicago, Illinois; Minneapolis, Minnesota; Paris, France; or London, England. The references to authors of quotations are seldom made by name unless they are world celebrities; we are told that "a famous historian recently said" or "as the papers pointed out not long ago" or "one of my friends, who is a distinguished preacher, told me." Intellectuals, particularly psychiatrists and college professors, are likely to be figures of either fun or menace. They spend a lot of time and money making studies that reveal what sensible people have always known. Alternatively they wickedly turn our young people against the ways of their parents. And yet, ambivalently, any formal evidence of learning is good. Even a certified psychiatrist can occasionally say something worth quoting. In 1971, both Graham and Barrows were much impressed by a new book on the second coming of Christ whose author was said by Barrows to be fully qualified to write it. One waited with bated breath to learn who could accredit a man to speak with authority on this subject. Barrows's answer: "He has two earned doctorates, one from Oxford University in England and one from Edinburgh University in Scotland."

But Graham and his associates speak in this fashion only when they are addressing a large American audience. Graham taught himself, after some painful early experiences, to adapt his style to his audience and has thereby been able to persuade many stiff-necked and originally dissenting people to become part of his continuing Crusade. When he first went to England, most of the established church and virtually all of the intellectuals disdained him. Before he was through, the Archbishop of Canterbury had said a prayer from the Crusade platform, and Graham had been invited to speak at the Cathedral of Oxford.

Graham moves so frequently and familiarly among the great people of the world that he sometimes uses them for purposes of illustration. On the evening of Tricia Nixon's wedding in the White House, he told a Chicago audience about how the rain had stopped that afternoon just in time to permit the service to be held outdoors, at which point Red Skelton came up to him and said, "Thank you, Billy." You know and I know that Graham is not divine, but isn't it funny that so many people pretend he is? Although he knows the leaders of the world, he is careful not to presume on that acquaintance. At a sermon I attended, he commented, "Of course, I have been to Buckingham Palace many times, but I don't say 'Hi, Queenie.' I bow and say 'Your Majesty.' I have called the President of the United States by his nickname for twenty years, but one hour after he was inaugurated and we were having lunch together, I called him 'Mr. President.' " He now uses such references more sparingly than in earlier years. Perhaps he has fewer such contacts than before, and certainly some of his friends (especially Richard Nixon) have wounded him by their actions. But it may also be true that he has realized that his familiar reference to his friends might seem to skeptics to be name-dropping, a charge that his own growing eminence makes it especially necessary for him to avoid.

Graham does not read his sermons. Notes either have been left for him on the lectern or are communicated to him there by some electronic device. He glances frequently at them. The lectern itself would be worth study. Among other things, it must contain complex timing and signaling devices; he no longer peeks surreptitiously at his wristwatch as he used to do. And while the lectern feeds information of various sorts to him, he must sometimes signal back again, for now and then his long fingers flick toward its face. Perhaps these devices help him meet the exacting demands of television while still seeming to be spontaneous and responsive to his present congregation. Actually he gets relatively little immediate response from his audience. For the most part, it is so quiet and orderly that if it gives him cues or responses, only he, at the focal point of its attention, can sense them. He does little to play to the crowd or to whip it into reaction. Even when demonstrators chant in the distance, as they sometimes do, he pays little formal attention, although on such occasions he is tighter and more nervous than at other times, and the amplification of his voice may be louder than usual.

V

His sermons are relatively loose in construction. There is some of the "firstly, secondly, thirdly" structure of the divines of an earlier age, and there is always an underlying theme; but it is the embroidery that counts. It seems likely that he builds each sermon on an outline but that he also jots down a number of phrases, quotations, and illustrations that he can use as they seem appropriate.

One sermon given in 1971 was based on the Ten Commandments. The modern meaning of each one was expounded. Since the laws of God are more subtle and searching than the laws of people, we can break the commandments against murder, adultery, and other sins merely by our thoughts and not necessarily by our actions. Every person listening to Graham's voice, and Graham himself, has broken every one of the Ten Commandments. They set an impossible standard of achievement. What are we to do? We are to ask God for forgiveness of past sins and for help in preserving us from future ones. He will answer our prayers.

A second sermon, on a youth night, was built on the story of Absalom, who, it developed, wore long hair, rejected his father, and "had immorality simultaneously with ten women in the presence of the whole city." At that point, the thoughts of one listener gave way to fantasy. When they wandered back, Graham was making the point that while the use of drugs, crime, rejection of authority, and fornication are all especially prevalent just now, some young people have always committed such sins. His hearers were then invited once again to contemplate the wickedness of Absalom, although not that of the ten women. It was pointed out that he came to a bad end because of his long hair, a fact that in 1971 did not surprise the elders in the audience. Absalom did not repent—and that is where the sinful youth of today have a great advantage. They can turn to Jesus and He will infallibly hear them and forgive them.

A third sermon was based on passages in the book of Matthew, which serve as a basis for Graham's belief that the world is moving toward a climactic end. Christ said that when that time approached, there would be twenty-seven premonitory signs—but unfortunately Graham had time that evening for only four of them: widespread use of drugs, growth of violence, obsession with sex, and an increasing disparity between the gluttonous and the starving. Some cataclysm will occur; we will be cleansed by fire. After that will come a time—and it will not be in heaven but on this earth—when there will be a new Jerusalem, and those who have prepared themselves for that day will become the rulers in "the kingdom age."

Whatever the specific text or reference, Graham's central message is clear. The Bible is the word of God, but He has not revealed his whole truth to us, perhaps because of our sins, perhaps because to know the truth would make us more than mortal. He has promised us, however, that someday He will send new revelations. People will then move into a far richer and more rewarding life. For the present, we must use our reason to ponder the meaning of what the Bible says, for much of its truth is veiled in mystery. If scientists think they have disproved any of its assertions, they are mistaken. Either they have not understood what it says or the crucial evidence has not yet come to light. The Bible is right, the scholars wrong. Therefore all of us must take it as a guide both for our lives here on earth and in our quest for immortality. In particular, we should seek to follow the example of Jesus. This same aim should suffuse the work of all our institutions and be evident in all our social actions. If we try hard enough to follow the revealed teachings, we will be redeemed, our evil thoughts or acts will be forgiven, and we shall be received into the kingdom of heaven.

If this message is true, it is clearly the most important communication human beings can receive, and it is therefore worth repeating as often as may be necessary for it to be heard and heeded. Certainly it has been said often in centuries past, can be heard in person every Sunday morning from pulpits throughout the world, and is programmed around the clock on television. Why then is Graham so much more successful than anyone else in attracting the multitudes who come to hear it yet again?

The most profound answer to this question is that he is the chosen instrument of God. A serious point of view, held by millions of people and with no data to disprove it, holds that he has been selected to help us, to warn us, and to give us the message intended by that deep and powerful principle of good that humans, in their stumbling and various ways, believe to exist somewhere deeply hidden within the seamy and complex manifestations of their experience. Our rationalistic age tends not to accept explanations of this sort. Even religious people may doubt that God would single out one man as his emissary, and at least a few would say that if He did choose somebody, it would not be Graham. But it may be worth noting that as I wrote that last sentence on a stormy morning, a bolt of lightning struck a tree just outside my window.

The brief answer that worldly people give when asked how Graham attracts the multitudes is "organization." The *Christian Century* observed of a New York Crusade that "canny experienced engineers of decision have laid the tracks, contracted for the passengers, and will now direct the traffic which arrives on schedule" (Pollock, 1966, p. 173). Every meeting has impressive evidence of the truth of this assertion. People who have been working for eight months to a year on a Crusade are introduced from the platform. The ushers and counselors bear evidence of flawless training. The handling of the crowds is impeccable. The electronic equipment is extraordinary: Lights go on and off with marvelous precision, and the sound of Graham's voice is clear and vibrant throughout the enormous hall, with none of the hum and feedback with which everyone is so depressingly familiar. The Graham organization asks for no religious discount at the places where meetings are held. The full fee is paid, and no less than perfection is demanded of the facilities and local staff. If they prove to be inadequate, special experts and equipment are brought in.

At each session of the 1971 Crusade in Chicago, the program listed the delegations present, usually about five hundred of them, of which only a fifth came from Chicago. The others were from all over Illinois, Indiana, Iowa, Michigan, Wisconsin, and from even more distant states, such as Minnesota. Most of these organized groups are from churches, but others come from service clubs, schools, and other community organizations. When one reflects that there were about 5,500 such delegations in the eleven days of the Crusade, it is clear that many people have been out winning the support of pastors and elders and helping to set up arrangements. Further study reveals that a hierarchy of geographical areas and districts and neighborhoods has been created and staffed. Circles to pray for the success of the Crusade have been organized by the thousands, and volunteers by the tens of thousands go to homes to spread the word of Graham's coming.

This intricate and detailed work has been enhanced by the power of the mass media. A Graham Crusade is big news, which starts even before the dates are set and builds to a crescendo a year or so later when the meetings start. Even the perennial exposés of the Graham organization's procedural techniques merely help to reinforce the central ideas that will be expressed in the sermons. They show to the discerning that God's messengers are using the printing presses and the television and radio stations that He put on earth for the purposes for which He intended them. Graham's national career was launched in 1949 by William Randolph Hearst and was furthered by such sponsors as Henry Luce, Sid Richardson (the Texas billionaire), and every president of the United States since Dwight D. Eisenhower. It seems clear to Graham's supporters that it was the will of God that such men should help his great crusade.

But every advertising person knows that a campaign will not succeed if it does not have a worthy product to sell. Graham's magnetic presence and performance must satisfy those who come or they will not return, and, very soon, the word will go forth that he has lost his power. In the best-researched book yet written about him, Marshall Frady traces his career from the time he was a skinny, angular, effusive youth, wearing pastel-colored, flapping suits, through the period when he was "a kind

of straightforward Eagle Scout of the American conscientious-
ness, wholly unpretentious and refreshingly open-natured, as
simple and honest as a sunflower" (1979, p. 321), and on to the
graver and more stately figure of today, occasionally spectacled,
impeccably dressed, and gaunt. During his long career, many
people have said that he is a has-been, but he has constantly
confounded them and gone on to triumph after triumph with
few failures.

One reason for his success is that Graham has pursued his
career with intelligence and with a rectitude that cannot have
been easy, particularly in his early hungry and uncertain years.
He has withstood the fact that he is anathema to many non-
believers and liberal Christians. The ranks of the fundamental-
ists have many schisms, and he has had to thread his way
through constant conflict and attack, launched even by those
who might seem to outsiders to share his own views. He had no
profound theological education and has had to seek learning
wherever he could find it. He has been constantly bombarded
since his teenage years by people who were eager to use him, to
trap him, to profit by his publicity, to discredit his views, or to
catch him in some indiscretion. In all that time he has seldom
slipped. When he has, he has confronted the issue as straight-
forwardly as the situation allowed and has made such amends as
he could. He has remained wholly free from personal scandal,
lives simply, and has amassed no fortune. He has been ahead of
his time on such matters as race. He now lives every day of his
life with the memory of Martin Luther King, Jr., and King's
mother, both of whom died violently, and with the constantly
present possibility of violence in his own life. His home is
shielded by high chain-link fences topped with barbed wire, by
radio-controlled electric-eye gates, and by patrol dogs day and
night. Yet during the meetings of his Crusades, he exposes himself freely, openly, and for extended periods to millions of
people.

Whether he is inspired by God or merely favored by nature with a striking and magnetic presence, he has never felt
that his gifts were sufficient but has constantly sought to improve them. Presumably his chief method for doing so is prayer.

But his official biographer (Pollock, 1966) stresses the fact that from the beginning of his career his concern about the poverty of his theological education has led him to have a deep hunger for learning. The results are evident in his sermons. If a Crusade lasts ten days, he must speak for about five hours, and he must try never to repeat himself. When he goes on to the next Crusade, he must start the whole process all over again, for his new audience will already have heard his earlier sermons on radio and television. Accompanying these stellar events are the demands for content imposed by his special appearances and publications and by the constant outpouring of *Decision* magazine, his radio shows, his newspaper column, and his books and motion pictures. To be sure, he has help in finding sources and making first drafts, but he is said to issue over his name nothing that he has not personally scrutinized. Even though much of what he says is exhortation, the sheer volume of information and illustration required to sustain its flow is phenomenal.

During a Crusade, he monitors closely the responses that come to him about how his actions are being interpreted or his message is being received. When a newspaper writer once commented on how vigorously Graham slammed the Bible against the pulpit, the Good Book was subsequently used more reverently. If an eminent divine complains (as Reinhold Niebuhr once did) that Graham devotes too much attention to a purely individualistic approach to God, subsequent sermons will deal more fully with social action. If a television interviewer suggests that the Crusade does not differentiate clearly enough between religion and the current administration in Washington, Graham will confess that he is aware of the problem and is working on it. All such changes, however, are merely refinements in the presentation of the central message, which never changes.

The most frequent criticism of his sermons is that they do not urge social reform or deal with the immediate sins and transgressions of the people. Perhaps so. It is true that Graham has no specific program of social action, militant or otherwise, and that he attacks only the lustier vices: murder, promiscuous sex, drunkenness, drug taking, violence, and war. These sins are probably not widely practiced by the people who come to a religious crusade. But his audiences show many evidences of personal indulgence and sexual allure: the use of cosmetics and perfume, carefully styled hair, pockets bulging with cigarettes and pipes, and, particularly in the summertime, the baring of much of the body by both men and women. An old-time evangelist would have thundered against these infallible signs of an already advanced progress down the sinful path of dalliance and indulgence. Graham does not do so. Perhaps he does not believe that they are bad, either in themselves or as they lead to deeper ills. Perhaps he attacks only the major vices as a way of warning or titillating his audiences. Probably, however, there is an even deeper reason. He wants to ignore the trivial and thereby draw closer the bonds of communion among the people who come to him so that they can collectively face with stouter hearts the real evils of the world around them.

VI

Here perhaps we get a clue to as much as we can ever know about Graham's effect on the people to whom he preaches. If the test of a political orator is the adoption of policies advocated, the test of the traditional religious orator is the number of souls saved. Such evidence is not revealed to human assessors —or, at any rate, not to this one. Taking a more mundane approach, we can count the number of people who come to hear Graham, and we know that, of this number, 2 to 4 percent will come forward to make evident their personal decisions for Christ. If subsequent attendance at churches is an index, we know that the figure will rise after a Crusade and then trail off again. This depressing decline does not necessarily indicate any fault of Graham's. His organization tirelessly points out that local congregations and their pastors do not adequately guide and nurture the recruits who come to them. The Graham staff itself cannot remain behind to help in this task. In any such action would lie the seeds of a new religious denomination that would threaten existing ones and thereby destroy the basis of future Crusades. In the absence of quantitative data, therefore, evi-

dence of success or failure has tended to be anecdotal—the influence of a Crusade on the personal thoughts and lives of individuals who attend it.

So uncertain and variable an evaluation cannot satisfy
those who contemplate the whole vast experience of Graham's
evangelism. Perhaps out of the 360,000 people who attend a
Crusade or the 12,000 people who come forward, a transcen-
dent figure or group of such persons will eventually emerge,
whose conversion will, in time, make Graham seem merely a
facilitator of the future. We must wait to see whether that happens. Meanwhile the very numbers of those who attend and
who make open profession of their belief are inherently important. Such people by their actions have taken at least one positive step to strengthen an existing community of Christian belief, to bear witness to their new or continuing membership in
that community and the principles that guide it, and to demonstrate to themselves and others that they are trying to make
their own lives more purposefully religious.

The whole complex means of instruction used by Graham suggest that his goal is different from that of earlier mass
evangelists. Despite the rhetoric he sometimes uses, his purpose
is not to win converts from among those who have had no previous contact with God or who rebel against Him. A Crusade is
not an arena for wrestling with the devil or a stage on which lost
souls are dramatically saved. The people who attend are not
urged to go into states of exaltation, and the few who do so are
sheltered, not displayed. Graham's central aim is to strengthen a
wavering belief, to give the final encouragement to those who
stand on the brink of conversion, or, as he quoted the Pope as
saying, "to evangelize those who have already been baptized."

Until we have available the evidence that can be provided
only by time or by supernatural intervention, we must conclude
that Graham, unlike some great orators of the past, has not
broken across any frontiers or been the instrument of dramatic
change. His great gifts, unparalleled in his time, are ultimately
devoted not to creation but to renewal, and it is on this basis
that he must be judged as a teacher.

References

Conway, M. D. *Autobiography*. Vol. 1. Boston: Houghton Mifflin, 1904.

Faust, C. H., and Johnson, T. H. *Jonathan Edwards*. New York: American Book Company, 1935.

Frady, M. *Billy Graham: A Parable of American Righteousness*. Boston: Little, Brown, 1979.

Lodge, H. C. *Daniel Webster*. Boston: Houghton Mifflin, 1883.

Morgan, G. *The True Patrick Henry*. Philadelphia: Lippincott, 1907.

Newman, J. H. *University Sketches*. Dublin: Browne and Nolan, no date. (Originally published 1856.)

Oliver, R. T. *History of Public Speaking in America*. Boston: Allyn & Bacon, 1965.

Pollock, J. *Billy Graham: The Authorized Biography*. New York: McGraw-Hill, 1966.

6

Florence

Studying the Resources
of a Center of Culture

I

Is foreign travel worth undertaking for the sake of education?
The best general answer, summing up the voluminous literature
of the last twenty-five hundred years, seems to be that sometimes it is and sometimes it is not. The elaboration of this answer provides the general theme of this chapter.

II

Those who believe that the answer is always affirmative
may be surprised at the depth and vehemence of the negative
responses. The belief that journeying into foreign lands is inherently evil was vigorously expressed near the end of the seventeenth century by an obscure Scottish bishop, Gilbert Burnet.
He pointed out, with choleric disregard for consistency, that
such travel led to little profit, an undesirable curiosity, exposure to commonplace people, the contempt of worthy people,
unnecessarily polished good manners, finery of clothing that
could never be worn out at home, atheism or the influence of a

foreign cult, femininity of manner, uncleanliness and vulgarity of speech, exposure along the way to duelers and robbers, poverty, and a dislike of home and country (Clarke, 1914).

A surprising number of distinguished people have expressed ideas similar to these. In 1787, Thomas Jefferson wrote a long letter to his nephew saying that travelling "makes men wiser, but less happy" and spelled out many reasons why this fact was true (1904, pp. 327-328). Ralph Waldo Emerson was vehement on the subject, particularly in his best-known essay, "Self-Reliance," in which he said, "Travelling is a fool's paradise. We owe to our first journeys the discovery that place is nothing." He observed that truth always comes from within the person or from places near at hand, and although travel may be used "for the purposes of art, of study, and benevolence," it can never have a major influence to help a man find anything greater than he knows. If he tries, "he carries ruins to ruins" (1841, pp. 66-67).

A strong argument against travel is that it wastes time and is unnecessary. Many broadly cultured people have stayed at home or journeyed only short distances. "I have travelled a good deal in Concord," Henry David Thoreau wrote in *Walden* (1906, p. 4), and, as was illustrated in Chapter Four, he demonstrated the universal values that a sharp and penetrating gaze can perceive although restricted to a narrow geographical compass. Sixty years before, Gilbert White, an English curate, observing only his immediate neighborhood, wrote *The Natural History of Selborne,* a book that has been issued in many editions and still delights the modern reader. Jean Henri Fabre, the French entomologist, brought the powers of a brilliant and trained mind to bear upon the insects of a single village, and Gregor Mendel founded the science of genetics in the garden of his monastery. Some of the most brilliant, sophisticated, and perceptive literary artists never went far from home; Jane Austen, Emily Dickinson, Alexander Pope, and William Shakespeare serve as examples for hosts of others.

A widespread body of opinion has asserted that if travel for education is undertaken it should not occur during youth. Charles W. Eliot, in his inaugural address as president of Harvard

College, said that travel is a "foolish beginning but excellent sequel to education" (1898, p. 2). An unkind (and probably unfair) critic might argue that such a statement would be natural from a man to whom the custodianship of an institution of higher learning was being delivered and who saw foreign travel as competition to that institution. Adam Smith would have agreed with such a critic: "Nothing but the discredit into which the universities are allowing themselves to fall, could ever have brought into repute so very absurd a practice as that of travelling at this early period of life. By sending his son abroad, a father delivers himself, at least for some time, from so disagreeable an object as that of a son unemployed, neglected, and going to ruin before his eyes." (1776, Book V, Part III, Article II).* John Locke, not much in favor of travel at any age, did concede that young children, under the careful control of disciplinarians, might go abroad to polish their pronunciation of foreign languages, but he felt that they should be brought safely home before the later stages of youth, "that boiling boisterous part of life," during which they are sure to fall into all sorts of evil ways so common in the wicked societies on the wrong side of the English Channel (1693, paragraph 212).

Comments of the foregoing sort were repugnant to Henry Peacham, who cynically observed that anybody who made them was like "one who hath filled his owne belly, and denieth the dish to his fellow" ([1634], 1906, p. 235). For the values of travel as a learning experience have been as ceaselessly advocated as they have been attacked. Alexander the Great was tutored by Aristotle and kept the works of Homer on his bedside table, but he was quoted as saying that he had found out more with his eyes than other kings were able to comprehend in thought (Peacham, [1634], 1906, pp. 235-236). Justus Lipsius, the neo-Platonist writing in 1578, observed that "humble and plebeian souls stay at home, bound to their own piece of earth; that soul is nearer

---

*Many editions are available of the writings of Smith, Locke, Bacon, and Newman, all of whom are quoted in this chapter. Rather than refer to page numbers in a version the reader may not have available, quotations by these authors are identified by specific, easily located sections or numbered paragraphs in the works cited. Only the original date of publication is given for works by these authors.

the divine which rejoices in movement, as do the heavens themselves. Therefore almost all great men from earliest times to our
own time were travellers" (Parks, 1951, p. 264). And in 1351,
the government of Florence wrote to Francesco Petrarch bidding him to come home to teach in the new university, saying,
"Surely you have traveled enough, and the manners and cities
of foreign peoples are an open book to you" (Parks, 1951, p.
264).

The further proliferation of comments and arguments
both for and against education by foreign travel appears to be
pointless. One can sum up the matter by quoting a piece of
doggerel by Thomas Hood, the nineteenth-century English
poet: "Some minds improve by travel, others, rather, / Resemble
copper wire or brass, / Which gets the narrower by going farther!" (p. 50). This casual dismissal of the topic suggests that
the educative effect of travel lies not in the experience itself but
in what the traveller brings to it.

Some people drift as they are moved by impulse or as
they are blown, like tumbleweeds, by forces external to themselves. They are like the girl in the folk ballad of whom it was
said, "She was the wanderin' kind." Such people, in the words
of Cardinal John Henry Newman, "abound in information in
detail, curious and entertaining, about men and things; and, having lived under the influence of no very clear or settled principles, religious or political, they speak of every one and every
thing, only as so many phenomena, which are complete in
themselves, and lead to nothing." Then there are other people,
Newman said, who are forced into travel by their work. "Seafaring men, for example, range from one end of the earth to the
other; but the multiplicity of external objects, which they have
encountered, forms no symmetrical and consistent picture upon
their imagination; they see the tapestry of human life, as it were
on the wrong side, and it tells no story" (1852, Discourse VI,
Part V).

Self-guided educative travel, however, to continue with
Newman, encourages not only:

> the passive reception into the mind of a number of
> ideas hitherto unknown to it, but in the mind's

energetic and simultaneous action upon and
towards and among those new ideas, which are
rushing in upon it. It is the action of a formative
power, reducing to order and meaning the matter
of our acquirements; it is a making of the objects
of our knowledge subjectively our own, or, to use a
familiar word, it is a digestion of what we receive,
into the substance of our previous state of thought.
[And therefore it may be said that] what is called
seeing the world, entering into active life, going
into society, travelling, gaining acquaintance with
the various classes of the community, coming into
contact with the principles and modes of thought
of various parties, interests, and races, their views,
aims, habits and manners, their religious creeds and
forms of worship—gaining experience [of] how
various yet how alike men are, how low-minded,
how bad, how opposed, yet how confident in their
opinions; all this exerts a perceptible influence upon the mind, which it is impossible to mistake, be
it good or be it bad, and is popularly called its en-
largement [1852, Discourse VI, part 4].

III

The balance of this chapter focuses on people who vigorously seek to learn by foreign travel. Attention is paid primarily
to self-directed study undertaken alone or with others but remaining under the control of the would-be learner or learners.
Formal study and organized tours are excluded, except periph-
erally, not because they are wholly different from self-guided
travel but because they are usually so highly regularized by
guides and tutors that they either are classroom instruction or
greatly resemble it. Students in such situations go to Oxford,
Heidelberg, or New Delhi to absorb the products of foreign cultures much as other students back home attend lecture series,
go on field trips, or work in laboratories. Formal study abroad
can lead to self-directed learning but often only during an inter-

session in an organized course, or because the student lives intimately with resident families and can therefore observe the customs of home and family life. Otherwise, organized study abroad often seems to the observer to resemble dormitory life or study in a continuing education center back home.

IV

The purposes and curricula of foreign study may be broadly generalized, but in specific terms they always relate to the setting where they occur. One who visits the upper Amazon will seek different benefits than will one who visits Tokyo. This chapter therefore focuses upon a place rather than upon a learner or a teacher, as was the case earlier. No single site can adequately represent all the locations to which a traveller might go for enlightenment, but for the broad cultural purposes that Newman suggested perhaps no place is more manifestly significant than the Italian city of Firenze, which English-speaking people call Florence. This ancient town was the cradle of much of our modern life and displays with profusion the wealth of its culture. It would be hard to think of another place that, for so long a time and in such a concentrated fashion, has been visited by so many people with the desire to learn.

Other cities may possess higher evidences of civilization, but their riches do not dominate and penetrate life so overwhelmingly as is true in Florence. Painting and sculpture, science and engineering, government and religion, banking and social service, music and literature—seek for manifestations of great moments or eras in these or other aspects of the growth of culture and you will discover them either in the streets of the city or inexpensively accessible in more than forty major museums and innumerable minor ones. Architecture reaches a peak of achievement not only in great exteriors and interiors but in the blending together of the parts of the ancient town. People who are born there usually do not leave, although a few, such as Amerigo Vespucci, go away for a time, and local artisans once went to India to teach Shah Jahan's workers how to make the inlaid stone that decorates the Taj Mahal. The Florentines are marvelously good at craftsmanship. From Giotto to Gucci, they have designed objects admired by the whole world. But, although proud of their past, they constantly usher in their future. An old market place near the Arno has been in business since it ceased to be the Roman forum near the beginning of the Christian era, but not far away is a supermarket that is highly advanced in the variety, design, and merchandising of its wares.

The Florentines generally display a cold but correct reserve to visitors, except occasionally to one who comes unusually well introduced or with a great deal of money in hand. The people of Charleston, South Carolina, are sometimes accused of believing that their city is the oldest and most aristocratic cultural center of the universe, the place where, as one inhabitant is said to have remarked, the Ashley and the Cooper rivers join to create the Atlantic Ocean. The Florentines have somewhat the same feeling, and they have had it for six centuries longer than the Charlestonians. To those who penetrate the surface, Florentines can show a warm and sympathetic affection; but, for those who come to the city as outsiders, Florence is no warm haven, and those who would learn from it get little help. A piece of sculpture may be mounted on a turntable so that it can be rotated to catch the light from every angle, but the wrath of a vigilant guard will be visited on anybody who dares to make use of this thoughtfully designed arrangement. The shops along the via dei Tornabuoni are alleged to require their clerks to treat customers with a high degree of rudeness. Since sufficient numbers of salespeople with this trait are hard to find, it is said that the shops must offer instruction to enable their employees to meet the required standards. Nor is the general ambiance inviting. The tile floors, as many people have remarked, look clean but seldom are. Tuscan cooking does not seem brilliant after two weeks of pasta, olive oil, veal, white beans, spinach, thick raw steaks, and nasty stews of not-usually-welcomed kinds of meat. The city can be glaringly hot, numbingly chill, or penetratingly damp; it is always noisy and often smelly; and one must pick one's way with care along its narrow, uneven streets. So it is; so it has always been. Until recently, automobiles and noisy motorbikes have added their modern

degradations, but Florentine pride has begun to win some battles against their aggressions.

Independence of thought and ludicrous contrasts are
richly provided. The most elegant hotel in the city fronts on a
square whose chief feature is a black marble statue of two
naked wrestlers, one of whom is bending over his almost supine
opponent. Presented with unmistakable emphasis to the view of
every person leaving the hotel is the most protuberant part of a
nude male seen from the rear. But then the visitor turns left to
the Arno, turns left again, and walks along its bank. Presently
high on a hill in the distance is seen San Miniato, the most beloved church of most visitors to Florence. At the entrance of
the Pitti Palace, guarding its incomparably priceless treasures,
is a statue so grossly obese that people avert their eyes from it.
And the visitor who enters the great hall of the Palazzo Vecchio
sees another statue of two nude wrestlers so designed as to emphasize the fact that one gentleman has firm hold upon a vital
part of the anatomy of the other. College sophomores, con-
vulsed with laughter, send postcards of this statue to their
roommates. Yet the visitor who walks to the back of the spec-
tacularly spacious meeting room will see, rather negligently displayed, Michelangelo's great statue of Victory.

V

In Florence, so much is to be learned that nobody could
ever master the city's total culture. Roughly characterized, however, there are certain layers of learning endeavor, some or all of
which may be found elsewhere, but which have long been visi-
bly present in Florence.

The deepest layer is made up of scholars who have come
from abroad to study there. The Florentines have long been
master archivists, and their written records and artifacts are
available in surprising wealth of detail. In a commercial city
long dominated by guilds, the masters needed to keep records
of their daily business; those accounts now provide a social history that ramifies far beyond the original intentions of the people who wrote them. (Double-entry bookkeeping was probably

invented in Italy and was well known to the Florentines by
1340.) But scholars do not need to depend solely on local ma-
terials. Leaders of all fields of learning have for centuries made
their way to Florence and brought their ideas and treasures with
them. In 1439, for example, a great Congress of Europeans and
Asiatics occurred there and left an enduring imprint. Manuscripts, documents, and other evidences of culture have long
accumulated, as have relics of the ancient past, for the land
around Florence is a famous archeological site. Great treasure
houses of knowledge have come into being, and scholars are
constantly at work in them. The flood of 1966 was a disaster. A
librarian said to me, "After World War II, we thought that the
danger would come from bombs from above. How could we
know that our enemy would prove to be that damnable ditch,
the Arno!" But after the grimy waters had been bailed out of
the underground vaults and bookstacks, scholars resumed their
work on the remaining and the restored documents.

The second group who learn from Florence are dedicated
amateurs, who study some aspect of the city's life and culture
only because they love it. Sometimes they are wealthy; sometimes they get remittances from their homes in other places as
long as they stay away from them; sometimes they live on pen-
sions; and sometimes they find a way to earn their keep if they
can discover a patron or find a job that a Florentine cannot do
better. Florence has been studied so much that only rarely can
an amateur scholar find a new topic, but always there is hope of
a revisionist interpretation, a new fact, or an expanded foot-
note. Van Wyck Brooks, dealing with the last quarter of the
nineteenth century, described a few of these amateurs: "There
were students from the Beaux-Arts in Paris who were making
architectural tours and others who were exploring 'Titian's
country.' . . . There were scholars who for fifty years had been
planning a book on Columbus that was to supersede all other
lives. . . . One young man [was] making a collection of Renaissance cloak-clasps, [and] another was studying the history of
the Malatestas" (1958, p. 195). Such dedicated amateurs as
these have lived in or near Florence for centuries; they live there
today.

The third group finds Florence to be a wellspring of creativeness. Many famous names crowd this category. "Italy was my University," said Robert Browning (Sharp, 1890, p. 56), and Florence was where he was most assiduously a student. Among the other people who refined their talents there were scientists Faraday and Humboldt, historians Gibbon and Macaulay, and philosophers Hobbes, Nietzsche, and Schopenhauer. There were novelists: James Fenimore Cooper, Dickens, Dostoevski, Dumas, Eliot, Hardy, Hawthorne, William Dean Howells, Henry James, Melville, Stendhal, Harriet Beecher Stowe, Thackeray, and the Trollopes, mother and son. There were musicians: Berlioz, Debussy, Handel, Liszt, Mendelssohn, Mozart, and Tschaikovsky. There were essayists: Addison, Matthew Arnold, Emerson, Hazlitt, Montaigne, and Ruskin. There were painters: Burne-Jones, Corot, Degas, Ingres, Millais, Reynolds, Rubens, Sargent, Turner, Van Dyck, Velazquez, and Watts. Most numerous perhaps were poets: Elizabeth Barrett Browning, William Cullen Bryant, Goldsmith, Thomas Gray, Heine, Lamartine, Longfellow, James Russell Lowell, Milton, Rilke, Shelley, Swinburne, Tennyson, and Wordsworth. And there were unique and unclassifiable people, such as David Garrick, Horace Mann, Mark Twain, and Oscar Wilde. On these few and on countless others, the study of some aspect of Florentine life made a profound impact, and the diversity of what the city has to teach can be perceived by appraising in their works the results of what they learned.

The fourth group—a large and pathetically ambitious company of people of which I am a casual and occasional member—are those who, often with guidebook in hand, try to acquire a general education about the city, seeking to find the times and places when crowds are not overwhelming or the forbidding *chiuso* sign has been removed, often only briefly. The portrait of this fourth group has been drawn with fidelity by E. M. Forster in his novel *A Room with a View*.

The final group are the quick trippers who cannot stay long in the city but want either a hasty immersion in its total culture or the opportunity to share some part of its treasure—perhaps to see the paintings of Fra Angelico or the laboratory

instruments of Galileo or to hear the music of the May Festival
in the city where, one evening in the final year of the sixteenth
century, opera was born.

Members of all these groups except the scholars are to
some extent engulfed in the multitudes of tourists that swarm
into Florence, particularly in the summer. Some are people on
vacation; their buses crowd the streets and their hordes flood
the Uffizi. In the Pitti Palace, their guides are loud in every language. Everywhere vendors have cheap wares to sell them. A
second kind of tourist—the unaffiliated young—crowd the center of the Ponte Vecchio, leading their own special and ritual-
ized life, complete with guitars, sleeping bags, and the scent of
marijuana. What do the two kinds of tourists learn? Sadly
enough, little or nothing.

Conversations with the first and reports from young emis-
saries to the second lead to the conclusion that most members
of both groups do not, in any real sense, know where they are
or what they have seen while in the city. Yet perhaps, for at
least a few of the members of both groups, a spark has been
lighted that will not be extinguished and that, on some future
day and in some unanticipated fashion, will burst into the flame
of intellectual inquiry.

VI

Using this place and the people who live in it as resources,
let us examine a few of the learning goals, particularly the goals
of those who try to acquire a general education about the city.
The scholars and the dedicated amateurs have their specialized
purposes, the seekers after inspiration use their own wellsprings
of creativeness, and the quick trippers organize their experience
around any of numerous goals. But the people here called the
generalists seek to develop their own potentialities or to master
aspects of the Florentine culture. The same desires may sometimes motivate members of the other groups. Scholars, for
example, may want to learn something unrelated to their work,
and quick trippers may stay for a longer and more purposeful
visit than originally planned. The goals of the generalists are

stated broadly here since they tend to be universal to many kinds of learning by travel, but the general statement is then made concrete by some reference to the life of Florence.

The most often expressed and most rudimentary goal is to acquire proficiency in a foreign language. For some people, this objective is apparently so easy to achieve that they feel it is hardly worth mentioning. In Milton's design for education, he notes, with an airy wave of the hand, that English schoolboys can easily learn "at any odd hour the Italian tongue" ([1644], 1963, p. 104). If they can do so while still at home, how much more readily and accurately can this goal be accomplished in the native place of the language. John Stuart Mill expressed the common view when he observed that "living languages are so much more easily acquired by intercourse with those who use them in daily life; a few months in the country itself, if properly employed, go so much farther than as many years of school lessons; that it is really a waste of time for those to whom that earlier mode is attainable, to labour at them with no help but that of books and masters" (1867, p. 20).

If this principle is sound, Florence is the best place to learn Italian. In the long centuries of the Dark Ages, as Latin fell into disuse, each Italian dialect flourished until the peninsula finally had no common tongue. Early in the fourteenth century, Dante argued the necessity of creating a literary language, constructing it from the common elements of all the dialects and discarding their localisms. Despite this idea, however, he wrote *The Divine Comedy* in his native Florentine, and his example was later followed by Giovanni Boccaccio and Petrarch, thus giving Italy its classic language pattern. It was soon understood that the people of Florence use the best Italian, a point which Oriana Fallaci made when she said, "Anything can be said about me but not that I don't write good Italian. I am Florentine" (*New Yorker*, Dec. 8, 1980, p. 46).

Many people, however, have reservations about the idea that a language can be learned—at least by adults—merely by living where it is the native tongue. Those who wish to study abroad must have "some entrance into the language" before they go, said Francis Bacon in his essay "Of Travel" (1625) and the best preparation is presumably a disciplined and serious study guided by a teacher who can correct, improve, and lay a basic groundwork of grammar and pronunciation. The idea that a language can be picked up, as it were, on the street is highly doubtful unless the learner is extraordinarily gifted linguistically. It is common to find people who have lived in a foreign city for many years and yet have never troubled to acquire more than a few essential phrases. Nor is it necessary to go abroad to find such people. Distinguished scholars on the faculties of American universities who have been in this country for forty years may retain such thick accents that it is a strain to discern the meaning of what they say. Their command of written English can be exquisitely subtle, but people wince when they begin to talk. And yet it is precisely the accent that direct experience in a foreign country is said to purify.

Probably the major lesson to be learned on this point is that most adults visiting most civilized parts of the world cannot learn the language by raw experience alone. Language acquisition requires expert tuition both before and during the time of foreign residence. As Bacon suggested, the learner must reach a sufficiently high level of accomplishment in the language to be able to start or continue a conversation upon arrival in the country. Then, for a fairly long time after residence begins, the aspiring student must have a teacher who can correct, explain, drill, identify rules and their exceptions, and, in general, provide a structure that can support the broad acquisition of vocabulary and the intricacy of nuance. A child has the same need for a combination of instruction and unguided experience but not in so great a measure, for adults must unlearn the physical habits of speech practiced for many years in their native languages before they can acquire the throatiness of German, the nasal and labial quality of French, or the soft, slurring liquidness of Italian. The adult must also acquire new habits of inflection and syntax that are often completely different from his or her native language.

A second learning goal for which travel is essential is to become sensitive to the harmony of a culture. In this respect, Italy offers unusual richness of both time and variety. As W. H.

Auden rhetorically asked, "Is there any other country in Europe where the character of the people seems to have been so little affected by political and technological change?" (1962, p. xiv). In this long-sustained tradition, the separateness of the city-states has made each of them unique. Truth to tell, anybody who greatly admires one of them is likely to have a distaste for the others. But endless and pointless comparisons that begin with discussion and end with rancor need not concern those who let the culture of the city they seek to understand gradually unfold itself as they wander through its streets or systematically seek out its treasures.

Florence is a city so impossible to describe that even the most ambitious authors are reduced finally to the use of vignettes. No better book about it is known to me than Mary McCarthy's *The Stones of Florence*, whose very formlessness and occasional opacity reflect aspects of the city. It is a place of art and beauty, of passion and cruelty, of commerce and cosmopolitanism, and of countless other traits and manifestations. Each person who seeks to understand it must begin a process of exploration of which there is never an end.

What is the best place to begin? Is it the Duomo, which dominates the city's skyline and which contains Michelangelo's rough-hewn Pietà? It was at the Duomo one Sunday morning, at the moment of the elevation of the host, that a group of high-born assassins gravely wounded Lorenzo de Medici and killed his younger brother, Giuliano; and it was also in that vast echoing space that modern electronic equipment cannot fill with intelligible sound that Girolamo Savonarola thundered forth the sermons that so influenced his listeners that he became, for a time, the dictator of the city. Or shall the visitor begin with the center of city government, the Palazzo Vecchio? Both Savonarola and the greatest of the Medici, Cosimo the elder, were imprisoned there, and it contains both in its interior and immediately outside its walls some of the greatest as well as some of the most embarrassingly bad works of art in the world. Or one might start with Giotto's tower or with the domed tomb of the Medici or with any of a hundred churches and museums.

Another place to begin is less conspicuous. It is the Bargello, so hidden away among its surrounding buildings that it cannot be seen whole and entire. The young Kenneth Clark, who was to become a renowned historian of civilization, began his own study of Florence at the Bargello because, his mentor told him, "its conversion into a museum [has] not destroyed its true Florentine character" (Clark, 1974, p. 130). Its construction was begun in 1255 as the city's first town hall, but in 1574 it became the police headquarters and such was its function through most of its history.

Although it is hardly visible from the outside, the visitor who enters from the narrow sidewalk will discover a spacious hall and see beyond it a magnificent courtyard with a monumental flight of stairs leading to the second floor. It is a place of awesome majesty that lifts the spirits of everyone who does not know its history, but, like the Tower of London or the Doges' Palace in Venice, it has witnessed so much horror that even on the brightest day a knowledgeable visitor feels an ominous aura. In the entrance hall, the courtyard, and the adjoining rooms have been enacted grim scenes of nightmarish ghastliness. The Bargello was the place of confinement of political prisoners and the workplace of men who carried the refinements of agonizing torture to heights that were probably not reached again until the twentieth century. The cold bulbous-eyed face of Cosimo I, as sculptured by Cellini, dominates the room in which it is located even as he dominated the Bargello and used it (as did so many other rulers of Florence) to achieve his purposes by pain and death made more exquisitely horrible by the fact that wives and parents and children were forced to witness the agonies and execution of those they loved.

It was not until 1857 that the Bargello was freed from its bloody past and turned into a museum containing many treasures of Florence's past, most notably its sculpture. Some of the greatest works of art in the world are to be found there. To move along the corridors and through the rooms that surround the great open court is to have a series of shocks of recognition as one comes face to face with the originals of long-familiar works by Michelangelo, Donatello, Verocchio, John of Bologna, Ghiberti, Brunelleschi, Cellini, Mino da Fiesole, Desiderio da

Settignano, the della Robbias, and many others. Around these great works, most of them created by Florentines, are other magnificent objects: chests, chairs, tables, altarpieces, miniature cast bronzes, tapestries, and other exquisite pieces. People who embroider often use the Bargello stitch, whose fame spread when it was copied from some chair seats in the museum. Many of its other treasures have also been imitated. Despite this overwhelming display, the Bargello is a good place to visit, for it is seldom crowded. Most tour buses do not stop there, and the guided groups are few and small. It sometimes happens that a visitor can be alone in a room with Michelangelos or Donatellos, without even a guard to destroy solitary contemplation.

A third learning goal is to study the original products of genius. André Malraux has developed the concept of the museum without walls, a society in which technology makes it possible for colors, sounds, textures, and other esthetic qualities to be so adequately reproduced that all people wishing to do so can have available the resources of the world's culture in their home environments. Nobody, said Malraux, would need to journey around the world to see, for example, all the paintings of such Florentines as Botticelli, Leonardo da Vinci, Filippo Lippi, or Bronzino. This concept is growing ever closer to achievement. Approximations of museums, opera houses, and concert halls are widely and comfortably available for those who have libraries, radios, televisions, videotapes, and cassette recorders.

The net effect of this ready supply, however, has been not to satisfy but to whet the appetite of those who acquire sensitivity to an art form. One may look again and again at reproductions of Raphael's paintings of his Florentine period, but the desire to see the originals in the Uffizi or the Pitti Palace is merely heightened by such secondhand contemplation. When the originals are seen, they burst with fresh splendor on the eye. And although Florence provides the greatest display of Raphael's work in the world, the thorough student who wants to examine it all would have to go to at least thirty-seven other locations, some of them far from major centers of culture. Thus the museum without walls has increased educational travel, not diminished it.

It is also true that if an original work of art is seen in its
home setting, it comes alive in ways not otherwise possible.
Mary Sheldon Barnes (1896, p. 31) has illustrated this point:

> Ten to one we know all we see beforehand;
> but now our knowledge enters through the senses,
> —the common highway of human spirit, the same
> for all times and places,—and a breadth of elevation
> of life itself, a widening of the personality, result. . . .
> For instance, as soon as we reached Rome we went
> to see Raphael's Transfiguration, a canvas famous
> through the world; but in our secret hearts, we
> only wondered before it, and had dim suspicions
> that the genius of Raphael was a kind of myth kept
> sacred by a tradition that no one dared attack. But
> day after day passed, and not a day without its
> vision of high art. The antique, in all its simple ma-
> jesty, took us in hand; silently the great gods and
> heroes of the Vatican and Capitol stood before us
> and said "Look, look!" and we looked until, little
> by little, their beauty grew alive in our souls. At
> last, after two months of such schooling, we went
> again to the little upper room where the Transfig-
> uration stood; and lo, the canvas was blazing with
> life and motion and color, and we knew that Ra-
> phael was in deed and truth the Raphael men said
> he was,—an archangel of high art.

Painting and sculpture are the greatest products of the
genius of Florence, perhaps, but many people go there to study
other works as well, such as artifacts of classical antiquity, tools
used by scientists, magnificent churches and other buildings,
one of the loveliest bridges ever built, jewelry, inlaid stone, elegant furniture, and, to include modern products, the best-
known leather work and high-fashion clothing that Italy pro-
duces. The educational appeal of much that is to be seen in
Florence is now vocational in nature; designers and craftsmen
study, adapt, and borrow its old designs. So it has always been

and will probably always be until the Arno or some other malignant enemy finally destroys all that the city possesses.

The fourth goal of educational travel is to gain perspective on one's own culture and way of life. John Gardner has put the case for this objective with his usual felicity: "Travel is a vivid experience for most of us. At home we have lost the capacity to see what is before us. Travel shakes us out of our apathy, and we regain an attentiveness that heightens every experience. The exhilaration of travel has many sources, but surely one of them is that we recapture in some measure the unspoiled awareness of children." Gardner concludes his long passage on the subject by suggesting that, "unlike the jailbird, we don't know that we've been imprisoned until after we've broken out" (1963, p. 9). If the trip is successful, nothing at home will seem quite the same again, for it will be seen in the perspective of a larger experience.

In seeking to achieve this goal, some people pervert it. The comparison of two cultures is almost never undertaken without some sense of relative evaluation, and, in gaining a perspective on their own country by visiting another, some people move so far from their antecedents that presently they can find nothing good to say about them. Such a course of action is not necessarily bad, although the Italians have long had a saying that "an Italianate Englishman is the devil incarnate." But to make a change of nationalities or cultures is, in a sense, to turn the fourth objective inside out, for then the newly created foreigner must revisit his or her original home in order to regain an identification with it.

A fifth goal is to help establish a sense of history. All of the other goals contribute in some way to this one. Although the pervasive influence of history is less deep in Florence than in such other living cities as Athens, Rome, or Cairo, the evident antiquity of Florentine institutions is significant enough so that it exerts a constant influence and extends the mind into realms far more ancient than any that can be afforded by the American experience. Travel is essential to the gaining of this sense of the lines of development of civilization. It is possible to acquire all the facts about history from books and other sources, but if its remains are constantly seen and lived with, they come alive in ways not otherwise possible.

In Florence, many avenues of human activity either began or were widely broadened. The Medici were the first great modern bankers and the evidence of their existence is everywhere. At the Or San Michele are traces of the long-continuing importance of the guilds in Florentine life. Voluntary charity of a highly organized sort was institutionalized in the city; the Misericordia, in continuous existence since the thirteenth century, has thousands of volunteer members who help the poor and ailing, and every one of them has made a vow to do so for at least one hour a week for life. Halfway up a very steep hill is the home of Galileo, and not far away are exhibited the scientific instruments his hands shaped and used.

Above all else, Florence displays the history of European art, which cannot be fully comprehended without going to see the seminal masterpieces visible there. Of all the sights of Florence, the most universally viewed are the doors to the Baptistry just across the street from the cathedral. (I have seen people studying them at two o'clock in the morning when they were illuminated only by streetlights and a full moon; during the day they never cease to draw a crowd.) They were designed by Ghiberti beginning in 1425. In making a first set, in the years 1403–1420, he was helped by many craftsmen, possibly including Masaccio. The doors are in bas-relief so that the varying levels of metal give depth to the scenes they portray.

Masaccio was basically a painter, and in helping to build the doors he perceived what no earlier painter known to him had understood: Techniques could be used to create a sense of depth in painting instead of the flatness that until then had been its characteristic in contemporary art. When he was given the commission to design the Brancacci Chapel in the church of the Carmine, he worked out his principles in the murals he painted. Since he died at the age of twenty-seven, this chapel contains almost all of his independent production. The paintings he did there, as Schevill, the magisterial historian of Florence points out, have become "the basis of all modern painting down to the threshold of the twentieth century," although art historians, despite constant efforts, have not yet succeeded in analyzing Masaccio's "revolutionary contribution" (1963, pp. 427–428). Clark agrees, calling the Brancacci paintings, along with some bronze reliefs of Donatello, "the bed-rock of European art" (1974, p. 161).

A sixth goal is to identify a new and absorbing personal interest. Everybody's home environment contains many cues and introductions to the knowledge of people and of nature, but they are hidden from view by a personal provincialism derived from routine pathways and habits. In a foreign place, the comforts of the familiar are stripped away, and we see places and customs and names that excite an interest that can deepen into a thoughtful and sometimes lengthy study.

For example, the street that runs between the Ponte Vecchio and the Pitti Palace is named the via Guicciardini, and the visitor to Florence comes across the name again and again in other places. Who or what was Guicciardini? Educated Florentines who are asked that question shake their heads in disbelief that the visitor would not know, for, to them, Guicciardini was a great historian and political scientist, often paired with another son of Florence, Machiavelli. For generations the reputations of the two men glowed equally brightly. In the nineteenth century, however, Guicciardini went into an eclipse from which he is only very slowly emerging. His work, Schevill says, was not only "the first thoroughly realistic history of modern times, but ... has the further merit of being the first clear exposition of the European political system as it emerged in Guicciardini's time and has continued without break to the present day" (1963, p. 503). Such a remark as this one whets the appetite and may lead to an absorbing interest in the man, his writings, and the nature of the political system that he described.

A seventh goal of travel is to acquire self-confidence. To live among a foreign people, dependent on one's own resources to secure even the simplest needs of life, is to gain a sense of self-reliance and a ready capacity to handle routines and deal with emergencies. Such, at any rate, is the accepted contention, although in his research on organized programs of travel for college students, Dennison Nash has shown that "self-confidence tends to decline as a result of a year abroad" (1976, p. 199). This result may occur from overprotection by mentors, the particular stresses of the postadolescent years, or other causes. No similar study has been made of those who engage in self-directed educational travel in adulthood, but a good deal of anecdotal evidence suggests that some people cannot readily cope with another culture. Many people have gone home earlier than planned because the strangeness of a foreign place became too much for them. The term *culture shock* has now become a cliché as its symptoms have been more and more widely felt by people encouraged to travel by the growth of mass transportation and the alluring promises of travel folders.

The ability to achieve this seventh goal is not universal. Some people recognize that they need to gain greater assurance and go abroad to find it, just as some children are sent away to summer camp for the same reason. In both cases, bouts of inadequacy and homesickness may result, but often the hoped-for self-reliance is enhanced. For everybody, rough moments occur and usually they quickly pass. But for some people, home is best and always will be.

Florence is a poor place to begin the process of knowing how to get along in foreign settings. As already noted, the people of the city are well known for their quickness and impatience, their eagerness to get about the business of their own lives, their sense of being part of a living present and a future filled with challenges, and their feeling that, despite all the glories of the city, tourism is, as McCarthy puts it, "an accidental by-product. . . . There is no city in Italy that treats its tourists so summarily, that caters so little to their comfort" (pp. 10–11). Her long and brilliantly executed first chapter is built on the theme "How can you stand it?", the *it* being Florence.

And yet, even as it is a poor place to learn to be self-reliant, it is a magnificent place to enjoy the advanced stages of independence. As McCarthy concludes, "This lack of cooperative spirit, this absence, this preoccupation, comes, after a time, and if you are not in a hurry, to seem one of the blessings of Florence, to make it, even, a hallowed place" (p. 13). Visitors are left alone there, the beggars being far fewer than they

used to be. And the Florentines are so accustomed to their city
that they no longer notice it, and therefore they seldom get in
the visitors' way. Twenty-five yards from the Bargello is a leather
shop; its proprietor, a man of forty who had worked there since
he could first toddle in with his father, from whom he later inherited the business, told me he had never been inside the museum—and neither had his father. Because there are so many
Florentines like him, many of the treasure houses and churches
of the city can be studied at leisure; experienced persons know
when often-crowded tourist sites are least likely to be cluttered
with other people. As for more esoteric places, the rules of
availability, if there are any, change from day to day. Even hotel keepers and travel agents shake their heads in despair when
asked to help a visitor discover when a building is open or
whether space in a theater is available. Those who can successfully make their way in Florence can do so anywhere in Western
Europe.

VII

Those who have argued for the educative value of travel
have usually held that it should be preceded and followed by direct and specific study. It is well to know at least the rudiments
of the language, topography, and history of the place to be
visited and to have reviewed the books that will serve as companions during the visit itself. Some authorities suggest that the
traveller begin a visit to a city or region by taking a comprehensive conducted tour in order to grasp its general geographic pattern and to locate the places to be visited later. Perhaps the only
kind of person who may have no need of any advance preparation is the painter or the impressionistic writer who wants to
capture and record personal images and who believes, for example, that it is possible to provide, after all the centuries, a fresh
interpretation of the red-tiled roofs of Florence or the combined squalor and elegance of the Ponte Vecchio. However,
such artists seek not to learn but to perform and therefore are
not true exceptions to the general rule.

For people who have specific goals in mind, advance

preparation is usually not a duty but a pleasurable necessity. Even a professional architect might do well to review the nature and history of the construction of churches before going to Florence or any other city noted for them. The nontrained generalist must either do some advance study or lose most of the value of the visit, for behind the specific examples to be viewed lies a long-established tradition of styles, processes of construction, forms, and conventions. Ephraim Emerton pointed out that "even a slight acquaintance with these technicalities immensely increases the enjoyment of architecture, and there is no form of art so pregnant with suggestions of the highest educational value. In the presence of a Gothic cathedral one is brought into relation not only with the miracle of its beauty and its constructive skill, but with the vast historical development for which it stands, with the social order that made it possible, with the religious feeling it embodies and expresses, and with the currents of active present life in which it has a part" (1921, p. 223). To visit the cathedrals of Milan, Florence, and Orvieto is to experience three differing sensations, but the impression of each cathedral will be greatly heightened if the mind is aware of the deeper resemblances and differences among them.

Of course, as Emerton noted, one can go too far. He cites the case of "an American college professor who said that he had found everything in the Eternal City exactly as he had worked it out from books, except that the Mamertine prison lay a few feet farther to the south than he had calculated" (1921, p. 209). For such a man travel was not a way of learning but of checking up on what he had previously learned.

While actually present in a foreign place, some plan of procedure is helpful, even if it be to follow Forster's advice concerning Alexandria that "the best way to see it is to wander aimlessly about" (Morris, 1976, p. 37). At the other extreme is the plan suggested by Francis Bacon in his essay "Of Travel," (1625), a schedule of activities few people would care to follow

> The things to be seen and observed are the courts of princes, especially when they give audience to ambassadors; the courts of justice, while

they sit and hear causes; and so of consistories ec-
clesiastic; the churches and monasteries, with the
monuments which are therein extant; the walls and
fortifications of cities and towns; and so the havens
and harbours, antiquities and ruins, libraries, colleges, disputations and lectures, where any are;
shipping and navies; houses and gardens of state
and pleasure near great cities; armories, arsenals,
magazines, exchanges, bourses, warehouses, exercises of horsemanship, fencing, training of soldiers,
and the like; comedies, such whereunto the better
sort of persons do resort; treasuries of jewels and
robes; cabinets and rarities; and, to conclude, what-
soever is memorable in the places where they go.
. . . As for triumphs, masks, feasts, weddings, funerals, capital executions, and such shows, men
need not be put in mind of them; yet they are not
to be neglected.

According to Lord Bacon, a traveller should have a guidebook,
keep a diary, and change lodgings from time to time in order to
learn various parts of the city; and a traveller should "sequester
himself from the company of his countrymen, and diet in such
places where there is good company of the nation where he
travelleth."

As for study after travel, it may or may not be serious
and sustained, but for one who has truly seen a foreign place,
not merely passed through it, a permanent sense of relationship
has been established, and it will almost always be reinforced by
subsequent experiences. One who has come to know Florence
will find its name or words associated with it leaping out from
the printed page so that a body of knowledge continues to ac-
cumulate, reinforcing and deepening the original bond to the
city. If travel uncovers a new learning goal, study of some sort
is almost certain to follow. In any case, the serious traveller will
join the enormous company of people who must decide whenever they go abroad whether they should visit new places or
deepen their knowledge of familiar ones.

The assessment of what has been learned by foreign travel depends in large measure on the situation in which a person who has had such experience finds himself or herself. Many of those who engage in self-guided educational travel care only about their own estimates of what they have learned, and their evaluation of progress is often made at the time of the travel itself. If their goal is to learn a language, they feel pride or dejection in their ability to deal adequately with daily encounters. If their purpose is to study original products of genius, they gain a sense of mastery as, with deeper appreciation than they ever felt before, they study, say, the strange and haunting works of Piero della Francesca. And if their aim is to establish a sense of history, they feel gratification as they grasp the various counterbalancing forces at work in the government of the Florentine city-state.

Some of those who wish to learn from foreign travel and residence seek not only a sense of personal accomplishment but also the esteem of a wide or elitist public for the results of their study. The scholar, the dedicated amateur, and the artist are judged by the profundity, insightfulness, or esthetic quality of what they have produced as a result of their sojourns. In such cases, the judges may differ greatly in their opinions. The best-known of all presumably scholarly books on the Medici family has been subjected to the scornful laughter of some critics ever since it was first published, but a half-century later it is still in print. Other books that scholars crown with laurels and are enjoyed by the few nonscholars who read them never find large audiences.

VIII

The question raised in the first paragraph of this chapter may now be given a summary answer that is a bit more explicit than the one provided there. The educative influence of travel is determined largely by the ability and sharpness of focus of the traveller. Some people avidly seek to learn, others are frightened by strange places, and others drift through them with no thought of a resulting change in their knowledge, skill, or sensitivity.

Travel is a way of learning that has unique advantages, but they can be fully achieved only when combined with such other methods as reading, formal instruction, tutorial guidance, and supervised practice. The creative combination of these methods is at once the cause and the result of the breadth and clarity of purpose that so greatly influence the educative effect of travel.

References

Auden, W. H. "Introduction." In J. W. von Goethe, *Italian Journey*. New York: Pantheon Books, 1962.

Bacon, F. "Of Travel." (Originally published 1625.)

Barnes, M. S. *Studies in Historical Method*. Lexington, Mass.: Heath, 1896.

Brooks, V. W. *The Dream of Arcadia*. New York: Dutton, 1958.

Clark, K. *Another Part of the Wood*. New York: Harper & Row, 1974.

Clarke, J. *Bishop Gilbert Burnet as Educationist*. Aberdeen: Aberdeen University Press, 1914.

Eliot, C. W. "Inaugural Address as President of Harvard College." In *Educational Reform*. New York: Appleton-Century-Crofts, 1898.

Emerson, R. W. *Essays*. Boston: James Munroe, 1841.

Emerton, E. *Learning and Living*. Cambridge, Mass.: Harvard University Press, 1921.

Gardner, J. W. *Self-Renewal*. New York: Harper & Row, 1963.

Hood, T. *Poetical Works*. London: Ward, Lock, no date.

Jefferson, T. *Works*. New York: Putnam's, 1904.

Locke, J. *Some Thoughts Concerning Education*. (Originally published 1693.)

McCarthy, M. *The Stones of Florence*. New York: Harcourt Brace Jovanovich, no date.

Mill, J. S. *Inaugural Address at St. Andrews*. London: Longmans, Green, 1867.

Milton, J. *Of Education*. London: Macmillan, 1963. (Originally published 1644.)

Morris, J. *Travels*. New York: Harcourt Brace Jovanovich, 1976.

Nash, D. "The Personal Consequences of a Year of Study Abroad." *Journal of Higher Education,* 1976, *47,* 191-203.

Newman, J. H. *The Idea of a University.* (Originally published 1852.)

Parks, G. B. "Travel as Education." In R. F. Jones (Ed.), *The Seventeenth Century.* Stanford, Calif.: Stanford University Press, 1951.

Peacham, H. *The Compleat Gentleman.* Oxford: Clarendon Press, 1906. (Originally published 1634.)

Schevill, F. *Medieval and Renaissance Florence.* New York: Harper & Row, 1963.

Sharp, W. *The Life of Robert Browning.* London: Walter Scott, 1890.

Smith, A. *An Inquiry into the Nature and Causes of the Wealth of Nations.* (Originally published 1776.)

Thoreau, H. D. *Works.* Vol. 2. Boston: Houghton Mifflin, 1906.

7

Edward Everett

Establishing a Formal System
of Education

I

Both the construction of the American educational ladder for young people and the foreshadowing of the concept of life-span learning occurred in the nineteenth century. The United States entered it with a few tiny colleges and academies, numerous dame schools, and various other casual and fleeting arrangements for the instruction of children and youth but with no organized system of formal schooling and no practical plans for achieving one. Three quarters of a century later, a pattern of elementary and secondary schools was in place, programs for teacher education had been developed, the research and the practical university had each been firmly conceptualized, and examples of both kinds were beginning to be established. The idea that education should be continued throughout adulthood had been formulated and to a modest extent institutionalized. These results had been brought about by many clusters of leaders, but modern historians who examine these groups with the perspective of hindsight will note that one man, whose lifetime almost exactly spanned the seventy-five years of educational innovation, appeared again and again, usually in a dominant or leading role.

II

Edward Everett was born in 1794 in Dorchester, Massachusetts, the descendant of a long line of farmers and mechanics who had been in America since about 1635. Edward's father, one of nine children, had, by great sacrifice, made his way through Harvard, not receiving his degree until the age of twenty-eight. He was then successively a clergyman and a judge and died at the age of fifty-seven, leaving his young wife to support their eight children, first with her father's aid and later with the help of Edward, who throughout a long life was never free of the burdens of caring for various members of his extended family.

Edward was graduated from college at the age of seventeen, acclaimed as the most brilliant student who had ever attended Harvard, whose president also said that Edward's physical beauty resembled that of the bust of Apollo. After two years of theological study, the young man was installed at the age of nineteen as pastor of the Brattle Street Church, which had the largest and most fashionable congregation in Boston. He occupied this post for a little more than a year, becoming a celebrated preacher and writing a 500-page treatise on *The Evidences of Christianity*. The editor of the *Edinburgh Review* considered him "the most remarkable young man I have seen in America" (Long, 1935, p. 62). Everett did not remain a pastor long; he soon accepted the Eliot Professorship of Greek at Harvard, on condition that he be allowed time to prepare himself adequately for his new work by study in Europe, where he spent the next four years.

Returning to Harvard from these foreign travels, he began to display the fruits of European civilization and German scholarship. Ralph Waldo Emerson, who had had an adolescent crush on Everett during the Brattle Street Church days and subsequently was a student of his at Harvard, wrote effusively on Everett's "radiant beauty of person, of a classic style," remarking also that to the "green boys from Connecticut, New Hampshire, and Massachusetts" he brought an intellectual rigor unknown to an "unoccupied American Parnassus" (1904, pp. 331–332). His fame, based on his earlier celebrity as a clergyman, continued to grow as students crowded into his classroom, and their parents came in ever-increasing numbers to his public lectures. Few art forms were actively practiced in the young nation but oratory was one of them, and he became perhaps its greatest practitioner. On hearing him, Henry Clay said, "This is the acme of eloquence" (Boston City Council, 1876, p. 57). In 1822, Everett secured his place among the Boston elite by marrying the daughter of Peter C. Brooks, a leading businessman. The young professor further augmented his scholarly distinction by accepting the editorship of the *North American Review*.

Soon, however, it was time for him to go on to national leadership, for which he had laid an earlier foundation. As a young preacher, he had traveled south to Washington, taking along letters of recommendation, one of which concluded:

> Mr. Everet is respectable in every Vein; in Family
> fortune Station Genius Learning and Character.
> What more ought to be said to Thomas Jefferson by
>   John Adams
> [Frothingham, 1925, p. 31]

Later, on returning from Europe, Everett had received great acclaim for a sermon delivered in the chamber of the House of Representatives in Washington. John Quincy Adams, a connoisseur of such matters, said it was the best sermon he had ever heard, adding that "it abounded in splendid imagery, in deep pathos, in cutting satire, in profound reflections of morals, in coruscations of wit, in thunderbolts of feeling" (Brooks, 1936, p. 74).

After five years of teaching at Harvard, Everett decided to return to the scene of this earlier triumph. He was elected to Congress in 1825, serving for ten years in the House. He then became governor of Massachusetts for four one-year terms.

After a period of rest and travel, he was appointed ambassador to Great Britain, a post he left after four years to become president of Harvard. He stayed in that position only until 1849, after which he performed various services for the government, including an appointment in Washington as Secretary of State. His most notable accomplishment in that post was to bring to a conclusion the often-attempted opening-up of Japan, a success shared by Matthew Perry's gunboats and Everett's persuasive eloquence in his letter to the Emperor. In 1853, he became a senator from Massachusetts but resigned after little more than a year because he was passionately devoted to the Union and feared that the policies his constituents wished to impose on the South would inevitably result in war. They could say contemptuously that threats of secession were "the barkings of a dog that would not bite," but he did not agree (Frothingham, 1925, p. 417), and, in the end, he proved to be right.

During the next few years he remained a private citizen, lending his talents to many causes. He developed and repeatedly delivered an address on George Washington that established for contemporaries and for posterity the mythic character of the great American hero. The fees received from the delivery of this lecture paid one third of the cost of Mount Vernon so that the estate could be turned over to the nation. When war came, Everett devoted his efforts to mobilizing support for the government, and then, when the Union victory began to seem inevitable, to urging moderation in the treatment of the South and the reestablishment of fraternal feeling with the Confederate states. His last address was at Faneuil Hall in Boston on January 12, 1865, where he urged that aid be sent to the sufferers at Savannah, which Sherman's army had just ravaged. Everett did not recover from the exertions of his address; he left the hall, he said, "with my extremities ice, and my lungs on fire" (Boston City Council, 1865, p. 52). Three days later he died from what was called "a sudden attack of an apoplectic nature" (p. 18).

President Lincoln announced Everett's death to the American people, and later the Boston City Council published a large memorial volume, containing many speeches, tributes, memoirs, and proceedings. On the day of his funeral, public and private businesses closed, government buildings were draped in black, and the route of his funeral procession was lined with mourners. The senior Oliver Wendell Holmes wrote an ode for the occasion, calling Everett "Our First Citizen" (Boston City Council, 1865, pp. 189–191).

Thus ended a dazzling career. The man whom most of his contemporaries thought to be brilliant, powerful, and magnificent spent a lifetime at center stage in the United States and in Europe. From boyhood until death, he was an associate of advanced thinkers and social luminaries. He knew all the great Americans of his time, and, in Europe, he was associated, on a more or less intimate basis, with (among others) Byron, Carlyle, Goethe, Lafayette, the Duke of Wellington, the Humboldt brothers, Walter Scott, Jenny Lind, Wordsworth, Pope Pius VII, Queen Victoria and her consort, the Czar, the Emperor of Austria, Napoleon III, the three nineteenth-century Bourbon kings of France, and the monarchs of Belgium, Hanover, Naples, the Netherlands, Prussia, and Saxony. However masterful his presence and his actions, he gave to the majority of those who observed him the impression that he had powers still held in reserve.

This radiant figure had also had perhaps more than his share of personal cares, some of which are noted elsewhere in this chapter. His diaries show that his public acclaim was matched by personal self-doubt. As a politician, he had taken part in all the great debates of the stormiest and most divisive period of American life and had acquired his due share of enemies. He had lost elections and had felt such distaste for the presidency of Harvard and the senatorship of Massachusetts that he had resigned both positions. He knew what harsh things were said about him in his lifetime and probably would not have been surprised by the negative comments in the biographies, diaries, memoirs, and collections of letters issued after his death. Was he vain, cold, calculating, and unable to conceal the artfulness with which he prepared his orations? Some of his contemporaries thought so. Did he care for honors but not accomplishment? Emerson, liberated from his early adulation, made that charge, calling Everett "a mere dangler and ornamental person" (Morison, 1936, p. 276). Was he too eager to assert the educational rights of black people? Such was the opinion of the students at Harvard. Was he too ardent an abolitionist? The Southern senators almost defeated his appointment as ambassador on that ground. Or did he fail to throw his full weight behind the antislavery cause as early and as fully as he should have? Some of the abolitionists thought so, and eventually he admitted that they might have been right. In his Gettysburg address, he said, "A sad foreboding of what would ensue, if war should break out between North and South, has haunted me through life, and led me, perhaps too long, to tread in the path of hopeless compromise, in the fond endeavor to conciliate those who are predetermined not be conciliated" (Everett, 1892, p. 652).

III

When Everett died, both he and his contemporaries would have had every reason to believe that he had established a prominent position in American history. Both his broadly based public acclaim and his location at the center of his nation's major controversies would seem to have assured such a position of honor for him. Such was not to be his destiny. Even he, who knew so much about the rise and fall of reputations, would probably not have believed how quickly he would be doomed to obscurity.

Evidence of the rapidity of that decline can be found in the observance of the centennial of his birth held by the Dorchester Historical Society one afternoon in 1894. It was a purely local affair, and few people of importance attended, not even Everett's son, who was currently occupying his father's former seat in Congress. The report of the proceedings (Dorchester Historical Society, 1897) describes a lackluster event. The major speaker, a local clergyman, began by saying, "I think far more highly of Edward Everett than I did thirty years ago" (p. 15), an opening that enabled him to explain the causes of his earlier dislike. The mayor of Boston sent a message in which he noted that Everett "hardly attained to the position of a popular favorite" (p. 7). Another speaker assured the audience that Everett's book, *The Evidences of Christianity*, was "not of the least worth among theological scholars of today" (p. 23). As the long afternoon wore on, most of the talks were trivial or irrelevant, expounding on some subject that the speaker had on his mind and usually only loosely tied to the theme of the occasion. Finally, Everett's young grandson concluded the meeting by saying that he was happy that the eulogies had not been "too fulsome" (p. 58). He apparently did not intend this comment to be ironic.

Thus it was clear that, less than thirty years after his death, Edward Everett was already well on his way to oblivion. His fame might have dwindled away almost entirely if it had not been for a single incident, one which was of scant importance in the panorama of his life but which could be made to suggest a moral and has therefore remained his major claim to whatever renown he still possesses.

The occasion was the dedication of the National Cemetery at Gettysburg, on the gloomy, chill day of November 19, 1863. Everett was the obvious choice to give the major oration, and the date was delayed for a month to give him time to prepare. The President of the United States was also asked to make some remarks. Shortly after noon, Everett advanced to the front of the platform, paused, and then began: "Standing beneath this serene sky, overlooking these broad fields now reposing from the labors of the waning year, the mighty Alleghenies dimly towering before us, the graves of our brethren beneath our feet, it is with hesitation that I raise my poor voice to break the eloquent silence of God and nature" (Everett, 1892, p. 622). He went on in lofty terms to describe what he called "the battles of Gettysburg," describing each military engagement within a broad context of place and time and strategy.

Behind him on the platform was a brilliant array of notables. Before him as far as he could see was a multitude, estimated by various observers as fifteen or thirty or fifty thousand people. His address had already been set in print, and reporters who followed its apparently spontaneous delivery found that

hardly a word was changed or out of place. He spoke for about
two hours. Carl Sandburg, summing up the observations of
those who heard Everett, reported that his voice never faltered,
adding that "his erect form and sturdy shoulders, his white hair
and flung-back head at dramatic points, his voice, his poise, and
chiefly some quality of inside goodheartedness, held most of his
audience to him" (1936, p. 468).

The Baltimore Glee Club then sang an ode written for
the occasion, after which the President unfolded his lengthy
figure, took out his spectacles and two sheets of paper and
walked forward. He started to read, but the audience hardly had
time to settle itself and prepare to listen when he finished and
resumed his seat. This sudden ending to the tumultuous celebration left most people uneasy. The President himself said, "It is a
flat failure and the people are disappointed" (Sandburg, 1936,
p. 472). The press reaction varied according to the political
views of the newspapers. The Chicago *Times* called the comments "silly, flat, and dish-watery utterances," but the Chicago
Tribune said, "The dedicatory remarks of President Lincoln will
live among the annals of man" (Sandburg, 1936, pp. 472-473).
As all the world knows, the latter judgment has proved to be
correct.

Everett was among the first to recognize the greatness of
the President's address. The sixty-nine-year-old man who had
stood in the open air on a raw November day projecting with
force and artistry a memorized two-hour speech to a multitude
did not then pause to rest and husband his strength to help him
through the remaining events of a crowded day. Instead, he listened closely to Lincoln and understood what he heard. The
next day he wrote to the President saying, "I should be glad if
I could flatter myself that I came as near to the central idea of
the occasion in two hours as you did in two minutes." Lincoln
responded: "In our respective parts yesterday, you could not
have been excused to make a short address, nor I a long one"
(Sandburg, 1936, p. 475).

As the fame of Lincoln's Gettysburg address spread, the
contrast between its simple sentences and the two-hour oration
that had preceded them seemed ever more ludicrous. In that

comparison, American social historians were not slow to find a lesson entirely at the expense of Everett: The plain, common speech of the self-taught American, expressed with conviction and brevity, endures far longer than does the elaborate, spacious oration of a highly polished scholar. This interpretation is unjust to both the brilliant rhetoric of Lincoln and the broad historic narrative of Everett. No matter. The anecdote is now set for all time. And so it has come about that, with all Everett's diverse talents and accomplishments, he, like many another person before and since, has been preserved in history's reckoning chiefly by an anecdote.

A realist might argue that such an outcome would be all that Everett might reasonably expect. The world of the past is so crowded that the few people who are remembered must have had special talents, high positions, or crowning achievements with which they can be identified. His talents were great, but they were spread in many directions. His reputation could not be comfortably hung on the peg of any one of his accomplishments; he is perhaps fortunate therefore that there was one event that helped him escape oblivion.

It should not be forgotten, however, that one paramount and dominant theme did govern his life. This fact was known to a few of his discerning contemporaries and is plain to those who examine the whole span of his career. To understand it fully, one must not focus on Pastor Everett, Professor Everett, Editor Everett, Congressman Everett, Governor Everett, Ambassador Everett, President Everett, Secretary of State Everett, Senator Everett, or even Everett the orator. One must examine instead what he tried to accomplish in these many roles as well as in the special causes in which he engaged as public officer or private citizen. Through all of them, he worked consistently at one task. His nephew, Edward Everett Hale, defined it when he said that his uncle's truly great contribution was the fact that "he stood, first, second, and last for public education, and that of the best" (Dorchester Historical Society, 1897, p. 69). The word *public* as used here was not an antonym for *private,* as it would be today, but implied a universal opportunity for education, however paid for. Everett was concerned with the spread of high-quality education to all who could profit from it, and to that task he gave his energies in many and diverse ways.

IV

His first contribution was to higher education. Until the middle of the nineteenth century, every American college began by imitating, directly or indirectly, one or another of the English colleges, taking it, however, out of the context of an overarching university. In an atmosphere of discipline and piety, the colleges taught the rudiments of a classical education. At Harvard, for example, the curriculum changed little during the first two centuries of the institution's existence. Class after class of students was taken through a series of textbooks almost entirely by instructors who had themselves been members of previous Harvard classes and had had no further formal preparation for their work.

As far as Harvard and its sister colleges were concerned, the professions did not exist as ordered and disciplined bodies of knowledge. Nor was liberal culture taught: The accomplishments of Charlemagne, Milton, Shakespeare, Bacon, Galileo, Michelangelo, Bach, Beethoven, Mozart, Voltaire, Rousseau, Lavoisier, Descartes, Adam Smith, and many another statesman and scholar were unknown to the curriculum. Unusually gifted students might learn something of the work of such people as these but only if they sought out that knowledge themselves. As Perry Miller has said, such students "were in actuality receiving two distinct and disparate educations: one in the classroom . . . and one in the dormitory" (1950, p. 12).

But although Harvard (and, indeed, all of New England) was provincial in outlook, a few people were dimly aware that in Germany the old universities had taken on a new life and were in the process of transforming themselves and that many European royal courts (particularly in middle Europe) were seeking to be centers of culture. Word had reached Boston of Goethe, Schiller, the Humboldts, Hegel, and a number of other men, some of them professors, who had achieved a certain measure of fame. Therefore, when Harvard offered Everett a professorship in 1815, it wisely allowed him to spend four years to study abroad before taking up his teaching duties. Germany seemed to be the right place for him to go. But how was he to learn German? No tutors or classes existed in Boston, and a ransacking of private libraries and bookstores produced no textbooks or grammars. Finally his brother found a book designed to teach German to speakers of French; that had to suffice. A pamphlet on the German universities also came to light, and Everett decided to go to Göttingen because the town, its university, and particularly its library seemed attractive to him. And so he, George Ticknor (with whom his life was to be entwined ever after), and several other young men set off for Europe.

Upon landing in England, they found that Napoleon had escaped from Elba and that the great final battles of his era were being fought. Instead of making a leisurely grand tour through the capitals of Europe, therefore, Everett and Ticknor went at once by a northern route to Göttingen. What they found there changed the lives of both of them, and they in turn had no little effect on the University of Göttingen. The new German university of the nineteenth century, centered on and steeped in research, came into being about 1810, reached its maturity by 1850, and remained in full flower for the rest of the century. Its central idea was scholarship, every topic being analyzed with a rigorous discipline that had never previously been so broadly institutionalized. But when Everett and Ticknor arrived, the new thrust of German learning was not yet well established, and the students, with relatively rare exceptions, were neither scholarly nor cultured. Most professors came from peasant stock and were used to drudgery, and it has been observed of the German students of that period that "their shirts were black with dirt; their leather pants were stained with tobacco juice and beer; they spat on the floor and had foul table manners; and they were grossly immoral and impious" (Tyack, 1967, p. 61).

The tradition being fostered, however, was one of hard work and long hours. Everett established for himself a Spartan daily regime: 5 to 8 o'clock, Greek; 8 to 9, German; 9 to 10, exegesis; 10 to 12, Greek; 1:30 to 4, Latin and French; 4 to 5, philology; 5 to 7, Greek; 7 to 8, fencing and military exercises; 9 to 11, recreational study of Hebrew, Syriac, natural history, and a four-mile walk. As later generations of Harvard students found their German-trained professors trying to impose such schedules of study as this one, a piece of doggerel of the time seemed appropriate:

> Whene'er with haggard eyes I view
> This dungeon, that I'm rotting in,
> I think of those companions true
> Who studied with me at the U-
>   niversity of Göttingen.

["Song by Rogero," 1798, p. 238]

Evidence suggests that the arduous schedule must have been modified, but Everett and Ticknor attacked it initially with such vigor, recited their lessons with such perfection, and were so courtly to professors and their wives that they were soon accepted socially, admitted to the inner circles of both town and gown (particularly among people of their own upper middle class), and finally were held up as models to be imitated by Germans and foreigners alike. Letters of introduction were given to the two young men that they used to good advantage when they visited other universities and centers of culture. They established a pathway that their successors would follow in a constantly increasing stream during the rest of the nineteenth century.

George Bancroft, whose career was guided by Everett, followed him to Göttingen and soon thereafter wrote back to the president of Harvard, "Mr. Everett on leaving the university received the degree of doctor from the philosophical faculty in a manner particularly honourable to him. As a friend of his I am received with open arms by everybody, whom I visit, and enter into a possession of all the rights, which belonged to him, when he resided here" (Howe, 1908, pp. 55-56). At other universities, courts, and salons that Bancroft later visited, he had the same experience. Everett had become the model of the cultivated American, and the Germans were none too sure that they themselves had any such exemplar.

Emerson's opinion of the influence of Everett when he returned to Harvard has already been noted. Many other people offered similar testimony. In 1865, a Massachusetts state senator said that he had been a member of Everett's first class, adding, "I may almost say, that his lecture-room in the old Harvard Hall was the birthplace of my mind" (Boston City Council, 1865, p. 101). Thus Everett set a model at home as well as abroad. It must be said that he never did what the German university trained him to do. He was never a scholar in the deep Germanic sense; he produced no enduring books or monographs nor did he display the formidable techniques of scholarship acquired during the long hours of study at Göttingen. Perhaps he was as much a product of the salon as of the seminar. But he played to perfection the role of the learned scholar, perhaps even better than those who lived the part. Samuel Eliot Morison, the official historian of Harvard, said that Everett and Edward Tyrrell Channing together "created the classic New England diction—the measured, dignified speech, careful enunciation, precise choice of words, and well-modulated voice that (for men of my age at least) will ever be associated with President [Charles W.] Eliot" (1936, p. 216).

Those who followed the example of Everett, Ticknor, and the other young men who studied in Germany came back to Harvard and the other little American colleges determined to broaden them into universities. The task was long and hard, particularly since other conceptions than the German research model also developed, most notably the practical ideal established by the Morrill Act of 1862. In the great comprehensive universities of today, however, for good or for ill, the values established and personified by Everett and his colleagues still have a preeminent value.

His gifts as an administrator helped Harvard to begin its move from a small college to a great university when he served as its president from 1846 to 1849. He was the first of a long succession of short-tenured occupants of the position. The place was wild and ferocious. The students were out of control, breaking up classes with their drunkenness, yelling and carousing all night, setting fire to the houses of unpopular professors including Everett's, exploding bombs in the chapel and the library, and, as one prim author put it, "becoming known to" the fancy ladies of Harvard Square. The faculty was also out of control, and Everett's running account of its actions in his diary would strike a sympathetic chord in the heart of any modern university president. One entry reads: "Issued the notice for a Faculty meeting tomorrow evening, and thus ends all comfort for the next twenty-one weeks." At another time, he wrote, "Faculty meeting in the evening; the usual amount of miserable, tasteless, spirit-breaking detail" (Frothingham, 1925, p. 279).

The college president had few powers. He was a utility man for everyone—board, faculty, and students—and took care of routines that nobody else would bother with. Everett accepted the position only because he was strongly pressed to do so by those who thought that somebody with his great authority could bring about order. As it turned out, his past glories as congressman, governor, and ambassador meant nothing at Harvard. Everett paid a heavy price for his presidency, particularly since it was during this period that his wife began to manifest the nervous disorder that would lead to her insanity, a burden that had to be borne by Everett along with the death at various ages of four of his seven children.

Even in the troubled years at Harvard there were triumphs, although their full significance would not appear until much later when Charles W. Eliot consolidated and advanced the earlier gains during his forty-year term as president. Into the lawless situation, Everett brought some measure of order, establishing and enforcing rules and procedures that had hitherto been lacking or disregarded. Morison's history of Harvard notes that "suddenly, in 1848, the students quieted down," although no credit is given to Everett for that accomplishment (1936, p. 278).

He created the Lawrence Scientific School, which greatly strengthened Harvard's offerings in the sciences and would eventually broaden the curriculum in many directions. He established the baccalaureate in science and hired Louis Agassiz, first of the great American professors of science. He continued to foster the traditions of Germanic research and helped develop some of the greatest scholars in American academic history. Finally, he confronted directly the opposition to the entry of a young black man as a student, saying, "The admission to Harvard College depends upon examinations; and if this boy passes the examinations, he will be admitted; and if the white students choose to withdraw, all the income of the College will be devoted to his education" (Frothingham, 1925, p. 299). The potential student died before the matter could be put to a test, but even after Everett left the presidency, antiabolitionist students would sometimes demonstrate outside his house.

V

Everett was far from content with the effort to change American higher education; he wanted to reform the earlier schools as well. His own early instruction had been something of a jumble, although his brilliant mind, striking handsomeness, and happy disposition had led his teachers to offer him all that their own poor preparation allowed. One of them, Daniel Webster, taught him only briefly, yet a half-century later, in his last year of life, he wrote to Everett: "We now and then see, stretching across the heavens, a long streak of clear, blue, cerulean sky, without cloud or mist or haze. And such appears to me our acquaintance, from the time when I heard you for a week recite your lessons in the little school-house, in Short Street to the [present] date" (Webster, 1903, p. 542). But in Germany, particularly in Prussia, Everett had seen a school system that was highly organized and ably staffed, far superior to anything in the United States. As soon as he returned from his foreign studies, he began to take an active part in the development of a public education that would reach all children.

The desire for a comprehensive school system had long been an American hope, and the ambition to achieve it was already becoming intensified when Everett began his own efforts to create a system of common schools. Lecture series had become popular, and as noted in Chapter Four, the American lyceum was founded in 1826 both to bring the benefits of culture to all adults and to advance the cause of education for children. Everett had by then so refined his skill as an orator that, as one of his biographers notes, "by virtue of [his] intuitive dramatic sense, the grace of his language, the music of his voice, and above all the magnetism of his presence, he created an unforgettable impression" (Pearson, 1931, p. 223). Vast throngs would turn out to hear him, even as today's audiences attend the recitals of a great musical soloist. He used the public platform skillfully to speak again and again on public education, on the importance of scientific knowledge, on the benefits of a general diffusion of knowledge, and on the need for and advantages of popular education.

As professor and president at Harvard, he was so busy with higher education reform that he did not take part in organizational work or in agitation for public schools. In Congress he was bound by the fact that the Constitution had inferentially reserved all responsibility for education to the states, a distinction that was taken seriously in those days. But as soon as he became governor of Massachusetts, he was in a position of power that he proceeded to use in full measure. He believed state government to be the proper instrument of reform for the schools, and he used that idea with speed and vigor. He persuaded the legislature to create a State Board of Education, retaining its chairmanship himself. He prevailed upon the president of the state senate, Horace Mann, to give up his preoccupation with the penal system and temperance and to interest himself instead in education, a change of career that was eventually to make Mann the most celebrated American leader of school reform in the nineteenth century. Everett was particularly concerned with teacher training. To speed this process, he secured private financing and then public funding to create the normal school, an institution with a French name and a Prussian-inspired curriculum. As he left the governorship, he could be content that he had set in motion the establishment of public education for all children, a movement that others would carry out but for which he had set the course.

VI

As soon as Everett left the presidency of Harvard, he turned to the accomplishment of another educational goal. At Göttingen, he had seen the value of a great university library, at least ten times the size of that at Harvard. He was critical of the inadequate American collegiate collections, but he felt that an allied resource was completely lacking: the provision of books so that those who had had only a common school education could continue their studies throughout their lives. He therefore became a persistent propagandist for free public libraries with the mayor, the city council, and the state government. To the city council, he wrote: "The sons of the wealthy alone have access to well-stored libraries, while those whose means do not allow them to purchase books are too often debarred from them at the moment when they would be most useful. We give them an elementary education, impart to them a taste, and inspire them with an earnest desire for further attainment,— which unite in making books a necessary of intellectual life,— and then make no provision for supplying them" (Whitehill, 1956, p. 22).

After five years of agitation, the Boston Public Library finally opened its doors on March 20, 1854, thus setting in motion a movement that was eventually to sweep the nation. One of Everett's chief successes was in enlisting the support of his old friend, Ticknor, who had been with him at Göttingen and who had for some years been living elegantly on his inherited wealth. Ticknor found in the library a cause that could absorb his attention, and the two men greatly enjoyed their collaboration in creating this new institution. Everett was the first chairman of its board of directors, retaining that position until his death, when Ticknor succeeded him.

Although the library was Everett's main form of institutionalized adult education, it was not his major method of public enlightenment. In a society that relied heavily for its knowledge on the spoken word, he was the acknowledged master performer. Modern historians of education, most notably Lawrence

Cremin, have stressed the importance of pastors in shaping the ideas of their hearers, and Everett, as a young man, occupied one of the most distinguished pulpits in the nation. These early years, however, were no more than an apprenticeship for the elegance of his later artistry and the power of his presence. He was so perfect a rhetorician that every word and movement combined to create a unified whole based upon his theme, whether it be the importance of the common school, the nature of Washington as man and national leader, or the details of a historical event such as the battle of Gettysburg.

In seeking to foster adult education, therefore, Everett was not so much organizer as teacher, casting his net broadly, choosing many themes, and speaking to uncounted audiences. Ticknor said that he knew of nobody other than Everett "who has presented himself under such various, distinct, and remarkable aspects to classes of our community so separate, thus commanding a degree of interest from each, whether scholars, theologians, or statesmen, which in the aggregate of its popular influence has become so extraordinary. For he has been, to a marvelous degree, successful in whatever he has touched" (Boston City Council, 1865, p. 164). His educational contributions were recognized in his own lifetime by perhaps the keenest educational observer of the nineteenth century, Henry Barnard, who published an essay about them in 1859. The most remarkable feature of these contributions, Barnard said, was the fact that although Everett was an accomplished scholar of the highest and most abstruse order, he "never makes the mistake of recommending the impossible. He always adapts his requisitions to the circumstances of the community. . . . Among all the men who have taken a leading part in improving our systems of education, we have had no one who has more distinctly understood the character of the people to be educated, or the methods by which the systems were to be improved" (p. 334).

VII

To a modern eye, Everett's work in education can best be synthesized by stating that he was concerned with learning as it occurs at every age of life from youth to death. Life-span education was not a point he stressed; it was one he took for granted. It was his destiny to be an innovator, creating ideas and generating political support for them but not engaging in the specialized work of their later development. Mann and Barnard were known for the work they did in support of the common schools. Countless famous scholars are given credit for the American adaptations of German scholarship. Eliot harvested the glory of bringing the most famous American college into its full growth as a university. Ticknor and, later, Melvil Dewey and Andrew Carnegie were known as the founders of the public library system. Everett himself was a teacher, perhaps the most broadly influential of the nineteenth century, but there was then no way of recording for posterity the elegance of his artistry and the power of his performance. His accomplishments were separate and distinct, but they are unified by his belief that at every age of life education is so important to society that the means for providing it are a public duty.

In his lifetime, the various aspects of Everett's career could be readily understood, for they were constantly developing before the eyes of his contemporaries. But in the perspective of history he seems to be like the bulk of a mountain range undergirding many peaks of performance. He gave rise to supreme achievements, but they are spread across such a broad terrain that the eye cannot easily encompass them and the mind cannot understand their complexity. Today we see only the elevations that lift upward from the base he provided; we have lost sight of the massif from which they rose.

References

Barnard, H. "Edward Everett." *American Journal of Education,* 1859, 7, 325-366.

Boston City Council. *A Memorial of Edward Everett from the City of Boston.* Boston: A. Williams, 1865.

Brooks, V. W. *The Flowering of New England.* New York: Dutton, 1936.

Dorchester Historical Society. *The Centennial Anniversary of the Birth of Edward Everett.* (2nd ed.) Boston: Municipal Printing Office, 1897.

Emerson, R. W. *Lectures and Biographical Sketches.* Boston: Houghton Mifflin, 1904. (Originally published 1892.)

Everett, E. *Orations and Speeches.* Vol. 4. Boston: Little, Brown, 1892.

Frothingham, P. R. *Edward Everett.* Boston: Houghton Mifflin, 1925.

Howe, M. A. D. *Life and Letters of George Bancroft.* Vol. 1. New York: Scribner's, 1908.

Long, O. W. *Literary Pioneers.* Cambridge, Mass.: Harvard University Press, 1935.

Miller, P. (Ed.). *The Transcendentalists.* Cambridge, Mass.: Harvard University Press, 1950.

Morison, S. E. *Three Centuries of Harvard.* Cambridge, Mass.: Harvard University Press, 1936.

Pearson, H. G. "Edward Everett." In *Dictionary of American Biography.* Vol. 6. New York: Scribner's, 1931.

Sandburg, C. *Abraham Lincoln.* Vol. 2. New York: Harcourt Brace Jovanovich, 1936.

"Song by Rogero." *Anti-Jacobin; or, Weekly Examiner,* June 4, 1798, pp. 238-239. [London.]

Tyack, D. B. *George Ticknor and the Boston Brahmins.* Cambridge, Mass.: Harvard University Press, 1967.

Webster, F. (Ed.). *The Writings and Speeches of Daniel Webster.* Vol. 18. Boston: Little, Brown, 1903.

Whitehill, W. M. *Boston Public Library.* Cambridge, Mass.: Harvard University Press, 1956.

8

William Osler

Creating a Complete
Educational Plan for Professionals

I

Work is the center of most people's lives. By contemplating, analyzing, and improving it, they often discover ways to achieve personal fulfillment and growth. Self-enhancement of this sort can be found in any vocation, but perhaps it is most often a characteristic of those occupations whose members try, individually and collectively, to perfect themselves as professionals. They identify missions essential to the deep needs of people and seek to achieve these missions on a case-by-case basis through the use of a developed art that effectively combines knowledge gained from many sciences. The members of professionalizing vocations set high standards of ethics and competence for themselves and for the people whom they select as colleagues. They expect to have a special place in society (sometimes one whose privileges and exemptions are guaranteed by law), they present a united front to the public, and they collaborate in well-estab-

This chapter was previously published in *Perspectives in Biology and Medicine*, 1969, *12* (4), 561–583, University of Chicago Press. Copyright © 1969, The University of Chicago. Used with permission.

lished ways with other groups of people, particularly those whose work is akin to theirs. Their methods of operation require them constantly to use changing technologies and to adapt to new social influences, thus laying upon themselves a heavy but necessary burden to maintain and improve the quality of their performance.

Such, at any rate, is an established current conception, not less deeply held for being relatively modern. Although some professionals feel kinships that stretch back to Solon, Hippocrates, and the priests of the ancient Athenian temples, the highly ordered, self-disciplined, and socially favored professions as we now know them were created in the late nineteenth century and established in the twentieth by people who bent untiring efforts to achieve precisely those ends.

The very idea of a profession implies not merely that a person will enter it only when well prepared but also that preparation will be continued throughout life. In achieving the first of these goals, great strides have been made; professional schools are far better than they used to be. One needs only to reflect on the impact of the Flexner report on American medical education to be aware of that fact. But the question has been increasingly raised of late whether equal progress has been made in achieving the second goal, the continuing education of the professional, particularly in these times of great advances of scientific knowledge. Sir George Pickering, Regius Professor of Medicine at Oxford, once commented that "those doctors who completed their formal education a quarter of a century ago and who have not subsequently participated in educational activities are a dead load to the profession and a potential menace to the sick" (1967, p. 18). His voice is echoed in many professions. Perhaps somewhere in the making in one of them is a Flexner report on continuing education that will provide a compelling conception of life-span learning, harmonizing that which occurs in both youth and adulthood.

Much of the machinery for improved continuing education already exists in the familiar libraries, professional societies, journals, study circles, extension programs, and meetings that all professions arrange for themselves. These devices were first set in motion by the founders of the professions, even while they were at work improving the preservice curriculum. At least some of those founders, however, had far more in mind than has ever been worked out in practice, and present discussions of professional continuing education would gain greatly in perspective if they included some comments from the voices of the past. The purpose of this chapter is to demonstrate that fact by summarizing what was said on the subject by one of them, Sir William Osler.

Appropriately, he was a physician. Of all the professions, medicine has perhaps the greatest social acceptance and protection. It is used as an exemplar by those who work at many other callings. In fact, Everett Hughes, the distinguished student of such matters, believed that most people who think collectively about the professions today usually have medicine in mind, whether they realize it or not (1962, p. 39). Consequently, Osler's comments reverberate far beyond his own field. He was only one of the company of distinguished men who founded modern medicine, but, of all of them, he has left the most complete record of his acts and thoughts. Throughout his life, his energies were prodigious, his triumphs were brilliant, and when he wanted to speak plainly he knew how to do so. After his death, able people devoted years of labor to preserving the record of his work and his personality. "With more hope than self-assurance," three of them said, "we have tried to interpret the dream and to stage the pageant" (*Bibliotheca Osleriana,* 1929, p. xiv). Always, from youth to old age, in practice as in precept, he bore witness to the doctor's urgent need to continue to learn. At the age of sixty-three, he began an address to the young gentlemen of Yale with the words "Fellow Students" (Osler, 1915, p. 5).

II

Osler was born in rural Canada in 1849, one of nine children of migrant English parents. His father was a clergyman, his mother was a strong-willed woman who lived to be 100 years old, and four of their sons grew up to be nationally known figures. Osler intended to become a clergyman but changed his goal to medicine when he fell under the influence of Dr. James Bovell, a local physician—who himself then became a clergyman. Osler was graduated from McGill, spent two years of study in hospitals and medical schools throughout Europe, and returned to McGill, where he became professor of the institutes of medicine. Ten years later he went to the University of Pennsylvania to be professor of clinical medicine. After only five years there, he joined the faculty of Johns Hopkins University, where, as the first physician-in-chief of its hospital and one of the first professors at its medical school, he became a major cause of the world-wide luster of both institutions. A foreigner meeting a Johns Hopkins professor once asked, "And how is your Osler? He must be centuries old" (Cushing, 1925, II, p. 658). Despite his long stay in the United States, Osler never sought American citizenship, feeling greater kinship with both Canada and Britain than with his adopted country. In 1906, he became Regius Professor of Medicine at Oxford (a post first created in 1548 by Henry VIII); in 1911, he was made a baronet; and in 1919 he died.

In most people's lives, and certainly in those of people said to be tempered to a fine steel by experience, there are periods of self-doubt, despair, grief, illness, passion, or frustration. Not so with Osler. Even his few failures added to his eventual happiness. He was so mischievous at school that he was jailed and expelled—and was promptly welcomed home with open arms and congratulated on having high spirits. He could not readily master Greek or Latin and said that he had to climb Parnassus in a fog; half a century later, he was made president of the Classical Association of Great Britain. For most of his years in school and college he was a star athlete, outstanding student, and chief prefect. A radiance seemed to shine about his head, and it stayed with him all his life.

Osler's biography was written as a labor of love by his long-time associate Harvey Cushing, the best-known brain surgeon in the United States. This work—which won the Pulitzer Prize and sold more than 20,000 copies in its first ten years—stretches out to two massive volumes totaling almost 1,400 large and tightly packed pages. Yet Cushing makes it plain that he regards his biography as only a preliminary outline for a more worthy, later treatment of the subject by some other author. This modesty sets a barrier against pretensions by anyone else. Let it be said at once, therefore, that the present account examines no more than one facet of Osler's brilliant career.

He was a medium-sized but well-knit and spare man, with deep-set haunting eyes so dark his father said they were "burnt holes in a blanket." His complexion was darkly sallow; "olive green" John Singer Sargent called it. Even before his hair grew sparse, he had a broad forehead and, like his three distinguished brothers, wore a deeply drooping mustache that gave his face a deceptively gloomy air, heightening by contrast his chief observable trait, which was gaiety. He danced along the street or the hospital corridor, singing or whistling as he went, always informal, even in the classroom, full of practical jokes and fun, with a genius for friendship, a marvelous memory for names and associations, and a knack for making himself seem a crony even to people he met only briefly.

Some of those who knew him best felt that his manner overlaid a deep and inextinguishable melancholy whose cause no one could guess, unless it was the strain imposed on a warm and loving heart by the scenes of disease and death that were constantly before his eyes. He was a professed stoic. The major virtue that the doctor must cultivate, he said, was imperturbability, which he defined as "coolness and presence of mind under all circumstances, calmness amid storm, clearness of judgment in moments of grave peril, immobility, impassiveness" (1906, p. 4). In his personal relations, a good mask (if one were needed) was that of a warm, friendly, and fun-filled person, always seizing the initiative, seeing countless people each day and making each one feel that he or she was the focus of Osler's closest and warmest attention. A patient said of him:

> As he passed about, gallant and debonair, with a whimsical wit that left the air sweet and gay, with an epigram here and a paradox there, tickling the ribs of his colleagues, none felt frivo-

lous: there was a point to his rapier for all he
played with the button on. The deep, sad eyes of
his soul watched a little cynically the light humour
of his mind. It was not necessary for him to be sensitive to a social atmosphere, because he always
made his own atmosphere. In a room full of discordant elements he entered and saw only his patient and only his patient's greatest need, and in-
stantly the atmosphere was charged with kindly
vitality, everyone felt that the situation was under
control, and all were attention. . . . The moment
Sir William gave you was yours. . . . With the easy
sweep of a great artist's line, beginning in your
necessity and ending in your necessity, the precious moment was yours, becoming wholly and entirely a part of the fabric of your life [Cushing,
1925, I, pp. 420-21].

It is growing increasingly difficult, so many years after
Osler's death, to see him clearly through the clouds of incense
rising from the altars erected to his memory by his family, his
former associates, and his followers. He has been called "the
greatest physician in history," a "saint," and even, in all seriousness, "Christlike" and "Godlike" (Reid, 1931, pp. 291, 55-
56). Recognizing his own good fortune, he consciously set a
model for others to follow, and by performing that role as best
he could, he may have begun the creation of his own legend;
but he never thought of himself as other than a fortunately
gifted man who was dedicated to the life of a physician. The
Osler mystique does the greatest possible disservice to his deepest desire, which was to establish a modern profession of medicine. If only Godlike people can be great doctors, then mere
mortals must be excused from their sins of negligence or mal-
practice.

He had his full share of peculiarities and annoying traits.
Nobody has yet made a serious effort to explain him in psycho-
analytic or other similar terms. Cushing was so far from doing
so that he could not even understand why Osler became inter-

ested in dreams in 1911. But there were unexplained and quirkish elements in his character. He mentioned his father rarely. He created a full-blown alter ego named Egerton Yorrick Davis and constructed a complete family and community background for him; sometimes Osler suppressed his own personality to live and write and publish as Davis. All his life, in hours of strain or boredom, he compulsively wrote and rewrote the name of his mentor, James Bovell. At the time of his marriage, rather late in life, he commented, "I feel very safe." From what? Other actions and attributes were less interesting but more infuriating: When sick, he was an abominably bad and infantile patient; his reported practical jokes were both unfunny and tedious, and it has been suggested that the unreported ones (as well as some of his writings) were crude enough to startle even doctors and medical students; he was a poor sport about jokes played on him; he was jealous of his time, and his swift-moving progression often created problems for other people; and his formal speech was sometimes so baroque that its elaborateness obscured its message.

Not surprisingly, a few people found him not at all to their taste, calling him effusive, insincere, pretentious, theatrical, and repetitive. In conflicts, he always tried to find a middle way, thereby disappointing those who held more extreme positions. He felt that patients needed hope, and this fact made him seem overoptimistic. Perhaps, too, like Aristides, he was sometimes condemned by those bored by his acclaim.

But in his personal life, it was roses, roses almost all the way. In his last six weeks of life, he wrote to a friend, "Except in one particular, I have had nothing but butter & honey" (Cushing, 1925, II, p. 678). He was sixty-eight when the great blow fell. In August 1917, a German shell mortally wounded his only child, Revere, who was buried in a field in Flanders. Late that night, in his Oxford study, the Regius Professor of Medicine wrote, "We had expected it. The Fates do not allow the good fortune that has followed me to go with me to the grave— call no man happy 'til he dies" (Cushing, 1925, II, pp. 577–578). From then on, he who had helped so many people face their own deaths now had to help other people face his. In his last days he wrote on a slip of paper: "The harbour is almost reached, after a splendid voyage, with such companions all the way, and my boy awaiting me" (Shepherd, 1926, p. 158).

III

When Osler began his career, the intellectual world was locked in the battle over Darwinism. In his life span he saw established some of the greatest contributions to biology and medicine the world has yet witnessed, including those of Pasteur, Koch, Huxley, Virchow, Charcot, Lister, Roentgen, Leonard Wood, Ehrlich, the Curies, Wassermann, Walter Reed, Trudeau, and Freud. Around such major stars as these were constellations of other innovators. Speaking in the first month of the twentieth century, Osler said of the nineteenth: "Measure as we may the progress of the world—materially, in the advantages of steam, electricity, and other mechanical appliances; sociologically, in the great improvement in the conditions of life; intellectually, in the diffusion of education; morally, in a possibly higher standard of ethics—there is no one measure which can compare with the decrease of physical suffering in man, woman, and child when stricken by disease or accident. This is the one fact of supreme personal import to every one of us. This is the Promethean gift of the century to man" (1906, p. 230).

He did as much as any person to make sure that the benefits of that gift would be shared by all. To read the story of his life, particularly in his early professional years, is to realize how little even he, with his unparalleled opportunities to know and to observe, could do to prevent or cure illness. He wrote countless scientific papers on diseases, concentrating particularly on typhoid fever, pneumonia, tuberculosis, and syphilis; he observed closely the work on diphtheria, yellow fever, smallpox, and malaria; and, as author of the frequently revised and most widely used general medical handbook of his time, he kept up to date on every aspect of his profession. Yet death struck close to him again and again, and there was nothing he could do about it. Even when remedies were known, it was often difficult to get people to act. In discussing typhoid fever, he said to the Maryland Public Health Association: "The penalties of cruel neglect have been paid for 1896; the dole of victims for 1897 is nearly complete, the sacrifices will number again above 200. We cannot save the predestined ones of 1898. . . . These will be offered to our Minotaur, these will be made to pass through the fire of the accursed Moloch. This, to our shame, we do with full knowledge, with an easy complacency that only long years of sinning can give" (Jacobs, 1920, p. 77).

For the knowledge to solve a health problem, the sciences were essential; but it would not actually be solved unless there were enough well-trained physicians to put the remedy everywhere into effect. Osler saw himself and his whole profession as scientifically based healers. He made original investigations, such as his early study of blood platelets, but here is not where his contribution lies. "The practice of medicine is an art, based on science," he said (1906, p. 36). And again, "Every medical student should remember that his end is not to be made a chemist or physiologist or anatomist, but to learn how to recognize and treat disease" (1906, p. 214). When the medical student has mastered the needed sciences, it is still necessary to translate their "hieroglyphics . . . into the plain language of healing" (1906, p. 31).

But the physicians being trained at that time (at least in the United States) knew neither science nor healing. It made one's blood boil, he said, to consider how poorly equipped were the people being produced "who have never attended a case of labour, and who are utterly ignorant of the ordinary everyday diseases which they may be called upon to treat." This fact being true, it could scarcely be wondered that "there is a widespread distrust in the public of professional education, and that quacks, charlatans and imposters possess the land" (Cushing, 1925, I, p. 307). And so, if the Promethean gift were to benefit humankind, an essential task must be the complete reconstitution of medical education.

The essential idea of that education, as Osler shaped and reshaped it in his four professorships, was that from the beginning the physician must consider study a lifelong task. The most hurtful thing the practitioner can do is to fail "to realize, *first,* the need of a lifelong progressive personal training and, *secondly,* the danger lest in the stress of practice he sacrifice that most precious of all possessions, his mental independence" (1906, p. 297). It is not easy to learn to be a doctor, and "all the college can do is to teach the student principles, based on facts in science, and give him good methods of work. These simply start him in the right direction, they do not make him a good practitioner—that is his own affair" (1906, pp. 297-298). As Osler went about his consultative practice, he saw many consequences of the failure of practitioners to improve themselves. One old doctor was once, he said, a modern, "but he crawled up the bank, and the stream has left him there, but he does not know it" (1906, p. 149). In another case, "a physician living within an hour's ride of the Surgeon-General's Library brought to me his little girl, aged twelve. The diagnosis of infantile myxoedema required only a half glance. In placid contentment he had been practising twenty years in 'Sleepy Hollow' and not even when his own flesh and blood was touched did he rouse from an apathy deep as Rip Van Winkle's sleep. In reply to questions: No, he had never seen anything in the journals about the thyroid gland; he had seen no pictures of cretinism or myxoedema; in fact his mind was a blank on the whole subject. He had not been a reader, he said, but he was a practical man with very little time" (1906, pp. 221-222). Nor is the danger of such decay to be found only in the general practitioner. "We all know consultants from whom patients find it very difficult to escape without their favorite prescription, no matter what the malady may be" (Camac, 1906, pp. 200-201). Not even medical professors are immune to a relentless "intellectual staleness" (Cushing, 1925, I, p. 529). In reviewing a medical textbook, Osler said it "illustrated the difficulty a teacher has in escaping from the bonds in which a routine course, delivered year after year, tends to inclose him, . . . the thoughts and professional opinions of thirty years ago" (Harvey and McKusick, 1967, p. 1).

IV

To continue to build knowledge and skill throughout life is a difficult task requiring constant effort. In the largest sense, it is true, education is "a subtle, slowly-affected change, due to the action upon us of the Externals; of the written record of the great minds of all ages, of the beautiful and harmonious surroundings of nature and of art, and of the lives, good or ill, of our fellows—these alone educate us, these alone mould the developing minds" (Osler, 1906, pp. 100-101). But the nature and scope of these influences are firmly set by the control that the individual establishes over them, for "not from without us, only from within comes, or can ever come, upon us light" (1906, p. 109). Each person must make his or her own way, and what is learned is a result of the interaction of the total personality with the total environment. But there are guides to be followed, from the first day of medical school to the end of an active career.

A basic essential is to remain in good health. One might think that doctors, above everyone else, would know and apply this rule, but anybody who thinks so does not know doctors. They are constantly exposed to infection, perhaps much more so in Osler's day than now. Their lives are overbusy and strained, they forget to take care of themselves, and they may even subconsciously believe that they are above the rules they prescribe for others. "Among the good men who have studied with me there stands out in my remembrance many a young Lycidas, 'dead ere his prime,' sacrificed to carelessness in habits of living and neglect of ordinary sanitary laws" (Osler, 1906, p. 380).

Throughout life the doctor must deeply believe that education "is not a college course, not a medical course, but a life course, for which the work of a few years under teachers is but a preparation" (Osler, 1906, p. 418). This conviction is not readily adopted by beginners, nor is it easily maintained later on. No technique or device of continuing education will really work if the student does not believe in the necessity for study required by the nature of the profession.

The doctor must develop and mature a personal and systematic approach to science, to medicine, and to the best use of time. Since all three are interrelated and their mastery is influenced by both the capacities of the individual and the nature of practice, each physician must work out a personal plan. The beginnings of the sciences are ordered in courses and textbooks, but science is always changing in its methods and findings. Even less fixed is medicine. "Our study is man, as the subject of accidents or diseases. Were he always, inside and outside, cast in the same mould, instead of differing from his fellow man as much in constitution and in his reaction to stimulus as in feature, we should ere this have reached some settled principles in our art" (Osler, 1906, p. 37). Least subject to control of all is the doctor's time, on which there are many demands. It is all the more important, therefore, to establish as much system as possible. "A few brilliant fellows try to dispense with it altogether, but they are a burden to their brethren and a sore trial to their intimates. . . . Forget all else, but take away this counsel of a man who has had to fight a hard battle, and not always a successful one, for the little order he has had in his life; take away with you a profound conviction of the value of system in your work. . . . Let each hour of the day have its allotted duty, and cultivate that power of concentration which grows with its exercise, so that the attention neither flags nor wavers, but settles with a bull-dog tenacity on the subject before you" (1906, pp. 377–378).

The doctor must focus wholly upon each patient as both a problem of treatment and an exercise in learning. "The important thing is to make the lesson of each case tell on your education" (Osler, 1906, p. 111). From this full contemplation, the doctor grows not merely as a physician but as a person, observing and relishing human nature. "Amid an eternal heritage of sorrow and suffering our work is laid, and this eternal note of sadness would be insupportable if the daily tragedies were not relieved by the spectacle of the heroism and devotion displayed by the actors. Nothing will sustain you more potently than the power to recognize in your humdrum routine, as perhaps it may be thought, the true poetry of life—the poetry of the commonplace, of the ordinary man, of the plain, toil-worn woman, with their loves and their joys, their sorrows and their griefs. The comedy, too, of life will be spread before you, and nobody laughs more often than the doctor at the pranks Puck plays upon the Titanias and the Bottoms among his patients" (1906, p. 423).

The doctor must consider the hospital as the central institution of learning. The medical student's training should take place there. The active practitioner should insist that a central function of the community hospital is its provision of a postgraduate school, not merely by being so well managed and equipped that it serves as a constant inspiration, but also by becoming the local center for a comprehensive and continuous national system of "medical extension courses, which will enable physicians to supplement their knowledge without making heavy material sacrifices" (Osler, 1911, p. 238).

The doctor should keep constant records of his or her observations and reflect upon them. The start of this process is the immediate observation of the patient. "Carry a small notebook which will fit into your waistcoat pocket, and never ask a new patient a question without notebook and pencil in hand. . . . Routine and system, when once made a habit, facilitate work, and the busier you are the more time you will have to make observations after examining a patient" (Osler, 1906, p. 431). Then think back over these notes, observe rhythms and consistencies, look deeply into puzzling observations, and see whether a group of cases teaches more than any single case.

The doctor must keep up on professional reading, constantly comparing it with practice; neither suffices without the other. "To study the phenomena of disease without books is to sail an uncharted sea, while to study books without patients is not to go to sea at all" (Osler, 1906, p. 220). Such reading must become habitual, part of the doctor's basic system. "The driven and tired practitioner might plead that he could not find time to read. He could not unless he had formed the practice in less busy days; then the habit of reading, like any other habit, became his master" (Cushing, 1925, II, p. 184). But he must not be too studious. "A bookish man may never succeed; deep-versed in books, he may not be able to use his knowledge to practical effect; or, more likely, his failure is not because he has studied books much, but because he has not studied men more" (1906, p. 437). Here, as everywhere else in life, a balance must be struck.

The doctor must work constantly and intimately with his

or her fellows at the task of learning. The medical school should
foster many student organizations and groups, so that the student
gets into the habit of autonomous group study that reinforces
the established curriculum. It is essential for the profession to
have a highly organized and systematic structure of associations,
but what is truly important is that local groups should have life
and vitality. Nothing else so reinforces the individual's learning.
"Of the value to the local practitioner of a medical society and
of a library we are all agreed. How common the experience to
enter a cold cheerless room in which the fire in the grate has
died down, not from lack of coal, not because the coal was not
alight, but the bits, large and small, falling away from each
other, have gradually become dark and cold. Break them with a
poker, get them together, and what a change in a few minutes!
There is light and heat and good cheer. What happens in the
grate illustrates very often the condition of the profession in a
town or county; singly or in cliques the men have fallen apart,
and, as in the dead or dying embers, there is neither light nor
warmth; or the coals may be there alive and bright, but covered
with the ashes of discord, jealousy, and faction." The medical
society is the poker that, by doing three things, brings the members of the profession together. "It is the most important single
factor in the promotion of that unity and good-fellowship
which adds so much to the dignity of the profession." It can
provide postgraduate instruction through programs for its members. It can support a library (Osler, 1911, p. 237).

The doctor should devote some time each day, even if it
can be only its last half hour, to reading great literature. "Start
at once a bed-side library" to provide a "communion with the
saints of humanity. There are great lessons to be learned from
Job and from David, from Isaiah and St. Paul" (Osler, 1906, p.
384). Such reading also provides relief: "When the complica-
tions of pharmacology are unbearable, ten minutes with Montaigne will lighten the burden" (1906, p. 214). Particular attention might well be given to those works which marry medicine
and literature. "In the group of literary physicians Sir Thomas
Browne stands preeminent. The *Religio Medici,* one of the great
English classics, should be in the hands—in the hearts too—of

every medical student" (1906, p. 214). Osler owned many copies of this book; the first was bought in the autumn of 1867. Two weeks before he died, he wrote in a copy of it, "I doubt if any man can more truly say of this book *'comes viae vitaeque,'* " and it lay on his coffin at his funeral (Cushing, 1925, II, pp. 681, 686).

The doctor should develop an absorbing outside interest that itself requires learning. "See to it that you have also an avocation—some intellectual pastime which may serve to keep you in touch with the world of art, of science, or of letters. Begin at once the cultivation of some interest other than the purely professional" (Osler, 1906, p. 213). Osler's own intellectual pastime, arising logically from his interest in Browne, was the collection and study of works related to the history of medicine. Bibliography, or, as he called it, "bibliomania," became an increasingly absorbing part of his life, and, on his seventieth birthday, he referred to himself as "one the love of whose life has been given equally to books and to men" (Cushing, 1925, II, p. 660).

The doctor must acquire the capacity to move easily in nonmedical circles. "Success in life depends as much upon the man as on the physician. . . . You are to be members of a polite as well as of a liberal profession and the more you see of life outside the narrow circle of your work the better equipped will you be for the struggle" (Osler, 1906, pp. 212-213). Learning the social graces is not a part of formal study, of course, but it is something that does not come automatically. One must share in life, observe it, modify one's habits and practices—become, in short, a person who practices medicine, not merely a physician.

Finally, having in mind his or her particular goals and the balance of activities suggested by the foregoing rules, the doctor should confront each day as it comes and live it to its fullest measure. This advice to live in what he called "day-tight compartments" was often on Osler's lips, and he drew his authority from the Sermon on the Mount: "Take therefore no thought for the morrow: for the morrow shall take thought for the things of itself." He found many other quotations to support his view, which he expressed briefly or at length, early and late in his career, in as many ways as he could but never more forcefully than in his address to the students of Yale. "The load of tomorrow, added to that of yesterday, carried today makes the strongest falter. Shut off the future as tightly as the past. . . . The future is today,—there is no tomorrow! The day of a man's salvation is *now*—the life of the present, of today, lived earnestly, intently, without a forward-looking thought, is the only insurance for the future. Let the limit of your horizon be a twenty-four-hour circle" (1915, pp. 29-31). To those who demurred that a career cannot be carefully constructed in this way, he answered with a quotation from Oliver Cromwell: "No one rises so high as he who knows not whither he is going."

V

These enduring principles must be worked out somewhat differently at each of the stages of life, no one of which is more important than another—although it must be confessed that when Osler was talking to either medical students or young doctors, he tended to suggest that theirs was the crucial age.

For the student in medical school, the task was to practice all of these principles so steadily and persistently that they became ingrained habits. And all of them must be practiced, every one. Osler provided a list of the ten first books that should be in the medical student's library (1906, p. 475). He told such students that they must give due attention to their broad social development, and he constantly urged the formation of groups, whose members would get the habit of voluntary association. Probably his favorite audience was one composed of medical students, and, with many elaborations and much embroidery, he had but one central message for them: the necessity to acquire the habits that would establish a life of study.

To the teachers of those students, the message was everywhere the same: Construct the curriculum so that the student not merely learns but is ingrained with the habit of learning. "To cover the vast field of medicine in four years is an impossible task. We can only instil principles, put the student in the right path, give him methods, teach him how to study, and early to discern between essentials and non-essentials" (Osler, 1906, p. 210). Most particularly, the major lesson to be taught is the observation and treatment of the patient in the hospital. "In what may be called the natural method of teaching the student begins with the patient, continues with the patient, and ends his studies with the patient, using books and lectures as tools, as means to an end" (1906, p. 331). In this way, the great habit of continuing inquiry is begun, using the focus and the setting that will be familiar to the doctor throughout life. The establishment of this principle was the cause of the greatness of Johns Hopkins University, and, as Osler said in his farewell to his colleagues there, "I desire no other epitaph—no hurry about it, I may say—than the statement that I taught medical students in the wards" (1906, p. 407).

VI

The young doctor starting out in practice, often with limited means and a heavy capital expense to recover, has left the shelter and the supporting routine of the medical school, and the particular peril is that he or she may fail to accept a full measure of personal responsibility for continuing education. Young people enter practice with higher standards than they find exemplified in the field; they have built up a store of knowledge on which they can subsist for some time; they see around them doctors doing very well for themselves with little acquaintance with the latest methods and even a contempt for book learning; and they are often busy. Small wonder that life becomes less and less a student life. "Ten years later he is dead mentally, past any possible hope of galvanizing into life as a student, fit to do a routine practice, often a capable, resourceful man, but without any deep convictions, and probably more interested in stocks or in horses than in diagnosis or therapeutics" (Osler, 1906, p. 429).

If possible, the young doctor should travel before settling into practice. Himself a lifelong peripatetic, Osler was convinced that the observation of practice in a number of different settings gave a perspective to a practitioner's view of medicine

that nothing else could provide. The science and art of healing is
universal, said Osler, and he devoted a major address to a vigor-
ous attack on parochialism in medicine. The best way for the
doctor to avoid it, he thought, was to travel while young, into
other countries if possible but widely at home if not. "Travel
not only widens the vision and gives certainties in place of vague
surmises, but the personal contact with foreign workers enables
[the young doctor] to appreciate better the failings or successes
in his own line of work" (1906, p. 421).

As young doctors settle into practice, the most essential
requirement is to continue to learn from the constant analysis
of experience with patients. They will make errors of diagnosis
or therapy but must be neither too sensitive to them nor too
hardened by their occurrence. "Start out with the conviction
that absolute truth is hard to reach in matters relating to our
fellow creatures, healthy or diseased, that slips in observation
are inevitable even with the best trained faculties, that errors in
judgment must occur in the practice of an art which consists
largely in balancing probabilities; start, I say, with this attitude
of mind, and mistakes will be acknowledged and regretted; but
instead of a slow process of self-deception, with ever increasing
inability to recognize truth, you will draw from your errors the
very lessons which may enable you to avoid their repetition"
(Osler, 1906, p. 40).

Every patient has something to teach the doctor. "The
important thing is to make the lesson of each case tell on your
education. . . . Let nothing slip by you; the ordinary humdrum
cases of the morning routine may have been accurately described and pictured, but study each one separately as though
it were new—so it is so far as your special experience goes"
(Osler, 1906, p. 111). Without this kind of conscious thought,
the doctor can acquire new facts but cannot truly educate himself or herself. "Many grow through life mentally as the crystal,
by simple accretion. . . . The growth which is organic and enduring, is totally different, marked by changes of an unmistakable
character. The observations are made with accuracy and care,
no pains are spared, nothing is thought a trouble in the investigation of a problem. The facts are looked at in connexion with

similar ones, their relation to others is studied, and the experience of the recorder is compared with that of others who have worked upon the question. Insensibly, year by year, a man finds that there has been in his mental protoplasm not only growth by assimilation but an actual development, bringing fuller powers of observation, additional capabilities of mental nutrition, and that increased breadth of view which is of the very essence of wisdom" (Osler, 1906, p. 112). Something else will have happened also: The doctor will have become established, celebrated, even famous. "Let him take heed to his education, and his reputation will take care of itself" (1906, p. 146).

Physicians should participate fully in the formal systems of learning set up by the medical profession and their own special fields. But that participation should not be simply a following of formalities: keeping up, going to meetings, reading the journals, and taking part in association work. It should be a creative endeavor in which one seeks not merely to learn by these means but also to build them up, giving them a life and vitality that they too often lack. Osler spoke for many a physician when he said, "We all have such hard work to keep up our interest in existing organizations" (Cushing, 1925, I, p. 406). He knew all about the rigidities of large associations, since he worked closely with both the American Medical Association and the British Medical Association, which, as Cushing cryptically put it, share "similar failings and virtues" (1925, II, p. 118). But one should work to change the machine, not criticize it. And, in local societies, the need for active sharing is particularly essential. "The daily round of a busy practitioner tends to develop an egoism of a most intense kind, to which there is no antidote. The few setbacks are forgotten, the mistakes are often buried, and ten years of successful work tend to make a man touchy, dogmatic, intolerant of correction, and abominably self-centered. To this mental attitude the medical society is the best corrective, and a man misses a good part of his education who does not get knocked about a bit by his colleagues in discussions and criticisms" (Cushing, 1925, I, p. 447).

Osler's own life, like that of the chambered nautilus, had ever more stately mansions, but in each his first efforts were the

same. Cushing observed: "It is interesting to see how consistently he began anew in Oxford with precisely the same projects as
those which had engaged him in Montreal, Philadelphia, and
Baltimore. A consuming interest in libraries and librarians; the
revivifying of an old medical society or the organization of new
ones; the establishment of a medical journal, the bringing together of discordant elements in the profession, and the raising
of money when money was needed" (1925, II, p. 69). As he began, so he ended. His last major effort, in the final year of his
life, was to help create a plan for the postgraduate education of
North American doctors stationed in England at the close of
World War I.

Although all methods of learning are essential, reading
was perhaps closest to Osler's own heart. He was sure that it
should be a cornerstone of continuing learning. "A physician
who does not use books and journals, who does not need a library, who does not read one or two of the best weeklies and
monthlies, soon sinks to the level of the cross-counter prescrib-
er, and not alone in practice, but in those mercenary feelings
and habits which characterize a trade" (Cushing, 1925, I, p.
448). The crucial years are those of early practice. "The kill-
ing vice of the young doctor is intellectual laziness." The physician who gets out of the habit of systematic reading will be
found, five to ten years after receiving a license, "knowing less
than he did when he started and without fixed educational purpose in life" (Osler, 1906, p. 351). The rewards of reading are
tangible. "It is in utilizing the fresh knowledge of the journals
that the young physician may attain quickly to the name and
fame he desires" (1906, p. 222).

VII

The later years of an established practice have their particular dangers—and Osler knew them all. A leader of the profession once told him that his own first ten years had been
spent getting bread, his second ten getting bread and butter, and
the rest getting cakes and ale. The fat years lead to self-satisfac-
tion, to prosperity, to a softening of the will to continue learn-

ing, and to other allied dangers. The senior doctor may come to rely on "the specious and seductive pamphlets issued by pharmaceutical houses" (Cushing, 1925, II, p. 180), "the bastard literature which floods the mail," and the traveling drug sellers who "are ready to express the most emphatic opinions on questions about which the greatest masters of our art are doubtful" (Osler, 1906, pp. 300–301).

Osler achieved world-wide notoriety with one of his views about life's stages. In his farewell address at Johns Hopkins, he expressed a long-held opinion (1906, pp. 397–399):

> I have two fixed ideas well known to my friends. . . . The first is the comparative uselessness of men above forty years of age. This may seem shocking, and yet read aright the world history bears out the statement. Take the sum of human achievement in action, in science, in art, in literature—subtract the work of the men above forty, and while we should miss great treasures, even priceless treasures, we would practically be where we are today. . . . My second fixed idea is the uselessness of men above sixty years of age, and the incalculable benefit it would be in commercial, political, and in professional life if, as a matter of course, men stopped work at this age. . . . As it can be maintained that all the great advances have come from men under forty, so the history of the world shows that a very large proportion of the evils may be traced to the sexagenarians. . . . It is not to be denied that occasionally there is a sexagenarian whose mind, as Cicero remarks, stands out of reach of the body's decay.

These remarks were coupled with a whimsical suggestion, derived from Anthony Trollope, that men over sixty should be chloroformed. When Osler's comments were picked up by the press, amplified by shocked editorial comment, and broadcast throughout the world, the whimsy was accepted as a recommendation. Suddenly Osler, already a great celebrity, was declared to be either a sinister figure or one showing signs of his own mental decay. He rode out the immediate storm in silence but, eighteen months later, reaffirmed his position. "The discussion which followed my remarks has not changed, but has rather strengthened my belief that the real work of life is done before the fortieth year and that after the sixtieth year it would be best for the world and best for themselves if men rested from their labours" (1906, p. viii). He lived the rest of his life with this special identification, which people expressed in needling remarks, sly references, and abusive letters. Many people knew him only as the doctor who wanted to chloroform old people. Just before he died, he said that he had attached to the manuscript of his last address on the subject "a note, the printing of which might be deferred a few years" (Cushing, 1925, II, p. 683). Cushing said that it had never been found.

What can the older person do to delay the inevitable decline in learning powers? A first essential is to work with younger people, taking them into practice as colleagues or in other ways seeing that associates "are not of his own age and generation. He must walk with the 'boys,' else he is lost, irrevocably lost; not all at once, but by easy grades, and every one perceives his ruin before he, 'good, easy man,' is aware of it" (Osler, 1906, p. 151).

A second essential is a "quinquennial brain-dusting, and this will often seem to him the hardest task to carry out. Every fifth year, back to the hospital, back to the laboratory, for renovation, rehabilitation, rejuvenation, reintegration, resuscitation, etc." On this special venture, all the doctor's accumulated notes should be taken along. Osler continues (1906, pp. 434-435):

> From the very start begin to save for the trip. Deny yourself all luxuries for it; shut up the room you meant for the nursery—have the definite determination to get your education thoroughly well started; if you are successful you may, perhaps, have enough saved at the end of three years

to spend six weeks in special study; or in five years
you may be able to spend six months. Hearken not
to the voice of old "Dr. Hayseed," who tells you it
will ruin your prospects, and that he "never heard
of such a thing" as a young man. . . . Watch him
wince when you say it is a speculation in the only
gold mine [in] which the physician should invest—
Grey Cortex. What about the wife and babies, if
you have them? Leave them! Heavy as are your responsibilities to those nearest and dearest, they are
outweighed by the responsibilities to yourself, to
the profession, and to the public.

All his life, inherently far more educative than most, Osler followed his own admonition, removing himself from practice for
periods of time to engage in study.

As for himself, as he grew older, Osler drew the pattern
for his own life from this passage, which he read in his fifty-
first year:

Conrad [von] Gesner, who kept open house
. . . for all learned men who came into his neigh-
bourhood . . . was not only the best naturalist
among the scholars of his day, but of all men of
that century he was the pattern man of letters. He
was faultless in private life, assiduous in study, dili-
gent in maintaining correspondence and good-will
with learned men in all countries, hospitable—
though his means were small—to every scholar that
came into Zurich. Prompt to serve all, he was an
editor of other men's volumes, a writer of prefaces
for friends, a suggester to young writers of books
on which they might engage themselves, and a
great helper to them in the progress of their work.
But still, while finding time for services to other
men, he could produce as much out of his own
study as though he had no part in the life beyond
its walls [Morley, 1854, pp. 152-153].

VIII

To some modern readers, Osler's thought on continuing education may sound obvious, even trite; if so, it is because his efforts helped so greatly to establish the pattern within which the modern professional has matured. He called William Pepper a "leader who sees ahead of his generation, but who has the sense to walk and work in it" (1909, p. 211). Osler himself was just such a leader. One must not expect from him the sophistication of today but the simple directness of a man who felt himself to be the spokesman for, if not always the originator of, the proper design of the physician's life. He could have no foreknowledge of the proliferation of specialities that were to come not merely into medicine but into all professions, but he helped set medicine on the scientific pathway that would lead it, through the growth of knowledge, to a scope and breadth he could not have foretold but which would not have surprised him.

In any discussion of life-span learning, Osler deserves to take part, even though his voice, like any other, makes comments with which some of the discussants disagree. He reminds us of what we were and how we have become what we are. More important, he still has a great deal to say that is relevant to our present condition. However the professions divide themselves up or group themselves for practice, highly educated people who relate their knowledge to complex practical problems will continue to exist and to help one another. They will learn their life's work, and then they will grow old in it. For them the shrewd worldly voice of Osler, recommending how they should act at each stage of life, can continue to suggest dangers, opportunities, and the best ways to react to both.

And Osler's remarks do not deal uniquely with medicine. He paid some attention to other professions, usually suggesting their vast inferiority to his own. Law and theology, he pointed out, were not progressive; moreover, they might disappear in time; how different they are in both respects from medicine. Only two other professions, nursing and librarianship, deeply interested him. He worked out a curriculum for a library school at Oxford, but it never materialized; and his attitude toward nursing was marred by an unconscious condescension that might well irritate practitioners of that profession. But his ideas were more universal than he thought, as the foregoing pages may have demonstrated. Other professions need only change his language; for *patient* and *hospital* the lawyer might read *client* and *law court* and the pastor *parishioner* and *congregation*. For all professions, the basic principles of a life of study are the same; the engineer and the architect need day-tight compartments and quinquennial brain-dustings quite as much as does the physician.

IX

Throughout his life Osler moved directly and rapidly to act upon impulse, and he held that unless goals were sought immediately they might never be attained. A quotation from *Macbeth* expressed this thought: "The flighty purpose never is o'ertook / Unless the deed go with it." His friends became familiar with the words "flighty purpose," often spoken over his shoulder as he departed rapidly upon some new mission. In the last year of life, he said to an old friend that the quotation expressed "the directing and guiding principle of his life" (Cushing, 1925, II, p. 613). In *Macbeth* the next lines are: "From this moment / The very firstlings of my heart shall be / The firstlings of my hand." To survey his career, observing his patterns and consistencies through all its transplantions and concerns, is to see how steadfastly he held to the idea that the physician must be a lifelong student and that the medical profession must be organized to foster learning. All professions and the people they serve have reason to be grateful that, throughout Osler's career, continuing education was a firstling of his heart and hand.

References

Bibliotheca Osleriana. Oxford: Clarendon Press, 1929.

Camac, C. N. B. (Ed.). *Counsels and Ideals from the Writings of William Osler.* Boston: Houghton Mifflin, 1906.

Cushing, H. *The Life of Sir William Osler*. 2 vols. Oxford: Clarendon Press, 1925.

Harvey, A. M., and McKusick, V. A. (Eds.). *Osler's Textbook Revisited*. New York: Appleton-Century-Crofts, 1967.

Hughes, E. C. "Education for a Profession." In P. H. Ennis and H. W. Winger (Eds.), *Seven Questions About the Profession of Librarianship*. Chicago: University of Chicago Press, 1962.

Jacobs, H. B. "Osler as a Citizen and His Relation to the Tuberculosis Crusade in Maryland." In *Sir William Osler, Bart*. Baltimore: Johns Hopkins University Press, 1920.

Morley, H. *Jerome Cardan: The Life of Girolamo Cardano of Milan, Physician*. Vol. 2. London: Chapman and Hall, 1854.

Osler, W. *Aequanimitas, with Other Addresses to Medical Students, Nurses and Practitioners of Medicine*. (2nd ed.) Philadelphia: Blakiston, 1906.

Osler, W. *An Alabama Student and Other Biographical Essays*. New York: Oxford University Press, 1909.

Osler, W. "Organization in the Profession." *British Medical Journal*, 1911, *1*, 237–239.

Osler, W. *A Way of Life*. New York: Paul B. Hoeber, 1915.

Pickering, G. *The Challenge to Education*. London: Watts, 1967.

Reid, E. G. *The Great Physician*. London: Oxford University Press, 1931.

Shepherd, F. J. "Osler's Montreal Period." *International Association of Medical Museums Bulletin* (Montreal), 1926, *9*, 153–158.

Traditional Conceptions, Goals, and Forms of Learning

I

The history of adult education, viewed in the perspective of thirty centuries, is a chronicle of pronouncements and episodes with but little continuity of conception or program. As has been illustrated in the preceding chapters, the idea that men and women can and should learn has been discovered again and again whenever it was required by human hopes and needs. Kings, nobles, priests, philosophers, citizens, serfs, and slaves have all at one time or another shared in the rewards of study, although usually it has been the right, the obligation, or the delight of only a privileged few. Some people have recorded their ideas about the values and means of learning, while other people have worked out ways of life to embody them. Both the ancients and the moderns have thought a great deal about learning processes and practiced them in many ways.

Although most of this great variety of experiences has been forgotten and much of the rest lies buried in documents, awaiting the attention of future historians, some peaks of thought or achievement have become parts of the established chronicle of culture. The purpose of this chapter, which broadens the inquiries presented earlier, is to identify some of the ends and means of adult education that had already emerged in Western civilization prior to the time when present institutions began to take their modern form. The sequence of presentation is not chronological but analytical, thoughts and practices being grouped because they are similar, not because they were contemporaneous. Where possible, ideas are expressed in the words of their original spokespeople, thus gaining the force and perhaps helping to give modern students of adult learning a sense of community with some of their distinguished forebears.

II

"You should keep learning as long as you are ignorant—even to the end of your life," Seneca wrote in one of his elegant epistles; and he went on to quote a proverb current in his day, " 'As long as you live, keep learning how to live' " (1930, pp. 147-149). The study of Seneca's life suggests that his statement was not merely a moralistic preachment. Although rich, he lived ascetically to keep his mind clear; although powerful, he moderated his strength with the humaneness that came from a study of philosophy; and although busy, he always found time to learn. But, even as he extols education, he confesses, "I persist in praising not the life that I lead but that which I know I ought to lead. I follow it at a great distance, crawling" (1932, p. 144).

Every thoughtful person has at some time considered this question: By what principle or principles should life be guided? For most men and women, perhaps, the question has never arisen with any seriousness; simple survival has had to be their highest hope. But wherever people have been freed from incessant labor for their livelihood and have not been content to conform to the established ways of the community, they have asked themselves how they should design their lives and have answered in various ways, sometimes in words, sometimes in action, or, as in Seneca's case, in both. At least some of these life patterns, including the most ancient, have included serious and persistent study. "The unexamined life is not worth living," Socrates insisted, until his fellow citizens deprived him of his own.

Although there have been many conceptions of how education could best be woven into an entire design of life, at least five major patterns have been perennially proposed.

Education as the Entire Purpose of Life. People who seek
a single principle to guide their lives, said Aristotle, usually
choose one of three: pleasure, glory, or contemplation. Those
drawn to the first two may study to heighten their pleasure or
enhance their glory, and manuals (such as those of Ovid or
Machiavelli) have been written to help them. But the third principle is that of learning for its own sake, accepting it as the ultimate road to happiness and thereby adopting a way of life
whose central activity is education. Thus René Descartes, as a
young man, decided that "I could not do better than continue
. . . in devoting my whole life to the cultivation of my reason,
and in making such progress as I could in the knowledge of the
truth" ([1637] , 1958, p. 114).

In a solitary contemplative life, a person usually retires
from active pursuits (often to a country estate or a cloistered
cell) and spends full time studying whatever is of most interest
or greatest availability. Aristotle defined the essence of such a
life: "Self-sufficiency . . . is preeminently a characteristic of the
speculative activity; . . . the wise man is capable of speculation
by himself, and the wiser he is, the more capable he is of such
speculation" (1892, p. 336). Many people have lived such a life;
although some have been scorned, many have won respect by
doing so. Sometimes, as was true of Montaigne, Thoreau, and
Darwin, the life of learning produced great works of thought.
When Isaac Newton was asked how he had discovered his laws,
he answered, "By thinking of them without ceasing" (Voltaire,
[1745] , 1835, p. 727). Sometimes, as with an Indian ascetic or
a Talmudic scholar, religious values are attached to scholarship,
particularly when pursued wholeheartedly. "He who leaves his
home in search of knowledge," said Mohammed, "walks in the
path of God," and "The ink of the scholar is more holy than
the blood of the martyr" (Ali, 1922, p. 361). Esteem for the
independent contemplative life is broadly felt; most thoughtful
people have at least a fitful yearning for such a life themselves
and therefore admire those who have the means and the cour-
age to choose it.

The contemplative life can be pursued with other like-
minded people as well as alone and perhaps to greater advantage. Even Aristotle, after praising the self-sufficiency of the

wise person who chooses the contemplative life, said, "It is perhaps better for him in his speculation to have fellow-workers"
(1892, p. 336). The classic example of such a life had been set
about two centuries earlier by Pythagoras, who, "of all men,"
Heraclitus said, "was the most assiduous enquirer" (Heath,
1955, p. 803). After spending his early manhood in travel,
Pythagoras established at Crotona his community of students
and fellow scholars, who made a secular religion of the pursuit
of knowledge. The value of such a life was neatly pointed up
by its end, for when the members of the community abandoned
their original intentions and decided that their wisdom entitled
them to rule their fellow citizens, those ungrateful people killed
or exiled them.

Although there have been many other examples of se-
cluded groups in pursuit of truth, perhaps the fullest expression
of collective contemplation was in the life of the monasteries in
the Middle Ages and particularly at the height of the age of
Scholasticism in the twelfth and thirteenth centuries. The earliest
universities provide another example; they were bands of scholars both young and old. "The medieval student might be of any
age," said Will Durant. "He might be a curate, a prior, an ab-
bott, a merchant, a married man; he might be a lad of thirteen,
troubled with the sudden dignity of his years" (1950, p. 936).
Only later did the university restrict its student body to
young people in the early years of postadolescence.

Education as a Way of Examining Life. Since the contemplative life, alone or with a group, is rigorous and usually costly,
most people will not or cannot choose it. Others find the idea
repugnant, embodying as it does a narrow approach to the rich
delights and responsibilities of humanity. Such people argue
that learning is essential to the good life but chiefly as a way of
refining it. Thought and action should be distinguished from
each other but not separated. Isidore of Seville, in the sixth century, captured the ideal of this conception in his often-quoted
maxim, "Study as if you were to live forever; live as if you were
to die tomorrow."

Again the ancient Greeks provide a model: the man of affairs, fully engaged in action and decision, who still finds time to give continuous thought to his own growth in virtue and wisdom, using for that purpose both introspection and study. Solon, the early Athenian lawgiver, said, "Ever as I grow old I learn many things" (Freeman, 1926, p. 212), and his words echoed through antiquity. The golden age of Greece found its leader in Pericles, whose love for art and knowledge were made manifest in his policies as statesman and who achieved from his studies with Anaxagoras, said Plutarch, "not merely, as was natural, elevation of purpose and dignity of language, raised far above the base and dishonest buffooneries of mob-eloquence, but, besides this, a composure of countenance and a serenity and calmness in all his movements, which no occurrence while he was speaking could disturb" (1882, p. 184). For such a man, as for everyone who tries to follow this model, study cannot be a substitute for experience in the world's affairs, but neither can the lessons of experience be learned without study.

Those who argue for the examined life know that it is not an easy one to lead. Study requires effort and makes demands; it suggests ideals that are hard to follow amid the pressures and accidents of life. Nicholas of Cusa knew well both the rewards and the perils of the examined life. Born in 1401, he rose to eminence as a cardinal and exerted great influence as administrator, reformer, and evangelist. Yet even in his overbusy existence, he remained a student. Near the end of his life, he said why:

> To know and to think, to see the truth with the eye of the mind, is always a joy. The older a man grows, the greater is the pleasure which it affords him. . . . As love is the life of the heart, so is the endeavor after knowledge and truth the life of the mind. In the midst of the movements of time, of the daily work of life, of its perplexities and contradictions, we should lift our gaze fearlessly to the clear vault of heaven, and seek ever to obtain a firmer grasp of . . . the origin of all goodness and beauty, the capacities of our own hearts and minds,

the intellectual fruits of mankind throughout the
centuries, and the wondrous works of Nature
around us; but remembering always that in humil-
ity alone lies true greatness, and that knowledge
and wisdom are alone profitable in so far as our
lives are governed by them [Janssen, 1896, pp.
3-4].

*Education as an Inherent Part of a Complex Pattern of
Life.* In a famous passage, Francis Bacon argued that "studies
serve for delight, for ornament, and for ability." Each person
should make an ordered design of life and consider how education can best serve each of its parts. In "privateness and retir-
ing" one delights in study for its own sake; in "discourse" one
needs the ornament of learning; and in "the judgment and disposition of business" one needs learning for ability. Too much
time in studies is "sloth," to overuse them for ornament is "af-
fectation," and to judge only by rigid intellectual rules is the
arid "humor of a scholar." But "crafty men contemn studies;
simple men admire them; and wise men use them" (1879, I, p.
301). Thus learning should be considered neither as a way of
life nor as a means of examining it, but as an activity that, in
varied ways, helps achieve the diverse goals of human existence.
       This controlled view of education, in which people study
as they need or desire to do so and abstain when they think
wise, has been expressed in many statements and many lives.
Those who argue the advantages of learning sometimes put forward other purposes than Bacon's, and analysts of this topic
have long argued about how best to introduce conscious learning into a personal plan. Joseph Addison reflected this familiar
diversity of approach in one of his essays on adult education
when he observed, "I shall not here engage on those beaten Subjects of the Usefulness of Knowledge, nor of the Pleasure and
Perfection it gives the Mind, nor on the Methods of attaining it,
nor recommend any particular Branch of it, all which have
been the Topicks of many other Writers" (*The Spectator,* No.
94, 1965, p. 398).

Education as Mastery of All Knowledge. At another time, Bacon expressed another view, thus reminding anyone who needs reminding that people are as changeable in their views of education as of other subjects. When his fortunes were at a low ebb, he wrote a letter, one of whose lines has echoed ever since: "I wax now somewhat ancient; one and thirty years is a great deal of sand in the hour-glass. . . . I confess that I have as vast contemplative ends, as I have moderate civil ends: for I have taken all knowledge to be my province. . . . This, whether it be curiosity, vain-glory, or nature . . . is so fixed in my mind, as it cannot be removed" (1879, II, p. 2).

The belief that one person can master all knowledge and become accomplished in life's many arts has been expressed or sought after in so many lives that examples come readily to mind. People of the thirteenth century marveled at Frederick II, the Holy Roman Emperor, called *stupor mundi,* the wonder of the world, because of the range and depth of his knowledge. His tutor, Michael Scot, was not thought to be acting entirely as a courtier when he said to Frederick: "O fortunate emperor! I verily believe that if ever a man could escape death by his learning, thou wouldst be the one" (Kantorowicz, 1931, pp. 355-356). Two and a half centuries later, another Holy Roman Emperor, Maximilian I, aroused almost equal admiration for his erudition and personal accomplishments. Both men sought perfection in everything, never letting brilliant achievement in one part of life deter them from seeking it in others.

This ideal had its fullest expression and perhaps its most nearly perfect realization in fifteenth-century Italy. The Renaissance man was one who took pains to develop all his capacities and become expert in every realm of knowledge while still remaining a bold and active leader and an accomplished performer of all of the arts, including love-making. Jacob Burckhardt thought that with "an acute and practised eye" one might be able to discern an "increase in the number of complete men" throughout the century. "Whether they had before them as a conscious object the harmonious development of their spiritual and material existence is hard to say; but several of them attained it, so far as is consistent with the imperfection of all that is earthly." To prove his point, he gives examples, culminating in the case of Leon Battista Alberti, who excelled "in all by which praise is won." But then, after two pages that enumerate these accomplishments, Burckhardt concludes, "and Leonardo da Vinci was to Alberti as the finisher to the beginner, as the master to the dilettante" (1958, pp. 147-150).

Education as a Way of Preserving or Perfecting the State. In still another comprehensive view, learning is set in a social rather than an individual context. Simply put, education is the way by which the state is preserved or perfected. The learners may be the rulers, the people, or both. Plato proposed that those who wished to be philosopher-kings should be rigorously tested in both theoretical and practical learning and, even after they assumed power at about the age of fifty, one of the rewards and necessities of their lives was to keep on learning. Aristotle argued that the purpose of laws is to educate citizens in virtue and that the wise statesman keeps that goal central to his thought.

All political systems have equal need for education, although its aims, content, and method are unique to each system. Thus the Athenians stressed the free quest for excellence and the responsibility of statesmen to guide their people to wisdom and virtue, while the Spartans emphasized simplicity, discipline, uniformity, and unquestioning obedience to the glory and advancement of the state through armed conflict. Both systems of thought, although at opposite poles, could be developed and supported only by the systematic reinforcement of education.

III

The comprehensive conceptions that have just been briefly presented (and others of the same order of generality) suggest the values that lifelong study is presumed to possess but state them only in broad terms. For example, *the contemplative life* describes a total pattern of existence but does not indicate whether it is chosen because of a passion to master some body of knowledge, because it offers refuge from the turmoil of the world, or because it is primarily a way of carrying out a congenial habit. Of the five conceptions described, only education as an inherent part of a complex pattern of life probes beneath the surface to identify the various and complex orientations that lead men and women to education.

Most people who have identified the values to be gained from learning have dealt with only one or a few purposes. Unlike the authors of the previously identified formulations, they did not give study a place in the total pattern of life but assumed or argued that it was so important that sensible people should find time for it. Why should they do so? The answers have been expressed in many forms: essays, historical or biographical passages, epigrams, *pensées,* single principles in larger structures of thought, or casual (often fleeting) comments. A synthesist can fit all these expressions of value together into a master plan or theory, but, as they were actually spoken or acted out, each had its own logic and its immediate urgency. A few of them are here loosely grouped in terms of the basic orientations that appear to underlie them, but their original flavor is preserved and they are not presented as a comprehensive system.

The Mastery of Knowledge as Delight and Passion. Of these values, perhaps the most common is the feeling that the enlarged understanding that results from learning is itself so conducive to happiness that it should be undertaken whenever circumstances permit. As minister to the Roman emperor, for example, Pliny had to give much of his time to administrative affairs, but he delighted in mastering knowledge. The rhythm of his habits was thus described by his nephew:

> He had a quick apprehension, incredible zeal, and a wakefulness beyond compare. He always began to work at midnight. . . . Before daybreak he used to wait upon Vespasian; who likewise chose that season to transact business. When

he had finished the affairs which that emperor committed to his charge, he returned home again to his studies. After a short and light repast at noon . . . he would frequently in the summer, if he was disengaged from business, repose himself in the sun; during which time some author was read to him, from whence he made extracts and observations, as indeed this was his constant method whatever book he read. . . . When this basking was over, he generally went into the cold bath, and as soon as he came out of it, just took a slight refreshment, and then reposed himself for a little while. Then, as if it had been a new day, he immediately resumed his studies till dinner-time, when a book was again read to him, upon which he would make some running notes. . . . Such was his manner of life amidst the noise and hurry of the town; but in the country his whole time was devoted to study without intermission, excepting only while he bathed. But in this exception I include no more than the time he was actually in the bath; for all the while he was rubbed and wiped, he was employed either in hearing some book read to him, or in dictating himself. In his journeys, as though released from all other cares, he found leisure from this sole pursuit . . . for he thought all was time lost that was not given to study [Pliny, 1915, pp. 199-203].

In most lives, the delight in study must be tempered by other passions or necessities. Many a person has been a sovereign, warrior, statesman, or courtier in youth and has turned to study only when middle age diminished the attractiveness of the world of practical affairs. Christina of Sweden did not wait. She had a great passion for knowledge, but while she was queen, she knew that she must restrain it. She arose early to receive instruction from her tutors before she turned to the affairs of state. (Descartes died of the pneumonia he contracted while tutoring her at five in the morning in wintry Stockholm.) But although John Milton said she was "fit to govern not only Sweden but the world" ([1638], 1834, p. 931), she herself could not be satisfied with her exalted position and finally renounced the throne so that she could live a wholly contemplative life.

Such a life is hard to live, and some authorities say that Christina later regretted her decision to do so. The other rewards and values of life are hard to repress. Thus Mme. du Chatelet, the mistress of Voltaire, thought that, "of all passions, the love of study is the one most necessary for our happiness; it is a certain resource against misfortunes and a source of inexhaustible pleasures." Then, rather inconsistently, she added that the love of another person is "perhaps the only passion which is able to make us desire to live," the only one to which even the pleasure of study ought to be sacrificed ([1796], 1961, pp. 23, 27).

Education as an Enjoyed Activity. Although some people have a passion to learn because they wish to master knowledge, others enjoy the activity itself, and the difference between the two motives is not always easy to determine. Some people are avid readers, some like to hear lectures, some enjoy being members of clubs and other groups, and some find satisfaction in travel. Any educational episode has its own distinctive purpose, which the learner sometimes insists is the paramount reason for participation. However, on reflection, he or she may conclude that it is not the succession of specific goals but the act of learning that is most satisfying.

Two quotations illustrate this concept. Addison believed that much of life, particularly that part of it spent in idleness, is long and tedious but that "those Parts of Life which are exercised in Study, Reading, and the Pursuits of Knowledge are long but not tedious" and therefore not merely lengthened life but also turned it to advantage (*The Spectator*, No. 94, 1965, p. 398). Isaac Disraeli said much the same thing but more directly: "The delight of opening a new pursuit, or a new course of reading, imparts the vivacity and novelty of youth even to old age" (1818, pp. 322–323).

Education as Self-Imposed Discipline. Another view of learning arises not from pleasure but from self-discipline. The compulsion to learn is imposed by the learner on himself or herself not for the sake of specific knowledge but because of the belief that study maintains or strengthens mental processes. "If I rest, I rust," said Martin Luther somewhere, and Leonardo da Vinci expressed the same idea: "Iron rusts from disuse; stagnant water loses its purity and in cold weather becomes frozen; even so does inaction sap the vigour of the mind" (1938, p. 96). *The Spectator* found yet another metaphor. "The Mind that lies fallow but a single Day," it observed, "sprouts up in Follies that are only to be killed by a constant and assiduous Culture" (No. 10, 1965, p. 44).

Since the mind has many dimensions and processes, anybody who wishes to retain or enhance its strength must give attention to many kinds of learning. As John Locke pointed out, "If men are, for a long time, accustomed only to one sort or method of thoughts, their minds grow stiff in it, and do not readily turn to another. . . . I do not propose . . . a variety and stock of knowledge, but a variety and freedom of thinking; . . . an increase of the powers and activity of the mind" ([1690], 1824, p. 356). Darwin provided a convenient example. Until he was thirty, he said, he loved poetry, drama, and music. But, in his autobiography, written near the end of his life, he observed: "I cannot endure to read a line of poetry: I have tried lately to read Shakespeare, and found it so intolerably dull that it nauseated me. I have also almost lost my taste for pictures or music. . . . My mind seems to have become a kind of machine for grinding general laws out of large collections of facts, but why this should have caused the atrophy of that part of the brain alone, on which the higher tastes depend, I cannot conceive. . . . If I had to live my life again, I would have made a rule to read some poetry and listen to some music at least once every week; for perhaps the parts of my brain now atrophied would thus have been kept alive through use" (1902, pp. 50-51).

Education as a Compulsory Activity. The compulsion to learn is sometimes not self-imposed but prescribed by those who hold that the values to be achieved by education are so great that anyone who will not willingly seek them must be required to do so. Such is the belief of those who wish to preserve present systems as well as of reformers who, upon gaining power, set out to reconstruct the social order. Cultural history is filled with stories of dictators and ruling elites who attempted to control thought, perhaps by requiring attendance at religious or civil gatherings where the truth could be explained or perhaps by setting such penalties for ignorance, however defined, that all prudent people would be compelled to seek the truth. Whether the requirement to learn is lax or stringent, those on whom it is imposed think of education as compulsory. They do not necessarily object to it on that account, for some people are willing or even eager to submit to the will of others or to conform to custom, but any such relinquishment of independence makes learning less voluntary than it would otherwise be.

One rather charming illustration is found in the biography of Alfred the Great written by Asser, a member of his court. The people of Alfred's kingdom often appealed to him to overrule the decisions of his judges. On looking into such cases, he sometimes concluded that the rulings had been unjust and would question the judges to "inquire whether it was from ignorance, or from ill-will of any sort, from love or fear of any man's money." Confronting these alternatives, the judges usually chose ignorance, whereupon Alfred would admonish them by saying, "I marvel greatly at this your insolence, since by the gift of God, and by my gift, you have assumed the duties and rank of wise men, but have neglected the study and exercise of wisdom. I command you, therefore, either to lay down here that exercise of earthly power which you enjoy, or to take care to apply yourselves with much greater zeal to the study of wisdom." On hearing these words, "the ealdormen and reeves" were terrified and "in a marvellous way" almost all of them, "who had been illiterate from infancy, studied the art of letters, preferring to learn an unwonted discipline with great toil than to lose the exercise of power." Unhappily some of them "were unable to make advance in the liberal arts, either from age or from the too great slowness of an unaccustomed mind," and therefore "considered themselves wretched since they had not in their youth learned letters nor were even able to do so in old age, though they ardently desired to do so." Asser concludes the story by saying, "Now we have set forth the zeal both of old and young in learning letters" (1908, pp. 88-91).

Education as Escape. Learning can also be escape. "Study has been for me," said Montesquieu, "the sovereign remedy against the disappointments of life, never having known any trouble that an hour of reading would not dissipate" (1879, p. 154). In this view the varied forms of educational activity are marvelously flexible. They permit escape from busyness into solitude—or from loneliness into conviviality. Wherever life binds or presses or pains, somewhere at hand there is a way out, one which is morally pleasing, socially acceptable, and ultimately rewarding, unlike drunkenness, the use of dope, or other dark forms of flight from life's frustrations.

Exile, isolation, and imprisonment have often stimulated study. One good example was Machiavelli at the time he lived in poverty in the countryside far from the glittering courts he loved. He rose early in the morning, walked in the woods, snared birds, read amorous poetry, chatted with passersby, ate a meager dinner at noon, and spent the afternoon at the inn playing at games with the tradespeople, loudly quarreling and wrangling. "Steeped in this degradation my wits grow mouldy, and I vent my rage at the malignity of fate." Then he went home at nightfall to his writing room, where "I take off the day's clothing, covered with mud and dust, and put on garments regal and courtly; and reclothed appropriately, I enter the ancient courts of ancient men, where, received by them with affection, I feed on that food which only is mine and which I was born for, where I am not ashamed to speak with them and to ask them the reasons for their actions; and they in their kindness answer me; and for four hours of time I do not feel boredom, I forget every trouble, I do not dread poverty, I am not frightened by death; entirely I give myself over to them" (1961, p. 142).

Education as the Distinguishing Mark of an Elite. In many cultures, knowledge has been considered to be the distinguishing characteristic of an elite. Only the ruling political or economic leaders or the priests and magicians had the right to learn. In some parts of Africa, tribal mysteries are carefully guarded; anyone who wishes to pass upward through the rites is subjected to severe tests and heavy costs. Oxford lore has it that more than a century ago Thomas Gaisford, in a sermon, observed that the advantages of a classical education are two-fold: It enables us to look down with contempt on those who have not shared its advantages and also fits us for places of emolument not only in this world, but in that which is to come.

The best-known expression of the idea in antiquity was that of Alexander. According to Plutarch, while Alexander was fighting in Asia, he heard that Aristotle, his former tutor, had published a treatise on metaphysics. At once the following letter was sent: "Alexander to Aristotle, greeting. You have not done well to publish your books of oral doctrine; for what is there now that we excel others in, if those things which we have been particularly instructed in be laid open to all?" Aristotle had no very good answer and responded by saying that the books were both published and not published, a comment Plutarch explains, speaking for the readers of these books in every later era, by saying that Aristotle's "books on metaphysics are written in a style which makes them useless for ordinary teaching, and instructive only, in the way of memoranda, for those who have been already conversant in that sort of learning" (1882, p. 578).

Education as Adornment. Wherever learning is prized as the distinguishing mark of an elite, it is likely to be taken up by the fashionable who esteem it as a form of adornment, wearing erudition as they would a jewel. In practice, it may be hard to draw the line between those who truly love knowledge and those who affect that love. The dilettante is scorned by the scholar. Often, too, what begins as genuine inquiry ends as pretentiousness. At the salon of the Marquise de Rambouillet, there were gathered together in an atmosphere of elegance and refinement many of the most distinguished men and women of the day (including more than a few scholars and artists), who took part in an elevated and graceful discourse. Gradually, how-

ever, the discourse became so self-consciously exquisite that
Molière satirized it in *Les Précieuses Ridicules.*

For purposes of adornment, any content or method will
suffice. Medieval knights, in the intervals between hunting and
warfare, learned the elegant code of chivalry and studied to be
romantic poets and troubadours just as some business people today acquire a deep interest in the fine arts. In the early days of
modern science, when it could be understood by those with no
more than a scanty formal education and required neither a specialized vocabulary nor complex instruments, topics that were
later to be developed into such disciplines as physics, chemistry,
and biology were often taken up by the aristocracy. Gentlemen
could display on their own bare arms William Harvey's proofs of
the circulation of the blood, and the possession of a chemical
laboratory, an air pump, or a microscope demonstrated the fact
that its owner was at the forefront of knowledge. However, in
science as in other subjects, the popular lecture has been the
chief recourse of the dilettante, particularly since in the lecture
hall the desire to learn can be prominently displayed along with
other adornments of person or dress. Oliver Goldsmith suggested as much when he observed in 1755 that in Paris "I have
seen as bright a circle of beauty at the chymical lectures of
Rouelle as at the court of Versailles. Wisdom never appears so
charming, as when graced and protected by beauty" (1966, p.
300). The descendants of that circle of beauty are still to be
found on prominent display at lectures, although chemistry is
less fashionable than it once was.

Education as a Way of Achieving Specific Goals. Perhaps
the most widespread conception of the value of education in
the Western world today is that the knowledge it conveys is of
practical use to an individual or to society. A person studies because of a goal: to gain pleasure or glory (as Aristotle said); to
be a better farmer or business leader; to serve more effectively
as citizen, elected official, or government employee; to get
ahead in a profession or to advance or protect it; to solve the
personal problems of marriage, family life, or social participation; or to know how to use leisure wisely. Such mundane goals

are far from the refined or arcane aims of education as they were classically conceived, and abstract knowledge and pure science still hold the highest place in the esteem of scholars; but practical needs and problems have always given rise to learning activities and thus to the idea that education is the way by which specific and tangible goals are reached.

People in earlier days needed practical knowledge quite as much as people do today, although, in a world that had a relatively small amount of tested knowledge and that was often governed by supernatural lore and superstitious belief, all too little hope could be entertained that any help could actually be derived from instruction. Henry V of England learned how to use an astrolabe so that he could chart the sky—but also so that he could work out horoscopes that would enable him to predict the future. The Greeks and the Romans had manuals to teach them the arts of the citizen, the statesman, the worker, and the lover. The waging of war has been studied by military leaders in every age, and the young officers of ancient times like those of today read Thucydides with fascination and profit.

With the growth of science, people learned better than before how to control themselves and their environments. In 1730, for example, Charles Townshend, an English viscount, worked out a system of crop rotation that was laughed to scorn by those who farmed the neighboring manors—until the evidence of its success on his estate led them to follow his example. A modern educator would say of him that he was one of the countless inventors of the demonstration technique, and a sociologist would say that he exemplified the theory of the diffusion of innovation, for, as a member of the aristocracy, he was a legitimizer. The other lords of the realm condescendingly called him Turnip Townshend, but they studied his practices and followed his example.

Since the deepest personal and social needs of people tend to be universal, the conception that education should be devoted to such specific ends leads idealists to believe that everyone should share in its benefits and that they should not be reserved solely for those who have leisure and wealth. Many a reformer or philosopher of medieval times caught the vision of a broadly based system of education that ultimately might teach everyone. However, it was not until the religious zeal of the Reformation was joined with the development of the printing press that an exalted aspiration and a mighty instrument of learning made feasible for the first time the hope that universal education might actually be achieved.

The original major impetus for widespread education was the belief that all men and women should seek God directly by turning to the Bible; and if they could not read, then the only road to salvation lay in learning how to do so. The consequence of ignorance might well be eternal damnation; the personal imperative for learning could scarcely have been clearer. In 1560, John Knox proposed a comprehensive system of parish schools for Scotland, holding that "this must be cairfullie provideit, that no fader, of what estait or conditioun that ever he be, use his children at his awin fantasie, especiallie in thair youth-heade; but all must be compelled to bring up thair children in learnyng and virtue" (1848, pp. 210-211). Although in Scotland as elsewhere reformers believed that the spread of schools for children was the paramount educational task, it seemed only logical to them that a second chance at salvation should be granted to those who had been denied a first. Sometimes this evangelism led to drastic countermeasures. In 1401, the English followers of John Wycliffe were declared subject to burning as heretics on the ground that "they hold and exercise Schools, they make and write Books, they do wickedly instruct and inform People" (*The Statutes of the Realm,* II, Henry IV, c. 15, 1816, p. 126). This was not the first time, nor would it be the last, that the main thrust of an educational program was directed toward adults, for the soul of an ignorant parent was as much worth saving as that of a child, and how would children ever learn if parents remained ignorant?

Beginning as a means, literacy became an end. As the use of printed and written symbols spread, learning, recreation, and the transaction of affairs came to depend on the ability to read and write; this ability gradually became so important that it could no longer be thought of only as a road to salvation. It became instead a basic requirement for all adults. Civilized people now take literacy so much for granted that they sometimes wonder why primitive people often do not respond readily to elementary education when it is offered to them. The answer, of course, is that such people feel no need to use it as a way of saving their souls or advancing their standards of life and therefore never accept it as either means or end. Men and women can spend their whole lives in a jungle or savage village without ever encountering print.

Although the hope of salvation provided the powerful stimulus for the first major reform movement in organized education, other goals eventually appeared, first rather slowly and then, in the nineteenth and twentieth centuries, with increasing rapidity. The educated person had economic and social advantages denied to the ignorant; and yet access to learning in childhood was everywhere so restricted that most people were condemned to a shallow development of their potential. Why should not everyone have the benefits granted to only a few? Can a good society be based on ignorance? Can those who have only a few skills, mostly rural, build a strong and complex economy? Can uninformed people be allowed to judge the complex questions of their own political destiny?

Such questions, once raised, cannot be ignored for long. The history of modern adult educational movements consists of an account of all the many ways by which answers are proposed and worked out in practice. Visionaries who have hope for a more rational and happy life and have gone forth to do battle for it often have held, with one of their twentieth-century counterparts, that "prejudice, superstition, fear, ignorance must be attacked in their strongholds, the adult mind" (Cary, 1962, p. 98). These reformers often thus become the schoolmasters of their contemporaries. The urgent themes of modern social improvement are reflected in the history of adult education: Economic leaders advance their various viewpoints; political leaders drive toward an order based on the rights of the many rather than the privileges of the few—or the reverse; rationalists hold with almost religious fervor that the evils of this life can be overcome by the growth and spread of objective knowledge; founders of the cooperative movement bring the principle of brotherhood into the production and consumption of goods; and unions struggle for the workers' right to share in the decisions that control their livelihood. By such massive efforts as these, put forward in generation after generation, the conception that education should exist chiefly to meet specific personal and social needs has so established itself that perhaps most people today would agree with James Froude that "the knowledge which a man can use is the only real knowledge, the only knowledge which has life and growth in it, and converts itself into practical power. The rest hangs like dust about the brain, or dries like raindrops off the stones" ([1867], 1908, p. 168).

To these varied views of the value of education others could be added, ranging from the broad or sublime to the rigid or meager. Perhaps these will suffice to show, however, that as modern institutions of adult education emerged and established themselves, they built upon an old and rich tradition. In the long history of culture, however beliefs in fundamental values were shaped, either by an individual designing a personal life or by a nation forging a common creed, the idea has been present that people should constantly study throughout their lives in order to realize their own potential and to strengthen their social institutions. An ultimate expression of this idea occurs in the constitution of the United Nations Educational, Scientific, and Cultural Organization: "Since wars begin in the minds of men, it is in the minds of men that the defenses of peace must be constructed."

IV

As earlier chapters have shown, the learning processes used to achieve these values emerged in antiquity from individual enterprise or group association. As those methods were used through the years from prehistoric to modern times, they have undergone many modulations while still keeping their central form. Some were forgotten and had to be reinvented. Some were remembered but reapplied in such a way that they seemed new. Thus in the middle of the nineteenth century, Bishop N. F. S. Grundtvig, in founding the Danish folk high schools, said that they should teach by means of what he called "the living word," by which he meant the oral presentation of content, usually suffused with emotional emphasis. Although Grundtvig must have been aware of the antiquity of this method, he was convinced that he was giving it a fresh and immediate currency for his time and place. His followers shared that belief.

As adult education has grown and become institutionalized, it has found ways of using these ancient processes of teaching and learning, often putting them together in new ways, adapting their specific applications, and adding refinements. In earlier chapters, these methods were examined as they occurred simultaneously or sequentially in the lives of learners and teachers or in educative settings. Now some of the most widely used processes will be identified and subjected to brief analyses.

Self-Directed Study. The paramount means of learning is and always has been self-directed study. The systematic observation of some aspect of nature must have been the earliest such activity, and modern archeologists have discovered that occasionally its results were carried to a high level. Interpretations of the ruins of both Stonehenge and Monte Alban, for example, suggest that in two widely separated cultures the study of astronomy resulted in impressive accomplishments. As such symbols for experience as the alphabet and number systems were evolved, resources for independent study were enlarged. Printing, libraries, an inexpensive and dependable postal service, motion pictures, radio, television, and the computer have further enhanced the process.

Individualized self-teaching is constantly being rediscovered in one way or another, as the surge of interest in programmed learning in the 1960s demonstrated. Most of the people in the world who seek to learn must still rely on the old method of direct observation of nature, but, in those countries in which civilization has had the greatest advances, symbolic resources for those who wish to direct their own learning are so great that the essential problem is not scarcity but wise choice.

Independent learning occurs naturally and to some degree in the life of everyone. Often it is a casual, almost random, scarcely planned activity arising out of a question. What makes these plants thrive and those die? What does the word *shrove* mean? Who was Wolsey? How can I learn the most from this museum before I get too tired? But individual autonomous study has also served as the basis for a sustained way of life; as Thomas Carlyle put it, "The man who cannot wonder, who does not habitually wonder (and worship), were he President of innumerable Royal Societies, and carried . . . the epitome of all Laboratories and Observations with their results in his single head,—is but a Pair of Spectacles behind which there is no Eye" (1831, pp. 46-47).

Tutorial Teaching. Tutorial teaching was as well known in antiquity as it is today, and, at those times in history when formal learning was restricted to the elite, such instruction was often the prevailing method. Its essence is the careful guidance of a specific student by a teacher who pays full attention to the student's abilities and requirements. Because it is expensive, highly skilled tutoring has ordinarily been available only to rulers, rich people, or the members of a governing class. "My rank is that of a scholar, and I need masters" was the motto adopted by Peter the Great in 1697 (Waliszewski, 1900, p. 52), and other kings and emperors have had a like feeling, either engaging learned scholars to teach them or owning them outright as slaves. The instruction was not always successful even with the most exalted students. Poor Charlemagne never could learn to write; and Voltaire had little luck in teaching Frederick the Great to compose poetry.

In the world of work, the method has been used in simple and humble ways throughout history—the farmer taught his son to plow; the mother helped her daughter to learn household arts; and the experienced craftsperson showed the novice how to use tools. But the method is also used for conveying the most complex and subtle skills, as when a master violinist, pianist, or singer seeks advanced instruction in a performing art. Because the tutorial method allows attention to be paid to the unique needs of the individual student (and perhaps also because of its expensiveness and its use by great people), it has often been suggested to be inherently the best method of teaching.

Scholarly Companionship. An even better method perhaps, although harder to contrive, is scholarly companionship—two or more people consciously making mutual learning a key element in their friendship. At one point in his life Benjamin Franklin undertook to learn Italian but was constantly interrupted in this pursuit by an acquaintance who kept tempting him to play chess. Franklin continues the story: "I at length refus'd to play any more, unless on this condition, that the victor in every game should have a right to impose a task, either in parts of the grammar to be got by heart, or in translations, etc., which tasks the vanquish'd was to perform, upon honour, before our next meeting. As we play'd pretty equally, we thus beat one another into that language" (1905, p. 347).

Sometimes scholarly companionship runs far deeper than this playful story suggests. In Chapter Two, an account has been given of the relationship of Montaigne and Etienne de La Boétie, a profound attachment based on constant study and scholarly discussion that was the most meaningful intellectual relationship in Montaigne's life. Another such friendship was that between the two great humanists of the early sixteenth century, Thomas More and Desiderius Erasmus, who for a third of a century continued their intellectual companionship, finding profit not merely in ridiculing the aridity of the Scholastic philosophers but also in studying together the liberal and humane accomplishments of humankind.

Voluntary Groups. The reader of cultural history and biography finds many records of groups of kindred souls who, recognizing a common need to learn, have banded together more or less formally for mutual instruction, while still being fully engaged in worldly affairs. The story of the Concord lyceum has been told in Chapter Four. To choose another example, John Stuart Mill was one of a dozen young men who met from half-past eight to ten two mornings a week in a borrowed room on Threadneedle Street in London to read and discuss "some systematic treatise." He had had perhaps the most advanced formal education in youth of anybody who ever lived, but he said of this group, "I have always dated from these conversations my own real inauguration as an original and independent thinker" (1883, pp. 119-123).

Many such groups try to do no more than master an existing body of knowledge or interpret for themselves either their own experience or the teachings of some religious or secular authority. Others hope to stimulate their members, usually a select company, to the exercise of their highest talents and potential. Galileo's thought was greatly influenced by the fact that he belonged to the Academy of the Lynx-Eyed, which desired "as its members philosophers who are eager for real knowledge and will give themselves to the study of nature, especially mathematics" (1957, p. 77). Ralph Waldo Emerson suggested the value of such an association by showing the consequences of its absence: "I cannot help seeing that Doctor Channing would have been a much greater writer had he found a strict tribunal of writers, a graduated intellectual empire established in the land, and knew that bad logic would not pass, and that the most severe exaction was to be made on all who enter these lists. . . . It is very easy to reach the degree of culture that prevails around us; very hard to pass it, and Doctor Channing, had he found Wordsworth, Southey, Coleridge, and Lamb around him, would as easily have been severe with himself and risen a degree higher as he has stood where he is. I mean, of course, a genuine intellectual tribunal, not a literary junto of Edinburgh wits, or dull conventions of Quarterly or Gentleman's Reviews" (1911, pp. 105-106).

Most mutual instruction groups rise, flourish briefly, and disappear, leaving little or no record of their existence unless noted people took part in them. Some, however, have matured into distinguished academies, centuries old, in which companies of scholars seek to advance their knowledge and that of the world. The Royal Society (of Great Britain) began as "a gentlemen's club for the discussion of scientific matters" (Stimson, 1939, p. 40), and the American Philosophical Society grew out of the Junto, a group of self-educating young men organized by

Franklin. Other such groups have achieved permanence essentially by replicating themselves, thus becoming modular units of structures that, in some cases, finally achieve great size. George Williams, a young workingman in London, created the same kind of voluntary group that Mill and Franklin found useful, but he and his followers went on to build it, with broadening purposes and programs, into the world-wide Young Men's Christian Association.

Disputation. In the passage concerning Doctor Channing, Emerson may have referred not to an actual gathering but to an interaction of scholars in public debate, correspondence, or print. Disputation, carried out privately or publicly, is a venerable means of getting at or communicating the truth; it was used in ancient Greece by both Socrates and the Sophists, and it was revived in the Middle Ages, most notably by the Scholastic philosophers.

Little about modern debate suggests the fieriness of its past. It has become for the most part a neatly ordered exercise for young students or a series of papers by those who hold opposing points of view. It was not always thus. Great issues might depend upon the outcome as was the case when Luther nailed his theses to the door of the church at Wittenberg. Disputation in earlier eras was usually a method of getting at the truth in the most fundamental realms of life, namely philosophy and theology. Thomas Aquinas expressed an essential spirit of adult education in 1270, when he hurled this challenge to his opponents: "If then anyone there be who, boastfully taking pride in his supposed wisdom, wishes to challenge what we have written, let him not do it in some corner nor before children who are powerless to decide on such difficult matters. Let him reply openly if he dare. He shall find me there confronting him, and not only my negligible self, but many another whose study is truth. We shall do battle with his errors or bring a cure to his ignorance" (D'Arcy, 1953, p. 35).

Masters and Teachers. The master-disciple and the teacher-student relationships, although similar in form, differ in essence. The master believes that he or she presents original truth and offers it to those who can carry it forth into the world; for the reasons Aquinas suggested, the disciples are usually adults, not children. In the Academy and the Lyceum of ancient Greece, the students were men, not boys, and so were those who first heard the messages of Jesus, Buddha, and Mohammed. Later on, when truths are accepted, the teacher explains them to students, who often present themselves in a group, partly because a classroom is more economical than tutorial instruction and partly because of the value of shared experience in learning.

For these reasons and because the classroom serves so well as the modular unit for a school, a college, or a university, it has become the dominant form of childhood and youth education and was early adopted by many adult educational institutions as their central or sole instructional setting. As a consequence of this widespread use, many people believe the technique used in the classroom to be the essential method of acquiring knowledge and feel uneasy when other processes are suggested. Thus a survey of the extent of adult education in a town may focus chiefly on the classes available, and a public librarian or museum curator, when asked about the institution's educational program, may dwell solely on the group instruction it provides.

Spoken Discourse. The form of spoken discourse is simple although its aims are diverse, as the examples of Billy Graham and Edward Everett have shown. One person addresses many people, speaking to them as a collective entity with no necessary knowledge of them as individuals. The comments expressed may closely follow a predetermined plan or they may be influenced by the response they arouse, but any such adaptation is to a crowd, not to an individual or group of individuals. Spoken discourse may have no other end than amusement or incitement, and, as Joseph Goebbels once remarked, propaganda has no need to be rich in intellectual content. But the purpose can also be to instruct, either directly or by narration or exhortation.

Spoken discourse had perhaps its most famous secular practitioner at the very beginning of its recorded history. Homer, the wandering poet-scholar, gave his illiterate or meagerly lettered hearers a recital that mingled poetic feeling, entertainment, history, and moral instruction. His method has been used ever since, with one or another of its basic purposes predominating. The folk tale, the ballad, and the oral chronicle have served to give primitive people a sense of their traditions and continuity. The sermon was for centuries the chief means by which people were instructed in virtue. Meanwhile a horde of forgotten or half-forgotten men and a much smaller number of women have served as lecturers, the retailers of learning. Sometimes lecture-going has achieved a great vogue, as it did in Renaissance and Elizabethan times.

The content of spoken discourse has broadened to include all knowledge, for this method has many advantages. It economically satisfies the desire of many people to learn. One speaker can have many hearers; motion pictures, records, electronic amplification, radio, television, audiotapes, videotapes, and videodiscs have enlarged the audience and thereby enhanced the usefulness of the method, particularly since it lends itself so readily to these adaptations of its original form. New knowledge not otherwise available can be presented, and old knowledge can be reordered into new frameworks. Spoken discourse does not require its hearers to demonstrate continuing participation as actively as do other methods, and therefore it can attract hearers who are not deeply interested in the subject or who feel unsure of their capacities. Most important, it presents knowledge from the viewpoint of one person and by exposure to a distinctive personality; this essentially is what Grundtvig meant by "the living word." These complex advantages give oral discourse in its various forms a prominent place in modern learning activities just as they did in earlier and simpler days.

The Collection and Use of the Instruments of Education. From the beginning of history people have gathered together books and other instruments of learning. The ancient Greeks did so, the Ptolemies established a museum (home of the Muses), the burning of the library at Alexandria has been recognized in every later age as a catastrophe for scholarship, and the Roman emperor Julian said, "Some men have a passion for horses, others for birds, others, again, for wild beasts; but I, from childhood, have been penetrated by a passionate longing to acquire books" (1923, p. 73).

Once assembled, books, works of art, or natural objects may serve many purposes, among them commemoration of the past, decoration, display, instruction, or the seeking of new knowledge. "If I were not a King," said James I of England on visiting the Bodleian Library, "I would be a University man; and if it were so that I must be a prisoner, if I might have my wish, I would desire to have no other prison than that Library, and to be chained together with so many good Authors and dead Masters" (Dick, 1949, pp. xxxviii–xxxix). Luther urged the German city councilmen that "no effort or expense should be spared to found good libraries" and suggested that the chief basis for collecting books should be their usefulness as tools of learning ([1524], 1931, pp. 125-129).

Separate Communities Based on Study. It has often been the case that those who believed most deeply in learning and wished to engage collectively in the contemplative life withdrew into communities for that purpose. Some of these communities had a religious orientation, as did monasteries, nunneries, and lamaseries, or they made a religion of study, as did the Pythagoreans. The medieval universities safeguarded their independence by a separation of the laws governing town and gown. Such centers as these engaged in learning not merely by preserving and using its instruments but also by maintaining study circles and by transmitting knowledge in a continuous human chain usually from older persons to younger ones, the entire group engaging in the lifelong pursuit of education. Some learning communities, such as those at residential social settlements, set themselves up as enclaves within a continuing worldly life. The actual forms of teaching and learning might include all those mentioned earlier (and others as well), but the fact that learning took place within the confines of a separate community added a new dimension to their use.

The Mass Media. Printing lifted the chains from the books in the Bodleian Library and carried the ideas they recorded to king and commoner alike. For a long while, efforts had been made to find ways to spread knowledge more widely. Modern drama has its beginnings in the cathedral mystery plays, painters told Biblical stories in pictures, and monks learned miniature writing so that more copies of manuscripts could be made by an economical use of vellum. But the development of movable type and the perfection of the printing press made new ways to popularize knowledge possible: books, newspapers, journals, tracts, pamphlets, posters, and broadsides. New instruments of learning were created, such as the dictionary, the encyclopedia, and the textbook. Most important of all for the spread of serious and sustained study, libraries ceased to be hoards of rare manuscripts and became collections of relatively inexpensive books. Where before there could be only a few libraries, now there could be thousands, and their resources could be used with great freedom and flexibility. The printing press became the major invention in the spread of knowledge, setting a pattern for all the mass media, whose later development helped make learning available to everyone.

Education by Experience. Throughout history, some people have insisted that the most profound learning results not from formal study but from the continuing flow of experience. The laws should teach virtue, and the city should mold its citizens by its harmony, beauty, and variety. Pericles, feeling it necessary to teach the arts as well as the moral virtues, set about the task of making Athens so beautiful and cultural events so frequent that the people would learn by their everyday life. When, on one occasion, he had difficulty in persuading the assembly to vote the necessary funds for centers of culture, he said that he would pay for them himself, adding that if he did so he would expect to put his own name on them. Plutarch concludes the story by saying that the assembly then "cried aloud, bidding him to spend on, and lay out what he thought fit from the public purse, and to spare no cost, till all were finished" (1882, p. 194).

Experience has also been thought to be the best teacher in adulthood even for those members of the elite who have had the benefit of schooling in youth. Traditionally the young Englishman completed his education by going on a grand tour of European capitals, often accompanied by an experienced tutor who could introduce him to all aspects of life in which a sophisticated man should be knowledgeable. Montaigne thought that at any age travel was the best form of education, provided one looked at new ways of life with an open mind and a discerning eye. "Someone said to Socrates, that a certain man had grown no better by his travels: 'I should think not,' he said; 'he took himself along with him' " (1967, p. 176). The world itself is the best instructor, Montaigne also said, since "so many humors, sects, judgments, opinions, laws, and customs, teach us to judge sanely of our own, and teach our judgment to recognize its own imperfection and natural weakness, which is no small lesson" (1967, p. 116).

V

One cannot conclude even a brief and incomplete account of the ruling conceptions and the varied methods of adult education without reflecting yet again on how limited was the access to learning in most of the eras of antiquity. In the Book of Ecclesiasticus, it is written that "the wisdom of a learned man cometh by opportunity of leisure," for "how can he get wisdom that holdeth the plough?" Those who work with their hands are essential, but "they shall not dwell where they will nor go up and down; they shall not be sought for in publick counsel, nor sit high in the congregation; they shall not sit on the judges' seat, nor understand the sentence of judgment" (38:24-25, 32-33). They shall not learn.

With the passage of time, two great changes have come about. First, as a result of a gradually broadening humanitarianism and the growth of inventions, there has been increasing insistence that ways must be found to carry knowledge to all men and women who seek it or might profit from it. Knowledge does not filter down through the ranks of society, although, as

Mary Ewen Palmer observed, "the more idealistic and patronizing leaders have always spoken of the pervasive quality of the education enjoyed by the more privileged classes as if it bestowed its benefits more or less automatically on the whole society" (1946, p. ii). Modern reformers believe (as did John Comenius) that everyone at every level of society must be given the opportunity to learn.

Second, the effort to achieve this goal has broadened the conception of what constitutes organized knowledge. It used to be thought that education should include only the formal disciplines such as the *trivium* and the *quadrivium*; anything else a person needed to know could be learned incidentally during the course of daily activities. But, as Roger Ascham wrote, "Learning teacheth more in one yeare than experience in twentie" ([1560], 1903, p. 61), and the application of this principle has constantly broadened as the increasing complexity of life has made it clear that experience alone is too slow a teacher to meet modern requirements. Those who need skill to work with their hands now learn it in ordered and systematic ways, and the skill itself is often supported by both theory and the results of scientific investigation. Also, since the common people have won the rights of citizenship, it is no longer sufficient merely to school aristocrats to become the guardians of the state. Now everyone shares in governing it, and everyone must learn how to do so.

The story of the gradual unfolding of these two great changes in adult education is a fitful one, full of advances and retreats, and with no indication that either is close to its full realization.

References

Ali, A. *The Spirit of Islam.* London: Christophers, 1922.

Aristotle. *The Nicomachean Ethics.* (J. E. C. Welldon, Trans.) London: Macmillan, 1892.

Ascham, R. *The Scholemaster.* (E. Arber, Ed.) Westminster, England: A. Constable, 1903. (Originally published 1560.)

Asser. *Life of King Alfred.* (L. C. Jane, Trans.) London: Chatto & Windus, 1908.

Bacon, F. *Works*. 2 vols. London: Reeves and Turner, 1879.

Burckhardt, J. *The Civilization of the Renaissance in Italy*. Vol. 1. New York: Harper & Row, 1958.

Carlyle, T. *Sartor Resartus*. London: Chapman and Hall, 1831.

Cary, J. *The Case for African Freedom, and Other Writings on Africa*. Austin: University of Texas Press, 1962.

D'Arcy, M. C. *St. Thomas Aquinas*. Westminster, Md.: Newman Press, 1953.

Darwin, C. R. *Charles R. Darwin: His Life Told in an Autobiographical Chapter and in a Selected Series of His Published Letters*. (F. Darwin, Ed.) London: John Murray, 1902.

Descartes, R. "Discourse on Method." In *Philosophical Writings*. (N. K. Smith, Trans.) New York: Modern Library, 1958. (Originally published 1637.)

Dick, O. L. (Ed.). *Aubrey's Brief Lives*. London: Secker and Warburg, 1949.

Disraeli, I. *The Literary Character, Illustrated by the History of Men of Genius*. London: John Murray, 1818.

Du Chatelet, E. *Discours sur le Bonheur* [*Discourse on Happiness*]. Paris: Société d'Edition "Les Belles Lettres," 1961. (Originally published 1796.)

Durant, W. *The Age of Faith*. New York: Simon & Schuster, 1950.

Emerson, R. W. *Journals*. (E. W. Emerson and W. E. Forbes, Eds.) Vol. 6. New York: Houghton Mifflin, 1911.

Franklin, B. *Writings*. (A. H. Smyth, Ed.) Vol. 1. New York: Macmillan, 1905.

Freeman, K. *The Work and Life of Solon*. London: Humphrey Milford, 1926.

Froude, J. A. *Short Studies on Great Subjects*. Vol. 3. New York: Scribner's, 1908. (Originally published 1867.)

Galileo. *Discoveries and Opinions*. (S. Drake, Trans.) New York: Doubleday, 1957.

Goldsmith, O. "Of Polite Learning in Europe." In *Collected Works*. Vol. 1. Oxford: Clarendon Press, 1966. (Originally published 1755.)

Heath, T. L. "Pythagoras." In *Encyclopaedia Britannica*. Vol. 18. 1955.

Janssen, J. *History of the German People at the Close of the Middle Ages.* (M. A. Mitchell and A. M. Christie, Trans.) Vol. 1. London: Kegan Paul, 1896.

Julian. *Works.* (W. C. Wright, Trans.) Vol. 3. New York: Putnam's, 1923.

Kantorowicz, E. *Frederick the Second.* (E. O. Lorimer, Trans.) London: Constable, 1931.

Knox, J. "The Buke of Discipline." In *Works.* Vol. 2. Edinburgh: Bannatyne Club, 1848. (Originally published 1560.)

Locke, J. "Of the Conduct of the Understanding." In *Works.* Vol. 2. London: C. Baldwin, 1824. (Originally published 1690.)

Luther, M. "Letter to the Burgomasters and Councilmen of All Cities in Germany." In *Works.* Vol. 4. Philadelphia: Muhlenberg Press, 1931. (Originally published 1524.)

Machiavelli, N. *Letters.* (A. Gilbert, Trans.) New York: Capricorn Books, 1961.

Mill, J. S. *Autobiography.* New York: Holt, Rinehart and Winston, 1883.

Milton, J. "The Second Defense of the People of England." In *Prose Works.* London: Westley and Davis, 1834. (Originally published 1638.)

Montaigne, M. de. *Complete Works.* (D. M. Frame, Trans.) Stanford, Calif.: Stanford University Press, 1967.

Montesquieu. *Oeuvres Complètes* [*Complete Works*]. Vol. 7. Paris: Garnier Frères, 1879.

Palmer, M. E. "Characteristic Patterns of Adult Education in the United States, England, Denmark, and Germany." Unpublished doctoral dissertation, Harvard University, 1946.

Pliny. *Letters.* (W. Melmeth, Trans.) Vol. 1. New York: Macmillan, 1915.

Plutarch. *Lives of Illustrious Men.* (J. Dryden, Trans.) New York: S. W. Green's Son, 1882.

Seneca. *Epistles.* (R. M. Gummore, Trans.) Vol. 2. New York: Putnam's, 1930.

Seneca. "De Vita Beata" ["A Happy Life"]. In *Moral Essays.* (J. W. Basore, Trans.) Vol. 2. New York: Putnam's, 1932.

The Spectator. (D. F. Bond, Ed.) Vol. 1. Oxford, Clarendon Press, 1965.

Stimson, D. "Amateurs of Science in 17th Century England." *Isis,* 1939, *31,* 32–47.

Vinci, L. da. *Notebooks.* (E. McCurdy, Trans.) Vol. 1. New York: Reynal and Hitchcock, 1938.

Voltaire. "Elements de Philosophie de Newton" ["Elements of the Philosophy of Newton"]. *Oeuvres Complètes* [*Complete Works*]. Vol. 5. Paris: Chez Furnes, 1835. (Originally published 1745.)

Waliszewski, K. *Peter the Great.* (M. Loyd, Trans.) New York: Appleton-Century-Crofts, 1900.

10

Implications for Educators

I

A century and a half ago, Alexis de Tocqueville observed that "the philosophical method of the Americans" had certain principal characteristics: "to evade the bondage of system and habit, of family maxims, class opinions, and, in some degree, of national prejudices; to accept tradition only as a means of information, and existing facts only as a lesson to be used in doing otherwise and doing better; to seek the reason of things for oneself, and in oneself alone; to tend to results without being bound to means, and to strike through the form to the substance" ([1835], 1946, p. 3). In the inquiries reported in this book, something like this "philosophical method" has been used rather than conventional systems of data collection and presentation. For example, the persons studied were chosen not because they made up a representative sample of a defined universe but because each one illustrated some aspect of the central themes being explored. (Preliminary studies of about twenty other people were not completed because they did not appear to add new dimensions to the inquiry.) The historical review in Chapter Nine was presented not chronologically but by the clustering of opinions expressed by people widely separated in time and place. Other special approaches were made as they seemed necessary in seeking to accomplish the three goals of this book.

As identified in Chapter One, these goals are to explore some of the ways by which basic learning processes have long been provided and used, to suggest how knowledge of these pro-

cesses may enhance and diversify the modern practice of education, and to reexamine the concept of lifelong learning in the
light of a broader conception of method than has previously
been used. The first purpose served as the organizing principle
for Chapters Two through Nine, although the second and third
purposes were implicit throughout. Now, however, separate attention will be given to each purpose to determine whether useful insights may be gained from a retrospective view of all of the
previous narratives and analyses.

II

The educational methods described in some detail in earlier chapters have shown how sequences of experience have occurred in the lives of human beings as they sought to learn or to
teach. Some of these sequences were reinvented again and again;
thus Alexander Pope's eager use of mentors and his self-disciplined study of the principles of poetry did not follow any
models known to him. Some methods, such as spoken discourse, were carried forward from era to era largely by tradition
and lore. Only a few methods showed traces of historical continuity, as when Josiah Holbrook named his lyceum after that
of Aristotle although the processes used by the two institutions
were dissimilar and Holbrook showed no awareness of similar
ventures that had occurred in the twenty-two centuries that
separated his efforts from those of the great Athenian.

These basic recurring patterns have been supplemented
by other methods so original that one might almost venture to
call them unique. Michel de Montaigne's father seems to have
had a passion for finding unusual ways of learning and teaching,
as illustrated by his exercise with leaded canes, his early morning music, his placement of his infant son in a peasant family,
his effort to create a Latin-speaking household, and his selection
of an indulgent tutor for young Michel. These creative—some
may say eccentric—methods might well give rise to laughter if
one could forget that they had some part in shaping the talents
of a genius and, more profoundly, that they highlighted the actions of a father who cared deeply about education and was un-
fettered by preconceptions about how it should be carried out.

As the foregoing examples (and all the others used in this book) suggest, a learning method must ultimately be viewed as a special way of organizing experience so that it will help convey knowledge, skill, or sensitiveness. It is always an abstraction separated from all other aspects of life that may be occurring simultaneously and is given form by the mind of a learner or an educator. As John Dewey said, "Amid all uncertainties there is one permanent frame of reference: namely, the organic connection between education and personal experience" (1938, p. 12). Unless analysts of learning begin with that principle, their results are likely to be parochially rooted in the work of a single institution or cluster of institutions.

Although a method is an abstractly defined segment of activity, it is intimately related in practice to the whole range of human experience and is strongly influenced by that fact. For example, the theme of Chapter Six is educative foreign travel; concreteness is given to the topic by focusing on the city of Florence. The chapter deals with the kinds of people who learn by such travel, the purposes they seek to achieve through their activity, and the reasons why Florence is so admirable for the use of this method. Yet everyone recognizes that Florence is visited by people who do not wish to learn, that learners do many additional things while they live there, and that at other locations the resources, purposes, and processes of study are different. A firm boundary line can never be drawn that separates experiences intended to be educative from those that are not.

The processes of learning are difficult to classify since they are enduring or transitory, they range from the universal to the particular, and they are shaped in each usage by the mind of the learner or the educator. It is not hard to make a list of some of them, such as the one provided in the latter part of Chapter Nine, but as yet no convincing taxonomy has been developed to array all of them in categories according to an organizing principle. Great values would undoubtedly arise from the systematization of methods into a logical framework that would allow comparisons, distinctions, and appropriate combinations, but no such system is yet available.

Insofar as the study of specific educational processes is

concerned, many rewarding studies have been made. Purposeful reading provides perhaps the best example, for, from the second decade of the twentieth century onward, this method of learning has been widely studied in both natural and laboratory settings. Age limitations were transcended. Even such early investigators as Guy Buswell and William S. Gray analyzed the reading of adults as well as that of children. Other methods, particularly such interactive ones as lecturing, discussion, debate, and the cluster of organized relationships known popularly as group dynamics, have also been analyzed, although they were less subject to laboratory treatment than was reading.

The methods of education are linked reciprocally to its goals. In the theory of modern educational program design, the objectives desired in any episode of learning are first identified and the processes that will best achieve them are then chosen. In practice, an awareness of the methods available often precedes the choice of the goals and always modifies the extent to which they can be accomplished. The learning undertaken or provided by all of the men and women used as examples in this book was determined by the nature of the resources accessible to them. For most such people (as for most of the population of the world today), the means of education were few in number. It is interesting to speculate what many of the individuals studied might have made of themselves if they had lived at a time when knowledge was richly and freely provided. Would they have been helped by that fact? Alternatively, did the scarcity of potential ways to use the basic methods of education challenge them to a level of accomplishment that the abundant resources of today might have stifled?

In considering such questions, we should remember that the major methodological changes that have occurred between earlier times and our own have been in the adaptation and reinterpretation of ancient techniques, chiefly with the intent of making them available more rapidly and flexibly and to many more people than could earlier share in their benefits. A quill pen can record as profound a philosophical truth as can a computerized word processor. If the goal of an educator was to convey factual knowledge, the ancient methods were spoken discourse and the use of manuscripts. The invention of the printing press added books, which replaced manuscripts but created a far wider market than before for the content they had provided and also for the transcriptions of spoken discourse. Radio, television, and recording machines later gave new audiences to such discourse and were accompanied (to most people's surprise) by an enormous increase in the number of books published. Similar kinds of adaptation have occurred for the other basic methods. The most advanced forms of computerization, telecommunication, and other innovations turn out, on analysis, to be variants of ancient forms of learning, such as mentoring or discussion. Even the use of enhanced consciousness or inward-directed processes, such as transcendental meditation and biofeedback, have early precursors, although they have not been considered here. The most interesting question of all, perhaps, is whether any completely new method of learning is ever likely to arise.

The effect of a method depends not so much on its inherent efficacy as on the intent and the talents of its user. Most people have believed that because Billy Graham uses techniques made familiar by Billy Sunday and other earlier evangelists, his goal is identical with theirs; close inspection of his practice reveals, however, that his desired achievements differ from the ones commonly ascribed to him. Henry David Thoreau witnessed the delivery of a large number of lectures, but that experience did little to enhance his own effectiveness in the use of the method. Countless writers have engaged in the self-disciplined study of their craft and innumerable scholars have undergone the rigors of a nineteenth-century German university education but have not achieved the distinction of either Pope or Everett. This difference in the influence of a method is caused not only by the inherent ability or level of readiness of the learner but also by the intensiveness and sophistication of his or her interaction with the environment, a point elegantly made by Cardinal John Henry Newman in his comment about seafaring men, which was quoted in Chapter Six.

In the repetitive use of an educational method by a provider, success apparently comes from the choice of a basic structural procedure that remains the same although its components vary to fit the different situations in which it is used. Everett and Graham both employed the method of spoken discourse, but a comparison of Everett's Gettysburg address with the message delivered at a Crusade session shows wholly different patterns of preparation and delivery. Everett brought to full refinement a form of historical and philosophical discourse perfected through a lifetime of use. Graham's basic approach to his mass audiences has retained the same symmetrical form since he started to use it, but the presentation now depends upon the use of thousands of components, to each of which careful attention is given both before a Crusade begins and at every stage of its unfolding. Evidence on earlier users of spoken discourse suggest that they were no less careful than Everett or Graham in the development of their distinctive styles.

These differences tend to be blurred when a method is examined in general terms even though useful observations may still be made about its distinctive usefulness when compared with other methods. The Concord lyceum and other examples suggest that local discussion groups are initially valuable in providing reinforcement through interaction, but they usually do not have adequate resources within their membership to maintain their programs for long periods of time without the importation of external stimuli. Foreign travel appears to have inherent values and limitations both as to the goals sought and the intensity with which they are achieved. The advocates of any method usually emphasize its strengths, but the students of its application discover also its weaknesses and limitations.

The analysis of learning methods in this book has been characterized by three approaches that are not frequently found in modern treatments of the topic. Each approach deserves separate consideration.

First, the history of adult education considered as a whole is difficult to write because until the second quarter of the twentieth century, it was episodic in character. Countless institutions and movements grew up, some of which had long lives, but each was independent and not undertaken as part of a broad, overarching movement or as one aspect of a unifying theme. Consequently, even today, those who study or practice adult education often have little awareness of the history of previous manifestations of the work that engages their interests and guides their activities. They are pigeonholed in the present and lack the sense of a deep background that nourishes and gives direction to the leaders of other theoretical and professional fields. Scholars of mathematics, history, and the sciences are well aware of the traditions of their disciplines; lawyers and legislators are sometimes called Solons after the early Athenian lawgiver; and physicians are at least aware of Hippocrates, Galen, Harvey, and other pioneers of medical theory and science.

Since adult education has been discovered afresh in many times and places and has been widespread in its application to human needs and desires, it has had few continuities of thought and development. However, like people who engage in such other emergent disciplines and fields of practice as social work, public health, or journalism, educators of adults can look backward to people in earlier centuries who thought as they do and who used forms that can now be reinterpreted and employed in a modern age. These earlier episodes cannot be slavishly imitated, but they can serve as resources and inspiration. It is for this reason that the present analysis of methods and patterns of method has been cast almost entirely in the past, the one exception to this general rule being Graham. He would not have been included if I had been able to find a detailed description of an earlier use of the method of spoken discourse.

The anecdotes, episodes, and case studies of the past can often throw fresh light on contemporary problems or issues. In modern times, for example, many people argue that freedom of choice to participate in organized learning activities is the essential characteristic of adult education. Opponents of this view have argued that the safety of society demands that some of its members—such as physicians, attorneys, and accountants—be required to keep on learning if they are to continue to practice their crafts. The example of Alfred the Great, as described in

Chapter Nine, shows that this problem is not a new one, and his reasoning still has force today.

The astonishingly rapid growth of the lyceum in a sparsely populated country is another example of a recurrent phenomenon of American adult education, a field of work prone to sudden enthusiasms and the swift expansion of new institutions, often accompanied in each case by the idea that the novelty will ultimately prevail over all existing systems. In the 1930s and again in the 1960s, many programs appeared, chiefly as a result of funding by the federal government. The people who directed them in each of the two decades believed that such programs established the framework of all future adult education, but today few of them survive. They were widely practiced but not deep-rooted. On the other hand, the work of Everett and his associates, later bolstered by Andrew Carnegie's carefully qualified fund granting, secured the growth of the public library, the most broadly useful form of self-directed learning yet devised in American society. The century-long struggle to establish what became the Cooperative Extension Service (an effort not described in this book) is another example of solid and long-enduring growth. It is fascinating to speculate why some institutions perish and others outlast trends.

Perhaps the most profound influence of the history and lore of a specific field of work is its power to build a sense of community. The vision of the people employed in a single type of institution is often circumscribed by its procedures so that common underlying purposes, shared content, similar goals, and basic methods among many kinds of institutions are obscured. Such fields of practical endeavor as social work and librarianship have been far more successful than adult education in achieving this sense of basic unity. The life-styles, purposes, and processes quickly scanned in Chapter Nine undergird all systematic forms of education, but the failure to recognize such common foundations ultimately limits the service that might be provided to learners, particularly adults.

The second special approach used in this book is that the analysis of methods of learning has been based on unique exam-

ples in an effort to discover universals through a broadly refer-
enced study of specific cases. Since the history of adult education has, in truth, been episodic, the recounting of such cases is
more appropriate, at least at the present time, than would be
the effort to present a panoramic view that would have no other unifying theme than the sequence of time. As a result of further study, such themes will undoubtedly emerge, but the continuing analysis of individual episodes will help provide the
basis for their emergence.

In considering this point, a pair of terms used in the
study of psychology may be helpful. The analysis of the theory
and practice of adult education has usually been centered upon
nomothetic inquiry, the effort to establish abstract, general, or
universal statements or laws that apply to all people or to identified categories of people. Other scholarly fields, most notably
those that have to do with the application of knowledge to particular cases, have, in addition to nomothetic inquiries, also
made much use of *idiographic analysis,* the study of concrete,
individual, or unique examples in which generalized laws have
specific interactive applications. For example, both the teaching
and the practice of law are based on the reporting of cases that
embody principles or establish precedents. In medicine, the
diagnosis and remediation of individual patients permeates both
study and practice, being found in pathology clinics, grand
rounds, clinical presentations, and journal articles, as well as in
the close observation by the physician or surgeon of each of his
or her patients. In university teaching about the various places
where administrative theory is applied (such as in business, government, schools, or health care institutions) heavy reliance is
often placed on specially prepared case studies.

The field of adult education has used idiographic analysis
to some extent but almost always on an institutional basis. The
literature abounds in chronicles of organizations or programs,
ranging in scope from serious historical studies to simple how-
we-do-it accounts. But although countless nomothetic investigations of the learning processes of individuals, groups, and institutions have been made, idiographic studies of this sort have
been rare. In this book, a variety of approaches to such analysis

has been used. In the accounts of Montaigne, Pope, and Thoreau, attention is centered on learners, although in the third case, an institution is also described. In the descriptions of Graham, Everett, and Osler, the focus is upon providers of education. In the study of Florence, emphasis is on a geographical place as it influences the learners who come to it. Chapter Nine reports conclusions reached from the analysis of a large number of anecdotes and quotations. In addition to the values that these diverse kinds of probes present in and of themselves, they may provide precedents for other studies using the same or other general approaches.

The third distinctive approach of this book grows out of a realization likely to impress anybody who studies learning as it actually occurs in the lives of individuals: the great significance of the use by an individual of simultaneous or sequential patterns of learning methods. My own recognition of the importance of this point emerged only after the studies reported in this book were under way. In what now seems a naive approach, I intended initially to link each person described with a dominant method—Montaigne with reading, Pope with self-disciplined study, Thoreau with discussion groups, and so on. Even before the first study was completed, the fallacy of this approach was evident, and, as the title of the book suggests, the clustering of methods became the paramount emphasis. The significance of this emphasis will be explored in later pages.

III

This comparative study of methods of learning may be used by several kinds of persons to enhance and diversify the practice of education. The first is the program builder engaged in planning, guiding, and directing educational activities. Program builders range from the individual who designs and carries out a personal course of study to the staff members of a large institution who plan programs for a mass audience or who devise a cluster of activities for a diversified clientele. The second major architect of improvement is the person who does the research and data collection that produce the knowledge base of the applied field of education. In other, lesser ways, the comparative study of method may also be of significance for those who, in either degree programs or in-service institutional or associational settings, are preparing themselves to be educational leaders; those who have a general responsibility for education, such as the trustees, administrators, or members of academic senates of universities; and those who have a broad interest in the field, perhaps because they contemplate entering it, perhaps because they want to look retrospectively over their experiences in it, or perhaps because they simply have an intellectual turn of mind. This section of the chapter focuses on the program builders and researchers—those who are concerned with enhancing and diversifying the modern practice of education—since the activities of others tend to be based upon their work.

A major frontier of improved practice is in formal schooling itself. This structure of education with all its connecting links is so deeply embedded in modern thought that it is hard to realize how recently it has been developed. The careers of Everett, Osler, and their colleagues in the nineteenth and early twentieth centuries were devoted to the creation of essentially new institutional forms, although some of them grew up within old structures; but the full development of the interlocked network of schooling with which everyone is now familiar did not come into being until well into the twentieth century. Some linking components were not, in fact, well established until fairly recently; for example, it was not until after World War II that standardized college, university, and professional school admission examinations were fully developed and widely accepted.

In the nature of the instruction that occurs in the classroom, however, a striking resistance to change continues to prevail. Enemies of rigidity have always been present: some of them following the theories of Dewey and other philosophers; some of them engaging in the progressive education movement, the nontraditional education movement, and other similar crusades; some of them following one of the many carefully engineered plans for reform that have been brought forward; and some of them following the leadership of master teachers. The ultimate cumulative effect of all these endeavors has so far been minor if reports made in the early 1980s are accurate. Researchers, such as John Goodlad, have examined closely the processes used in many classrooms and found them astonishingly arid and lacking in interest. As a result, learning achievement is often low. Cross-national studies of educational attainment have suggested that in other countries much more is accomplished in the 15,000 hours of schooling available to each child who completes a twelve-year program of schooling than is true in the United States. Various commissions under both public and private auspices have concluded that although some schools reach a high level of accomplishment, the poor performance of others leads to low average achievement.

No easy answer to this problem will be found, but perhaps one major route toward improvement would result from the analysis and use of multiple methods of instruction. As the examples described earlier in this book suggest, each individual has a distinctive learning pattern. If emphasis in designing instruction could be placed on the combination of such patterns and not on the standardization of systems believed to be appropriate for everyone, the resulting achievements of the markedly heterogeneous young people in the nation's schools might be much greater than at present. The capacity to help young people learn flows from an understanding of each of them as an individual and from an awareness of the distinctive qualities of the various methods of learning.

The gaining of formal academic credentials without necessarily using standardized systems of teaching is already widespread among adult learners in the so-called nontraditional and experiential learning movements. It is evident to anybody who considers the matter that the general experiences of life are all educative to some extent and that the lessons they teach often correspond fairly closely to those conveyed by formal schooling. A first major demonstration of this fact was the administration of the test of general education developed during and after World War II to serve as a measure of the knowledge possessed by people who have achieved a high school diploma.

This test was not readily accepted by educational authorities, and its administration was for a long time restricted to adults, but it is now so common throughout the country that in the early 1980s about 14 percent of the people winning high school credentials did so by achieving a sufficiently high score on this test. In 1982, a total of 515,247 people passed, and 9.5 percent of them were under the age of eighteen.

The use of tests as a way of measuring learning not necessarily achieved by formal means was extended to the collegiate level by the College-Level Examination Program and the Advanced Placement Examination, both of which are based on conventional collegiate curricula. Also special tests, often called challenge examinations, were devised for various courses of study, many of them leading to professional credentials. The testing of learning by unconventional means was then extended to other ways of measuring such accomplishments. Mature students were permitted to submit portfolios, which demonstrated accomplishments in many different ways, and to have them evaluated for college credit. These portfolios were, at first, retrospective, showing what had already occurred, but it was not long before some educational institutions began counseling students about how they could embark on a monitored series of future experiences and thereby win recognition. Soon external degrees for adult learners were being devised by many organizations; a few colleges devoted their attention entirely to the awarding of such degrees. The growth of these new methods of recognizing formal learning by previously unconventional means has also encouraged many adults to enter traditional colleges because the length of the programs of study that would lead to a desired degree was drastically shortened by the advanced standing such students could win by unconventional means.

As far as adult education is concerned, the availability of a large number of methods of learning allows a freedom of choice and a precision of application that may greatly extend and enrich the goals achieved. All too often this opportunity is ignored. Large programs (such as those of general university extension divisions, museums, the training departments of industry, and state-wide Cooperative Extension Services) can become rigid and fixed in their processes, thereby limiting the goals they can reach or the clienteles they can serve. Movements based on a single method or cluster of methods (such as lecturing or group dynamics) can grow so strong that their proponents believe that all other ways of learning are inferior or invalid. Alternatively, movements aimed at the achievement of specific goals (such as literacy or the liberal studies) may overstress the values of the processes that are particularly suitable for such purposes. Individuals designing programs for themselves often restrict their activities because they do not know of other available options. In all such cases, the field of adult education, conceived as a whole, is narrowed and made less effective than it otherwise would be.

The same result may occur when new programs or episodes of learning are planned, unless the individual or the staff that is examining various precedents or possibilities has a broad conception of the range of goals and methods available to it so that the two may be meshed together in the best fashion possible. For example, a community college may identify an unserved occupational group that it wishes to help. The clarification of the specific goals to be attained and the development of the most efficient means for doing so then become twin tasks, each to be considered separately but ultimately to be blended together. The same kind of process occurs whenever an individual or an autonomous group plans a program; Montaigne's plan to devote his life to reading, John Stuart Mill's discussion group on Threadneedle Street, and Benjamin Franklin's use of chess to motivate his learning of Italian are examples of creativeness in meshing ends and means.

The heart of adult education lies in the ability of its program designers to perceive all of the relevant elements in situation after situation and to take them into account in planning and carrying out learning programs. In older professions, the generalist preceded the specialists; for example, the family practitioner antedated the pediatrician and the cardiologist. In many of the newer professionalizing groups, people who already possess specific kinds of expertise band together to seek the common themes that will broaden their horizons and enrich their competence. Thus public administration has grown out of the study of the tasks performed by various types of government officials, social work has been a coalescence of the many ways by which welfare needs are met, and business administration is centered on the responsibilities that must be carried by the managers of countless forms of money-making enterprises. In this way, adult education grew up as a practical field of both action and study because many institutions and programs with distinctive goals and methods existed to serve the learning needs of adults or of society.

To be fully successful, therefore, the professional educator of adults must be deeply conversant with the goals and methods of learning, gaining such knowledge from study in university graduate departments, from other organized training efforts, from self-directed programs of study, or from the contemplative examination of his or her own experience. Continuing educators are not exempt from the need for continuing education. This conclusion is true in part because of the great body of present knowledge about the practice of adult education, in part because the knowledge base that undergirds practice is constantly being enlarged, and in part because any general process of learning must always be applied afresh in specific situations. The circumstances of each application are always unique and (as is often not noted) so is each applier of a method. Two program administrators, although they may be people of similar background, experience, training, and ability, will have distinctive ways of conceptualizing and carrying out their work. They need not only to know the general nature of the methods they use and how such methods can best attain the distinctive purposes to be achieved but also to be aware of how each of them can best design and carry out a pattern of activities in accordance with his or her own preferred ways of work.

A mature awareness of method can often help the policy makers and general administrators of an institution to conceptualize its work more adequately. Many associations and organizations (such as museums, professional societies, and government bureaus) have initiated schoollike activities that they call their educational programs. In addition, they may conduct national and regional conferences, issue journals, undertake other forms of mass dissemination of knowledge, sponsor study conferences or seminars, and conduct testing programs that require self-directed study. These and other similar activities are often not considered educational, however. As a result, values that might be derived from a comprehensive perspective and the interactive improvement of the various parts of the total program are lost. The self-image of the institution and the perception of it by its publics does not disclose how pervasively educational its program truly is.

As the examples cited in earlier chapters indicate, many people who guide their own learning are capable of building the often creative patterns of methods that best suit their needs. Other people, particularly those who are initiating a program of study, have little awareness of the resources available or, alternatively, are unable to evaluate the profusion of opportunities that come, often insistently, to their attention. This manifest need for guidance has given rise to a number of adult counseling systems, offered by personal assistance, by print, or by interactive computer programs. Excellent books are also available giving general advice to would-be learners on how to develop their patterns of study. As yet, however, the services available are not adequate to meet the needs that exist; the theme of Thomas Gray's *Elegy Written in a Country Churchyard* is as valid today as it ever was.

It was noted earlier that one of the two major sources of improvement in education is the person who does the research and data collection that provide the knowledge base on which program designers and administrators can draw. General institutional statistics have long been available, and, as has already been noted, many studies have been made concerning specific processes of learning. Most such investigations have, intentionally or unconsciously, been based on the work of specific kinds of institutions. Therefore, however valuable they might be in program planning in those limited settings, they have tended to segment rather than unify thinking about patterns of learning as they exist at any given time or as they change throughout the life span.

Even the attempts to mark out the dimensions of the whole field of education at any given time of life have, until recently, been institution-centered and have therefore led systematically to a blurring of measurement so that it became virtually meaningless. As comprehensive statistics on adult education were collected beginning about 1930, the major method used was to add up the number of participants in programs defined as being adult educational. Thus total adult registrants in public schools, universities, public libraries, and industry- and labor-sponsored courses were added to attendance at museums, exhibitions, church-sponsored study groups, and so on, the limits being the availability of data and the inclusiveness of the definition of adult education. Although such studies showed the variety of forms of participation and built up impressive total figures that, for the first time, demonstrated the massive scale of adult education, the totals were meaningless because they were composed of noncomparable items and also because they omitted many crucial forms of self-directed individual and group learning.

Beginning in the 1960s, the nature of the measurement changed so that it focused on the kind and amount of activities undertaken by individuals. Most such studies were made of samples of various populations and required interviews of a number of persons to indicate the frequency or amount of participation in various kinds of activities. With increasing precision as later studies built on earlier ones, it was possible to measure the total amount of participation of each respondent, examine the patterns of learning in which he or she was currently engaged, and correlate these kinds of data with other statistics, including demographic and personality characteristics. Thus the focus tended to shift from institutions to individuals, from separate actions to patterns of behavior, and from formalized education to broadly based learning.

This line of research has not been extended, in any significant way, to deal with two central concerns of this book: what gives coherence to simultaneous patterns of learning, and how, in the life of a person, one pattern merges sequentially into another. Common sense suggests that methods reinforce one another. For example, it was noted in Chapter Six that the value of foreign travel is greatly heightened if it is preceded, accompanied, and followed by other processes of inquiry. Most of the knowledge of how such mutual reinforcement occurs, however, is the result of lore and is based on specific and often traditional learning programs. A high school course in the natural sciences, for example, may call for the judicious combination of reading, lectures, class discussion, laboratory work, and field experience. These combinations tend to be determined by custom as modified by experience and an awareness of the total time available. The established mixture used in a course may be the best attainable for all students, for most students, or for average students—but nobody really knows that it is. The research that would give practical insights into method combinations is scarce, perhaps because investigators have not found ways to conceptualize it, particularly in adulthood, when learning is provided by many institutions and must be integrated into the varied experience of an active life.

This problem is complex as far as the design of a single episode or sequence of learning is concerned, but it grows much more so when one examines the total learning that an individual may be undertaking simultaneously in pursuit of various goals or the series of patterns that flow sequentially, one following the other. Such studies can be descriptive (as the chapters on Pope, Thoreau, and Montaigne have shown), but the ways of going beyond idiographic treatment remain obscure.

Sustained analysis of the methods and patterns of learning may advance the development and testing of various kinds of typologies that would give order and system to the field of adult education. For example, several categorizations have emerged from the observations reported in this book, but they are all presented as hypotheses, not tested classifications. Are there basic conceptions of learning as part of a life-style other than those suggested in Chapter Nine? Do the goals of education outlined in that chapter conform to the motivations and orientations derived from other kinds of research? Are the categories of people who seek to learn by foreign travel and the goals they try to achieve accurately portrayed in Chapter Six? Such questions as these grow out of idiographic study. How can they be dealt with by nomothetic analysis?

IV

The central conception of education in the future is likely to be that of lifelong learning, although most of the specialists in both childhood and adult education do not yet fully recognize that fact. The examples embodying this idea that are listed in Chapter One have come into being for several reasons: because of the inherent nature of a sponsoring institution (the public library, the Cooperative Extension Service); because an authoritative employer or occupational group designed a career ladder that intimately included education (the armed services, systems of professional education); or because the people controlling a school or college sought to broaden its range of service. In most such ventures, expansion or alteration of programs occurred on an opportunistic or pragmatic basis. In others it has been guided by theory, sometimes arising from one or another of the conceptions put forward by international organizations and briefly stated in Chapter One.

The studies reported in earlier chapters suggest that if these conceptions were more clearly differentiated from one another, greater clarity would allow each one to be better understood and become the basis for practical action. *Lifelong learning* expresses the idea that learning never ceases from birth to death and that (until senility) educational programs can be devised for people of any age. At least three specific approaches to action are related to this general term. *Lifelong inquiry* (sometimes called *permanent education*) implies that learning is (or can be) woven into the fabric of experience as it occurs minute by minute throughout life. *Recurrent education* implies that at various times in life, a period of study occurs after intervals of nonstudy, with each episode of learning beginning afresh. *Life-span learning* implies the existence of some grand design or sequence of lesser designs of education as it relates to human experience. One such design (here called the *stages of life* approach) is constructed on the idea that all people or some defined category of people move sequentially through a series of stages that in its ultimate extreme spans the whole sweep of life. Once the stages have been defined, the next step is to inquire what kinds of education are most often found or are most relevant during each one. A second design (the one developed in this book and here called the *sequential patterns of learning* approach) is based on the observation that at any given time an individual is engaging in a complex pattern of learning activities. In this conception, life-span learning is centered on the analysis of how such patterns shift (or can be made to shift) with advancing age.

These terms are all illustrated in the life and writings of Osler. In seeking to discern the distinctive problems of every patient he saw and in suggesting the importance of "day-tight compartments," he was existentially carrying out lifelong inquiry. In his advocacy of "quinquennial brain-dusting," he was recommending recurrent education. In his analysis of the learning that should occur at the four stages of the physician's life, he was proposing one form of life-span learning, and in identifying a basic pattern of activities to be carried out at each age, he was proposing another form. In both word and deed throughout his life, he made manifest his belief in lifelong learning.

In considering how these terms and conceptions might facilitate a more complete idea of lifelong learning than now exists, distinctive applications of each of them may be suggested.

Adapting the formal educational system to lifelong learning. When Edward Everett and his groups of colleagues established or strengthened the formal institutions of education, including the public library as the means of continuing education throughout life, it was generally assumed that the opportunities thus afforded would be so inherently attractive that people would be eager to follow the pathway of learning prepared for them. But as graded and formally sequential education grew in size and scope to include kinds of students who had not previously been served, more and more young people slipped off the ladder or stepped away from it, with particularly heavy losses occurring at the points of transition between institutions, such as that from the secondary school to the college or university.

The major point of disruption of lifelong learning, however, occurs when individuals move from the laddered system of youth education (which gives structure not only to their learning but to their lives) into the broadly diversified world of adulthood. Their education is no longer carried forward in graduated steps. More than that, the credential-granting ceremonies of the system itself often tend to encourage the idea that the education of the graduate has now been completed, although the word *commencement*, often used on such occasions, would seem to indicate a contrary belief. Osler suggested that for the physician the greatest point of danger in the continuance of self-directed learning during the course of life occurred at the start of independent practice and was caused by a false self-confidence concerning the adequacy of the knowledge already acquired, by the observation of other physicians who were not continuing learners, and by the pressures of work in the establishment of a practice. Transition from school to practice in medicine is better today than it was in Osler's time, but his general point is probably still valid not only for medical doctors but also for most people ending their preservice education.

The one institution in that formal system that has most successfully incorporated lifelong education into its curriculum is the community college, which did not mature into its present form until after the modern idea of adult education had been well established. Universities have also found ways to create new programs especially for adults and also to attract them to activities originally established for young people with the result that the average age of students is steadily rising and there has been much talk about the graying of the campuses. Young people increasingly see their parents or other senior members of the community studying, and in university classrooms there is often a mixture of the generations, thus making evident the fact that learning continues throughout life.

The institutions not directly on the ladder of the formal instructional system are gradually incorporating the idea of lifelong education into their programs. Museums, for example, have always attracted people of all ages but are now redesigning their services in such a way as to have a greater and more universal educational impact. Such institutions as the Deutsches Museum in Munich, the Jeu de Paume in Paris, and the Exploratorium in San Francisco have been powerful stimulants to encourage museums to go beyond school-related and school-imitative programs; instead they offer learning experiences that are unique to a museum setting, not only using such devices as portable audio-tape players but, far more important, designing the exhibits themselves to be more educative.

Much attention is now being given to articulation among formal educational institutions so that the transition of a learner from one level of schooling to the next is accomplished with maximum efficiency. The nature and amount of learning that should occur during the transition to out-of-school adulthood is also being given some attention, particularly as it is realized in the professions that early preparation can do no more than lay foundations for future study, which must occur throughout a lifetime. In every advanced field of applied knowledge, the amount that must be learned is so great that it cannot all be conveyed in the collegiate years. Therefore some rethinking of the sequence of studies must occur so that topics that will not be needed until the later stages of a career will be learned at that time and removed from the preservice curriculum.

It is also being recognized afresh that changes in programs for early learning often follow changes made in programs for more advanced learning. The establishment of the university itself occurred prior to the systematization of the secondary school. Countless examples could be given of how content, method, and their combination in programming occurred for adult audiences before they were provided for young people. Significant books and works of art are usually created for adults and, only later, are introduced into the schools. Many of the university-based professional schools (such as those of social work, librarianship, nursing, and business administration) began as course sequences established to upgrade the work of people already in service in a field. This general process continues today, and if there is to be improvement in early schooling, it may well come from the adoption of activities pioneered with adult learners. As the example of the lyceum suggests, any such improvement cannot occur before those who have reached adulthood (and are therefore in control of society) inform themselves about the best kinds of education in childhood.

Most of the foregoing changes have been guided only by a generalized belief in lifelong learning, although the rethinking of curricula depends to some extent on the conceptualization of stages of life as they occur, either generally or in a professional lifespan.

Enhancing the zest for life-long inquiry. All of the individuals studied at length in previous chapters demonstrated a strong spirit of inquiry lasting throughout their lives. Each in his or her own way, using methods and patterns of methods unique to his or her own development, carried forward the processes of learning, sometimes alone, sometimes with friends, and sometimes by participation in organized educational activities. One of Osler's basic principles for the education of the practicing physicians was that each safeguard "that most precious of all possessions, his mental independence" (1906, p. 297). Amidst all the diversities of Osler's own learning, a central core of initiative and control was always present. The same thing was true for Montaigne, Thoreau, Pope, Graham, and Everett.

Although such men and women are exceptional in regard to learning, all normal people possess the desire to know, to understand, and to improve their skills. We vary greatly in the ways by which we respond to that desire and the control we exert over our own learning patterns. It is possible that this variance is related in some systematic way to the changes in an individual that occur during the course of life, but as yet both the changes and the variance are only dimly perceived.

It is true that stereotypic and often derogatory ways of considering the matter abound. Children are said to be naturally curious about many things. When they go to school, however, it is charged that they enter a lock-step system. Their motivation to learn is specific, but the goals of the school are generalized and grow essentially out of society's expectations. If the stu-

dents cannot match their aims to those of the school, they grow
either restless or passive, and, as time goes on and habits deep-
en, the chasm between expected accomplishments and actual
achievement grow ever wider. Thus the schools are said to diminish the natural curiosity of children, thereby creating a high
early dropout rate. Colleges and universities must also cope with
a high rate of change in major fields of study as young people
restlessly seek specializations that appeal to them. When they
leave formal schooling, the nature of their motivation continues
to be specific. If they study at all, they do so for concrete reasons that vary as they grow older. Some people continue to
have inquiring minds all their lives, while others gradually go
through a cooling-out process that eventually leaves them almost devoid of curiosity.

This late twentieth-century view, whatever its validity, is
based on the full development of a formal educational system
that has carried to a logical extreme the ideas of Everett and his
colleagues as they sought to achieve egalitarian schooling for
young people. Now, as that same mission is extended to provide
more and larger opportunities for learning in adulthood, it will
be appropriate to consider whether all the adjustments in both
formal schooling and later study can be carried out in such a
fashion as to enlarge the number of people who vigorously demonstrate their sense of inquiry as they move through appropriate patterns of learning throughout their lives. Without continuing learner-directed initiative, education cannot be effective in
achieving the fullest measure of human potential.

Fostering recurrent education. Periods of recurrent education do not necessarily have to be undertaken on a full-time
basis, but most of the writing and discussion on the topic tend
to assume that they do. Until recently the idea that people
should withdraw from work occasionally or periodically to engage in learning was carried out chiefly by highly trained people
on an individual basis. Institutionalization of the practice occurred chiefly in colleges and universities, and even these sab-
batical programs usually did not occur with seven-year regular-
ity. They were meagerly financed and, in practice, were often
granted as a reward for past accomplishment rather than as
preparation for future achievements.

In the mid-twentieth century, however, interest in systematic programs of recurrent education became evident in a number of places. As has been noted, professional military careers were designed to include alternating periods of service and study. In fast-developing industries, it proved to be necessary to retrain staff members to deal with successive generations of products. In collective bargaining, the right of workers to have paid study leaves became an issue. European governments enacted legislation to support recurrent education for various categories of workers, chiefly industrial and commercial managers. Public and private fellowship programs have grown up in profusion to enable selected people to engage in directed or independent study.

The general purpose of the foregoing efforts has been the normal advancement of career lines, but a social problem now gives great additional force to recurrent education. It is the urgent and growing need for people to be trained or retrained for new occupations. Technological obsolescence has been part of the life of industrialized nations for a long time, but only recently has it become clear that one of the major solutions to the problem of unemployment must be a period of study, often of lengthy duration, in which a new occupation is learned. An allied problem has been the need for education of adults, most often women, who want to enter the work force. Still another category of substantial size is made up of people who want to change careers but cannot do so without being retrained. If the word *recurrent* is used to describe events that happen time after time, then it is inappropriate to use it to describe the kinds of education mentioned in this paragraph. Another meaning of *recurrent*, however, is movement in a direction opposite to a former course; here the term seems to apply sufficiently well. In any case, in the span of a lifetime, a separate period of study is a notable event, one that must be planned with care and that is different from activities undertaken in other approaches to lifelong learning.

Designing education for the successive stages of life. The idea that education should be related to the successive stages of life has been a familiar one throughout recorded history, its best-known expression being that of Plato's *Republic*. The idea has come up again and again in the history of culture. The fullest treatment in this book is the expression of the ideas of Osler, who took as a basic principle for the practice of medicine "the need of a lifelong progressive personal training" (1906, p. 297). He felt that initial medical training could do no more than "teach the student principles, based on facts in science, and give him good methods of work. These simply start him in the first direction, they do not make him a good practitioner—that is his own affair" (1906, pp. 297-298). He went on to identify four stages in a physician's career: the medical student, the young doctor, the mid-career doctor, and the doctor in the later years of his practice. He defined the nature of each stage, pointing out the distinctive challenges of each and indicating how those challenges might be met by education.

In recent years, specialists in the various disciplines that are related to human development have given much thought to defining the stages of life. Gesell and his associates, for example, made careful studies of the successive phases of childhood and youth. Other scholars have carefully examined old age and middle age, and the literature of both biology and developmental psychology are richly filled with descriptions of the systematic patterns of passage through life. Most of these approaches have important implications for education and a large body of opinion and investigation has grown up relating to the ways learning should occur during specific segments of life, particularly childhood and old age. The further development of this approach to life-span learning appears to be promising for investigators and for practitioners.

Developing the study of sequential patterns of learning. In the special circumstances of his bitterly deprived life, Pope, by both self-direction and chance and without formal schooling, moved through a sequence of learning patterns that helped him to perfect his art and that occurred in a fashion that could be seen, retrospectively at least, to have had a kind of inevitability in their flow in the sense that later events could not have had their full effect if they had not been preceded by earlier ones. As other reports presented earlier in this book have also suggested, the influence of education, broadly conceived, upon the lives of most people has resulted not from a single form of study but from the use of a shifting pattern of methods. Chance plays a part in the designing of such patterns; Pope found circles of challenging colleagues whereas, as Emerson pointed out, Channing did not and was the poorer for it.

To suggest that the study of sequential patterns of learning may be a way to approach the theory and practice of life-span education is to embark upon an almost uncharted pattern of investigation. As this book has demonstrated, the idea can be described and illustrated idiographically. It was also pointed out earlier in this chapter that the extent of participation in adult education is now being measured by asking respondents to indicate the extent to which they take part in a variety of activities. Thus patterns of learning in the lives of individuals are emerging as still pictures reporting a cluster of activities at a moment in time. As yet, however, the way by which such patterns change during the course of life has not been generally studied nor widely speculated about.

One way to move beyond individual accounts to nomothetic analysis is to identify a complex goal and then study the patterns of learning of a number of people who have achieved it. In a pioneering study, whose full report is still being prepared,* Benjamin Bloom and his colleagues studied 120 persons who, before the age of thirty-five, demonstrated high achievement in artistic areas (concert pianists and sculptors), psychomotor areas (Olympic swimmers and tennis players), and cognitive areas (research mathematicians and research neurologists). These people, their parents, and their teachers were asked in lengthy retrospective interviews to describe the processes by which the talents of these outstanding achievers were developed. Many in-school and out-of-school processes were revealed, all of them familiar to the readers of Chapter Nine.

---

*Among already-published papers describing aspects of this study are: Bloom, B. S., and Sosniak, L. A. "Talent Development Vs. Schooling." *Educational Leadership*, 1981, *39*, 86–94; Bloom, B. S. "The Role of Gifts and Markers in the Development of Talent." *Exceptional Children*, 1982, *48*, 510–522; and Bloom, B. S. "The Master Teachers." *Phi Delta Kappan*, 1982, *64*, 664–668, 715.

These processes made up both simultaneous and sequential patterns, and, most important, a sequence of patterns was discovered that was common to all six categories of outstanding accomplishment.

As other investigations like Bloom's become available, they will move the analysis of life-span learning away from purely institutional reports and individual descriptions toward the awareness of generalized patterns of learning. This change in emphasis should provide a much greater richness and depth of understanding of the methods of learning than presently exists.

V

The study of education, particularly in adulthood (a far longer sequence of learning stages than that which occurs during youth) must ultimately rest upon the desire to discover and use new and better means of learning. It is essential to have systems and established procedures—based on theory if possible, but if not, derived from empirical experience. For many people, the following of such well-charted pathways may be sufficient. But the truly professional educator must transcend the dictates of any one theory, institution, or methodology and apply the total body of his or her knowledge creatively in each particular case; like medicine, education is an art based on science. In the course of this final chapter, many implications for both practice and research have been suggested as products of the studies reported in this book. But it is worth repeating that all of the ideas expressed here are intended to suggest ways to initiate thought, not to complete it. Each person who studies or works professionally in education has his or her own vantage point of observation. From it, the perspective on the nature or practice of learning is unique. This fact should lead to great diversity of programming, but only such diversity can meet the needs of a complex society.

References

Dewey, J. *Experience and Education.* New York: Macmillan, 1938.

Goodlad, J. I. *A Place Called School: Prospects for the Future.* New York: McGraw-Hill, 1983.

Osler, W. *Aequanimitas, with Other Addresses to Medical Students, Nurses and Practitioners of Medicine.* (2nd ed.) Philadelphia: Blakiston, 1906.

Tocqueville, A. de. *Democracy in America.* Vol. 2. New York: Knopf, 1946. (Originally published 1835.)

Index